The Richest Woman in America

The
RICHEST
WOMAN
IN AMERICA

Hetty Green
in the Gilded Age

Janet Wallach

NAN A. TALESE

Doubleday

NEW YORK   LONDON   TORONTO   SYDNEY   AUCKLAND

Book design by Maria Carella
Jacket design by John Fontana
Jacket photograph of street © Street Scenes, Fifth Avenue, 57th to 59th Streets,
ca. 1897, Museum of the City of New York, Byron Co. Collection;
inset image of Hetty Green courtesy of the Library of Congress

Library of Congress Cataloging-in-Publication Data
Wallach, Janet
The richest woman in America : Hetty Green in the Gilded Age /
Janet Wallach. — 1st ed.
p.   cm.
Includes bibliographical references and index.
(alk. paper)
1. Green, Hetty Howland Robinson, 1835–1916.   2. Women capitalists and
financiers—United States—Biography.   3. Millionaires—United States—
Biography.   I. Title.
HG2463.G74W35 2012
332.092—dc23
[B]   2012005657

ISBN 978-0-385-53197-9

MANUFACTURED IN THE UNITED STATES OF AMERICA

1   3   5   7   9   10   8   6   4   2

First Edition

To Bob

My Symphony

(a favorite poem of Hetty Howland Robinson Green)

To live content with small means;
To seek elegance rather than luxury,
And refinement rather than fashion;
To be worthy, not respectable, and wealthy, not rich;
To study hard, think quietly,
Talk gently,
Act frankly;
To listen to stars and birds, to babes and sages, with
      open heart;
To bear all cheerfully,
Do all bravely,
Await occasions,
Hurry never.
In a word, to let the spiritual, unbidden and unconscious,
      grow up through the common.
This is to be my symphony.

WILLIAM HENRY CHANNING

Contents

═══

Author's Note

Hetty Green left no diaries, journals, or correspondence, no personal jottings to serve as a key to her enigmatic ways. She did, however, leave behind thousands of articles and interviews published by newspapers and magazines around the world. They range from a few brief lines to lengthy accounts. Some of them are reliable, many are not. It took scores of hours to read these stories and scores more, combing through the myths, to begin to understand her. For these reasons, this is not a traditional biography: it does not have the precise images, the fine line drawings, that such a book requires: rather, it is an impressionist painting, a series of brushstrokes meant to shed light on a woman and her times.

Hetty Green respected reporters and enjoyed talking to them. She understood the value of newspapers, and, from childhood on, she read the evening news to her father and grandfather. As an adult, she used the news as a matter of course in her daily investing. But though she relied on newspapers, much of what was reported about her was smeared with the yellow journalism so popular in her day. Worse, the snarky stories were repeated again and again, changing and growing like Pinocchio's nose. And she too repeated her stories and changed her accounts, embellishing facts here, embroidering memories there. She liked to attract attention and she enjoyed saying outrageous things.

Hetty Green was a strong and independent woman who rejected the trappings of her upper-class background and avoided the glittery style of the Gilded Age. Instead, she broke new ground and set her own course for marriage, family, and a career. She encouraged girls to educate themselves about business; she urged women to manage their own money and take control of their finances. In her own investing, she ignored the emotions of the crowd and kept a cool head. I hope that reading about her wise financial ways will inspire others. And every once in a while, as Hetty no doubt would have wanted, I hope that her words make the reader smile.

The Richest Woman in America

———

Prologue

A pack of reporters swarmed around the woman who emerged from the heavy doors of the courthouse. A cape of black cloth wrapped her tall frame, a black bonnet obscured her thick gray hair, a frayed black purse hung from her wrist. A passerby might say she looked as poor as a church mouse, but her clothes were merely a costume to conceal her incredible wealth. Standing in front of the granite building was Hetty Green, the richest woman in America.

A twinkle lit up her blue eyes, a half smile appeared on her lips as she glanced at the eager men and shook her head in resignation. She was, admittedly, the smartest woman on Wall Street, a financial genius, a railroad magnate, a real estate mogul, a Gilded Era renegade, a reliable source for city funds. Wherever she went, whatever she did, reporters were lurking, ready to hound her: Where was she living? Where was her husband? What about her children? How many millions did she have now? How did it feel to be the richest woman in America? Did she win the case? Who would she sue next?

"I have had fights with some of the greatest financial men in the country," she said in her broad New England accent. "Did you ever hear of any of them getting ahead of Hetty Green?"

Pleased with her victory in court on that spring day in 1896, her rights affirmed by the judge, she assured the men she was content with her work, at peace with her life.

If it was true that her constant lawsuits filled court dockets and her mounds of dollars overflowed bank vaults, it was also true that she was devoted to her children, adoring of her dogs, loving to youngsters, kind to strangers, and generous to friends. But reporters and readers refused to acknowledge her softer side; they demanded something more of the nation's richest woman. They did not begrudge her the piles of money, if only she would allow them the vicarious pleasure of spending it. What was the point of being a multi-multimillionaire if she did not carry out the role, if she did not parade about in Worth dresses or reside in beaux arts mansions, if she did not appear at the opera and never dined at Delmonico's?

The public resented the somberness of her clothing, the plainness of her diet, the austerity of her home. Her starched New England values did nothing to enrich their impoverished lives. But Hetty Green refused to yield to the role of Gilded Age socialite. Indeed, she refused to comply with any stereotype. Defiantly independent, she made her own rules and lived by them, even if she sometimes changed them in midstream.

Whatever methods she used to make her money, however, she would not succumb to the tactics of other millionaires. She did not employ workers at slave wages, did not steal land from the public or outsmart stockholders or pay off government officials like some. She did not scheme with Wall Street or speculate with other people's money. No, she told a reporter, her formula for success was simple: common sense and hard work. Yet the press portrayed her as cruel. "I am in earnest," she said. "Therefore, they picture me as heartless. I go my own way, take no partners, risk nobody else's fortune."

Her holdings ranged from gilt-edged mortgages and real estate in New York to dozens of buildings in downtown Chicago; gold, copper, and iron mines out west; diamonds and pearls; railroads; and government bonds. She was considered the single biggest individual financier in the world. By the time she died in 1916 she was worth a minimum of $100 million, the equivalent of more than $2 billion today. She achieved the financial ranks of Rockefeller, Vanderbilt, Morgan, and Gould and would have made the latest *Forbes* Four Hundred list.

The image she saw in the mirror was a singular woman swimming against the tide, struggling to survive in a sea of hostile men. Even now, triumphant in her latest court case, she knew there were others trying to snatch away her fortune. She was a woman alone in a world of envious men. "I am Madame Ishmael," she proclaimed, "set against every man." She fought the battle all her life.

═══

Chapter 1

The Spirit Within

The rancid smell of whale oil pervaded the air and perfumed the purses of New Bedford, Massachusetts, in 1841. When Herman Melville arrived at the wharves in search of work, square-masted whaling ships flew Union Jacks and tricolors alongside boats flying flags from Russia and Spain, but the Stars and Stripes waved for the largest fleet of whalers in the world. The local sloop *Acushnet,* sailing for the Pacific, gave Melville a place on its crew, and he soon began the expedition that inspired his masterpiece *Moby-Dick.*

While his captain acquired provisions and assembled a crew, the writer strolled along the streets. On slippery cobblestones that sloped down to the river, he passed odd-looking sailors from near and far: dark-skinned men from Cape Verde, blond-haired boys from the Netherlands, swarthy sailors from Portugal, dreaded cannibals from Fiji, tattooed natives from the South Seas, and runaway slaves newly arrived on the Underground Railroad from the South. With time on their hands before their ships set sail and their last prayers at the Seamen's Bethel yet unsaid, they roamed the shops, packed their pouches with tobacco, purchased razors, blankets, and mattresses stuffed with straw, stopped at the public houses to down some shots of rum, paid visits to the brothels, and slept at the Swordfish Inn or the Crossed Harpoon.

Along the bustling waterfront hundreds of men toiled on the boats. Caulkers, riggers, carpenters, and other craftsmen slogged for adventure, escape, and a share in the profits. Sweat oozed from the pores of the sailors as they off-loaded the casks of whale oil that lighted America's homes, lubricated its tools and instruments, and primed its paint and varnish. Salty language flowed from their lips as they lugged the whalebone that corseted and hoop-skirted the women, perfumed the ladies with ambergris, stayed the men's collars, handled the buggy whips and walking sticks, and entertained the children with chess pieces and piano keys. Whale oil was as valuable then as petroleum is now.

While the sailors hauled the barrels, the captains inspected their ships. On the top decks they checked the brick furnaces: as soon as the whales were caught, their blubber was burned down until it turned into oil. Squinting up at the crows' nests the men saw the lookouts high on the masts where sailors at sea could spot the whales. They thrilled recalling the words "Thar she blows!" and prayed they had the right answer when they returned from their expeditions. "What luck? Clean or greasy?" the owners always asked, hoping the barque was slick with oil.

As Melville walked along the wharves he passed blacksmiths, ironmongers, sail makers, and warehouses filled with supplies. A whaling trip took five hundred barrels of fresh water; fifty barrels of salt; seventy barrels of flour; one hundred gallons of molasses; four hundred pounds of coffee; four hundred pounds of sugar; and enough dried apples, pork, rice, beans, beef, butter, cheese, codfish, corn, raisins, potatoes, onions, liquor, tea, and tobacco to satisfy the hunger of twenty-five men for as long as forty-eight months. In addition, a ship needed spermaceti candles, linseed oil, pine board, pine nails, oak nails, gunpowder, copper sheathing, cordage, flags, bricks, lime, cotton, canvas, twine, tar, and paint to keep it seaworthy, harpoon the whales, and, four years later, return with the prize to New Bedford.

At the countinghouses nearby, clerks perched on high stools and, pencils in hand, leaning over account logs, entered the whalers' expenses and income. At the trading firm on Pleasant Street, whaling owners bought and sold commodities, hedging bets on the future cost of provisions and the price they might get for their goods. Close by at the fresh oyster stand on the wharf, the whalers swallowed the slippery oysters and slurped the juice, joined at lunchtime by men who manufactured steam engines, boilers, sewing machines, candles, or leather shoes, who sold insurance or dry goods, served as lawyers, published newspapers, or ran the banks.

Heading up from the waterfront and the railroad station built in Egyptian Revival style, Melville edged his way along the narrow streets. Pink-cheeked women in horse-drawn carriages rode by, while freed colored men, white men in well-cut suits, and Quakers in dull coats and wide-brimmed hats passed one another on the sidewalks. Inside the granite banks, clerks and officers welcomed dozens of men making deposits and others seeking loans to sow their businesses. In the small wooden shops the atmosphere bustled with women buying brocades from France, tea leaves from India, and spices from the Middle East. At Polly Johnson's popular store, girls and boys licked whipped-cream cakes while the colored owner helped them decide over chewy ginger cookies or candy sticks. In the back of the shop Frederick Douglass practiced a speech on abolition.

Farther up the hill stood the Lyceum, where Emerson delivered his lecture, and buildings of every sort, from the Unitarian church with its crenellated towers to the Quaker meetinghouse, simple and square, called congregants to prayer. Streets shaded by elms and horse chestnuts boasted gracious gardens and stately homes occupied by sea captains and shippers, manufacturers and merchants, bankers and businessmen, many of whom were members of the Society of Friends, the first settlers of New Bedford. Inside the Federal frame houses and the granite houses in Gothic or Greek Revival style where Methodists, Baptists, Unitarians, Catholics, and even a few Jews lived, fancy furniture and vivid silks embellished the rooms. But the stone house of Edward Mott Robinson and the Greek Revival of his father-in-law, Gideon Howland Jr., avoided show of any sort—no stripes or florals or gaudy colors; like their clothing, their plain Quaker homes lacked adornment.

Everyone in New Bedford, white or black, worldly or Quaker, had an interest in whaling. Whether it was a quarter, an eighth, or a thirty-second, they all bought a share in the expeditions. New Bedford residents owned more whaling ships than the people of any other town, and though the voyages might end in disaster—the ships lost at sea, destroyed by mutinies, or downed by storms—more often than not they brought home a bountiful return. One journey alone might bring back $100,000 in whales. It wasn't only Americans who bought the by-products of the giant mammals: seven million gallons of whale oil and two million pounds of whalebone were exported every year.

But ships could not be built, sailors could not be hired, supplies could not be purchased to launch a voyage without money from the banks. The Howland and Robinson families were a mainstay of whaling and banking: their agency, Isaac Howland Jr. and Company, owned more ships than any other in town, their banks made more loans than most, and their personal wealth ranked near the top. To New Englanders of every sort, prosperity was a virtue. To those in the Society of Friends, wealth was the visible sign of election by God. For Edward Mott Robinson, wealth was an obsession, a relentless pursuit of righteousness.

The shrewd, sagacious businessman held his money closely, followed the Quaker precepts, and attended the Quaker worship. Almost everyone he dealt with was Quaker. He trusted his brothers in commerce and knew he could rely on them for honesty and goodwill, candor and rectitude.

Seven years earlier in a quiet Quaker ceremony, Edward had married his partner's younger daughter, Abby Slocum Howland. Like the Jews who lived in nearby Newport, the closely knit Society of Friends prayed together, transacted business together, and married within their circle. Howlands, Hathaways, Rodmans, Rotches, Grinnells, and Pells: it was rare to find a family in which these names were not entwined. Nor was it easy to find a family without the given names of Isaac, Moses, or Samuel, Rachel, Rebecca, or Sarah. The Bible had its place in every house and daily readings ensured that family members could quote the Scriptures chapter and verse. Indeed, the Quakers cited them at their special meetings where they quelled their members' anger and helped them resolve disputes. Anger, they believed, was the cause of war. As conscientious objectors, they promoted peaceful coexistence.

Through their method of dialogue, they kept their members out of the law courts and kept their quarrels from spiraling outside their sphere. Their ministers and arbitrators, women as well as men, mediated family arguments and settled business feuds. All were equal in the eyes of the Friends, and women played an important role in religious and business affairs. Independent and often outspoken, they ran their own meetings, made their own decisions, and frequently managed their own businesses.

As self-sufficient as they may have been, Quaker women were expected to be obedient wives, but even as a newlywed in 1834, Abby Howland Robinson was more diffident than most. She deferred to her husband, Edward Robinson, in every way. Other women may have voiced their opinions quietly, but Abby shriveled in his presence and quivered at his word.

Dressed in the dull, dark clothes and small white cap that distinguished her as a Quaker, she walked meekly beside him on Seventh Days as they went together to the meetinghouse. They entered the building through their separate entrances, took their places on the long, hard benches, Brother Robinson with the men, Sister Robinson with the women, and faced the small group of elders and ministers perched on a raised bench in the front. A blanket of quiet silenced the hall. No prayers were read, no reverend preached, no choir rang out. Restless children squirmed, their parents frowned, and the young ones settled down in the stillness. Heads covered and bowed, the congregants focused: they centered their thoughts, and searched for the light inside.

Slowly, someone rose and removed his hat; spurred on by the spirit within, he began to talk. Restrained at first, he spoke in a quiet voice, and as his courage increased, his voice grew firm, his words gained strength. Then, when the spirit faded and the words no longer flowed, he took his seat and covered his head again. More time went by. More stillness filled the air. More children squirmed. More parents frowned. Again a Friend stood up, spoke as the spirit moved him, and sat down. So it went: male and female, young and old. Sometimes the speakers trembled. Sometimes passion poured forth. Sometimes silence prevailed. Sometimes Edward Robinson spoke. Rarely would Abby utter a word. An hour later two of the elders stood and shook hands, the signal the meeting was over.

Afterward, it was the Quaker tradition for the Robinsons to join Abby's family for dinner at her father's house. A lively widower who had once captained a whaling ship, Gideon Howland had taken a cousin, Mehatable, as his bride, but she died soon after the birth of Abby, their second child. With no one to care for his young children, Gideon moved in with his father-in-law, Isaac Howland, and continued to live with the late Isaac's second wife, Ruth.

Gideon's older daughter, Sylvia, physically weak from a spinal problem at birth, had been spurned by Edward Robinson in favor of her younger sister. Strong-willed and outspoken, Sylvia remained a spinster in the house with Gideon. While the widow Ruth concentrated on running the household and overseeing the servants, twenty-eight-year-old Sylvia, well known for her quick tongue and lack of charm, fought for control. Every few years she changed her will.

The family slipped into their seats in the dining room and bowed their heads in silent grace, then dined at the polished wood table. New Englanders savored the fresh fish caught daily in their waters and the fruits and vegetables they stored all year: steamed scallops; fried clams; oyster chowder thick with pork, potatoes, onions, and peas; corn bread; and apple crisp thick with rich cream. Although the meal was plentiful, the talk at the Howland table was terse. Gideon's insobriety added to the tension. Emotions simmered under the Quaker silence. Below the smiles of serenity, Abby and Sylvia stewed over sibling jealousies; Ruth and Sylvia bristled over their turf.

While the family chewed in silence, Edward did little to ease the strain. He and Sylvia eyed each other suspiciously: he, certain she was trying to sabotage him; she, convinced he was after the family fortune. Consumed by wealth and the intent to increase his means, he admitted that "making money was the great object" of his life. He pursued his fortune like Ahab pursued the great white whale.

Ordinarily, he focused his thinking on commerce and calculated his talk: the new building his partner Gideon just put up on the riverfront; the arrival of one of their ships; the price that whale oil was bringing. But now with his wife in a family way, his dreams floated toward his future son.

They had no doubt their firstborn would be a boy and they would call him Isaac. He would carry with pride his father's deep Rhode Island roots and his mother's Mayflower ancestry. Robinson took satisfaction in knowing his son would inherit both the wealth and the pedigrees. It wouldn't be long before he would take the young boy down to the Howland wharves, where he would educate him in the intricacies of enterprise: he would teach him how to read the ledgers at the countinghouse; he would pat him on the back when the young man bargained well for a captain and crew; he would swell with pride when his son squeezed the profits as he did.

It was the duty of every heir, Robinson believed, to increase the family riches. With that in mind, he would teach his boy to loan at interest and tell him never to borrow a cent. "Never owe anyone anything. Not even a kindness," he always preached. Kindness rarely entered his world. How well his wife discovered this when, on November 21, 1834, instead of a son, Abby delivered a baby girl. They named her Hetty Howland Robinson.

Devastated by the birth of this child, Robinson insisted upon a male heir. Before the infant Hetty was nine months old, Abby's stomach swelled again with child. Once more the future danced before Edward Robinson, and this time his dreams came true. Once more he saw himself mentoring the future entrepreneur, teaching him the secrets of stocks and bonds, commodities, profit and loss. But if disappointment befell him when his firstborn turned out to be a girl, Robinson seethed when his second born, Isaac, died at a few weeks of age.

In the graveyard of the Quaker meetinghouse they buried their infant Isaac. But they could not bury Edward Robinson's anger. His wife, fearful of his rage and depressed over her loss, took to her bed. Edward fumed at his fate, Abby sobbed in her pillow, and both rejected their only child. Like the biblical Ishmael, the unwanted Hetty was cast aside. Dismissed from the house, she was sent to live with her grandfather Gideon.

Chapter 2

A Polished Reflection

A house is a tangible object, a stack of bricks or stone or wood; but home is ethereal, a sense of comfort and protection, a feeling of belonging. Hetty never belonged. Not in her parents' house. Not in her grandfather's dwelling. Gideon's stone house shivered with the frost of personal feuds that not even a little girl could melt. Backs stiffened, lips pursed, the dry-breasted women passed each other in silence and often ignored the child. Though they may have wanted to help her, they had little comprehension of her needs.

Like a wounded animal afraid of being hurt again, the girl snapped at the smallest slight and threw tantrums whenever she felt unloved. Her aunt Sylvia, who took on the role of surrogate mother, had neither the patience nor the physical strength to care for her; Ruth, older and worn from raising Isaac's daughters, became her grandmother and arranged a place in her room for Hetty to sleep. When she was sick, Ruth nursed her back to health; the rest of the time a servant sent by Abby looked after the child.

As Hetty grew up, a tutor schooled her in the ABCs. The girl was quick with numbers and good at reading, and she caught her grandfather's notice. A man with a fleet at sea needed the latest information, from shipping rates in London to the price that oil fetched in Peru, from yields on bonds to the price of common stocks. With his eyesight failing, he snapped open the evening newspapers, handed them to Hetty, and asked her to read aloud. In her child's voice she called out the stock quotations and commerce reports, warming her grandfather's heart. And sometimes when he needed help with his correspondence, he called on her. That was how she absorbed some of his business methods, she later said. That was when he told her she would inherit some of his money.

But "Uncle Gid," as he was called by all, had a penchant for drink and a thirst for fun that often kept him away. Hurt and in need of attention, young Hetty, her nostrils flared, her eyes burning, screamed and stamped her feet in fits of temper that threw the women into a tailspin. Most of the time they relented, but once in a while they refused, and the girl hobbled off like an injured bird and retreated to her parents' house, searching for love where none existed.

Quakers viewed anger as a distraction to be mastered. Along with music, dancing, theater, and romantic fiction, it diverted a person from the spirit inside. How lucky the men, whose anger propelled them in their pursuit of money. How unlucky the women, forced to suppress their rage; and how often it emerged in nervous conditions.

Too weak, too busy with doctors to pay attention to Hetty, Abby left it to her husband, who used the Quaker silence to rein his daughter in. Thrifty with words, thrifty with money, thrifty in spirit, he had little time for her temper. "Hetty, daughter, art thee angry?" he asked. If she answered, "Yes," he told her not to speak for fifteen minutes. At the end of that time he asked again. "Art thee angry?" If she said yes, he told her not to speak for an hour. At the end of the hour, if her anger remained, he told her to stay silent for three hours, and if she still proved stubborn, she was forbidden to speak until morning.

But her father's rebukes failed to keep her down. The admonitions may have stifled her mother, but they could not muffle her. Young Hetty's rage exploded when she was sent to the dentist alone. She howled at the unfamiliar doctor who ordered her into the strange chair, and she howled even more when he forced the cold metal instruments into her mouth. While another young patient, William Crapo, sat in the waiting room, she screamed for help and screamed to get out of the chair, but no family member rushed to her side; only a servant tried to calm her with a shiny coin, which he promised had come from her mother.

If money equaled affection, Hetty grasped the equation. At the age of eight, dressed in her plain Quaker clothes, she gathered the precious coins she had saved from her weekly allowance, asked the Howland driver to hitch up the horses, and rode into town. As they approached the big brick savings bank, the child jumped out of the carriage, marched up the steps to the building, poured out her money onto the cashier's desk, and opened an account. Not only did she earn compounded interest, she made her family proud. It was a story they told to friends in town and to those who gathered at Round Hills, the Howland farmstead.

Seven miles south of New Bedford, a well-trodden dirt path led away from the stench of whale oil and toward the briny air of the sea. Travelers passed farm fields and fruit orchards before they arrived at the high stone walls that protected the sheep meadows and grassy fields rolling down to the edge of Buzzard's Bay. The wooden house with gabled roofs and dormer windows that stood on a hundred acres was Sylvia's much-loved summer home and Hetty's favorite place to escape. Here she practiced driving a carriage, learned to ride side-saddle, and even splashed in the sea.

The highlight of every summer came when scores of Howlands gathered for a family reunion. The frugal Quakers, who all chipped in to share the costs of the day, drew deep breaths of fresh air and caught up with their kinfolk while they inspected the familiar grounds; Hetty and the other children raced one another across the silvery fields, rode through the paddocks, and barreled down the big hill. As the day progressed and their hunger built, the crowd of adults and youngsters moved to the top of the rise, where they listened in silence as one of their own read from Scripture. Then, making their way inside the big tent set up for the occasion, with the crockery paid for by the participants and the camp chairs donated by cousin Moses Grinnell, they sat down to a feast of good, substantial food—roast turkey, cooked beef, lots of bread and fruit pies—followed by cigars for the men and a round of postprandial speeches for all. The summers lingered in her memory, but the joy that Hetty felt disappeared in the fall of her tenth year.

There was no feast at Eliza Wing's establishment in Sandwich,

Massachusetts. But there was plenty of Scripture. It was painful enough that once again she was cast from the house. Now she was sent to the strict boarding school to keep her from being spoiled. The girl arrived to find a miserly course of fare. The money her family paid for her tuition helped cover the cost for the poorer girls who attended. There were no generous meals, or pretty clothes, or comfortable rooms. Quaker discipline and the Disciples ruled her nights and days.

The school required that she read three chapters of the Bible every day and five chapters on Sunday. At the end of the year, when she had finished reading it all, she could put down the book and close it. The regime was no less severe when she sat down to eat. At her first dinner, the food set before her looked dry, and when she asked for something to drink, she was given only a glass of skimmed milk. The outspoken Hetty remarked on the fresh food and thick cream on the Howland table and refused what was on her plate. "Skimmed milk," she recalled later. "Skimmed milk when pitchers of cream were set on our table at home as a matter of course." When the same plate of tasteless food appeared at supper, she was too hungry to turn it down and managed to chew half. When the remainder was put in front of her the following morning at breakfast, she swallowed hard and learned her lesson.

The classroom instruction did not go down any easier. The rote memorization and long lists of dates left her with little interest in literature, history, science, or even spelling. But the memories of the girls too poor to pay their own way and the Quaker values of justice and thrift stayed with her. She treated everyone, rich or poor, as equals, and guarded her pennies as others would guard their gold.

The only relief from the harsh routine at Eliza Wing's came during school vacations. Back in New Bedford her grandfather's zest for life kept the family alert. Yet even they were surprised when Gideon purchased the first piano in town. Music may have been forbidden by the Society of Friends, but like so many people, Uncle Gid made his own deals with God. In the dark of night, when the neighbors' curtains were drawn, he ordered the upright carried into the house and up to the third floor. Hetty found delight in running her fingers over the smooth ivory keys.

It was not to the delight of Hetty's mother, however. The dour Abby Robinson frowned at such frivolities. On a day when Abby was well enough to join the family and attend a Seventh Day meeting, Hetty invited some friends to gather at the house. While one of the girls played the piano, they all sang the words to a popular song:

The monkey married the baboon's sister,
Smacked his lips and then he kissed her.

Laughing uproariously, the girls heard no hint of Hetty's mother when, unexpected and fresh from the meetinghouse, she stamped up the stairs and rushed into the room. Her dull Quaker coat buttoned neck to hem, her hair parted flat, wrapped in buns capped in white crochet, she fixed her piercing blue eyes on Mary Swift and demanded that she stop. "Take thy music, thy person and thy furbelows and be gone!" she ordered. "When next we want music, we will call thee." Flabbergasted, the girl grabbed the music, gathered up her petticoats, and fled, the two other girls racing down the stairs behind her. Hetty suffered her mother's displeasure alone.

At least she could laugh with Grandfather Gideon. He joked with the local youths, teased them to catch him and tie his shoes, and tippled a little too much. But the laughter stopped when the old man took ill and died. They laid him to rest and wished him peace. But his Quaker daughter and mother-in-law, far from coexisting in the manner of Friends, wanted to live apart. With money from her inheritance, Sylvia bought Ruth's share of the house, the furnishings, and the horses and said farewell. The widow who had brought up Abby and Sylvia moved to a nearby town. Faced with the idea of living alone with her aunt, Hetty returned to her parents' house for school vacations.

The two main beneficiaries of Gideon Howland's estate were his daughters, Abby and Sylvia; Hetty's portion went to her mother. While Abby sobbed in her bed, Sylvia collected her share of the profits and, through her adviser Thomas Mandell, the third partner in the Isaac Howland firm, cannily invested some of her funds. When her cousin Joseph Grinnell, a congressman and successful merchant shipper, created Wamsutta Mills, she was one of his major backers. The first company to manufacture cotton textiles in New Bedford, it became one of the largest cotton producers in the country.

Intelligent and aware, Sylvia showed a concern for women and an interest in business and books. But confined primarily to her home, she resented her debility and used it as a means of control. Hetty rebelled against the restraints imposed on her and wrestled constantly for her independence.

The one who gained the most from Gideon's death was his son-in-law, Edward Robinson. The man whom one local called "the very Napoleon of our little business community" not only became the head partner of the Howland whaling firm, he also controlled his wife's money and her share of the business. With unrelenting aggression and astute investing, he increased their assets enormously.

For all her good works, Sylvia's dreary existence hardly served as inspiration for a young girl in search of a way of life. Instead, Hetty turned to her father. Though it was said he "squeezed a penny till the eagle squawked," he was known for his cunning and boldness. Called by the nickname "Black Hawk," Edward Robinson ran the company and controlled its affairs, and presided over the Bedford Commercial Bank. He was the one Hetty chose to emulate.

Despite his frugality, he took part in local activities and won the town's respect. When Joseph Grinnell ran for a third term in Congress in 1848, it was Edward Robinson who nominated him at the Whig convention in Worcester, Massachusetts. Following the convention, it was Edward who helped welcome Congressman Abraham Lincoln to New Bedford when he spoke at Liberty Hall. After they dined, Lincoln slept at Joseph's home.

As her father's anger subsided, the adolescent Hetty stayed closer to his side. Sometimes she nestled next to him in his sleigh, a buffalo blanket covering them both as they ripped around New Bedford, her father making their horse go faster than any other in town. Other times, dressed in worn old clothes with nary a hint of their riches, they walked together through the warehouses. She watched him closely as he assessed the inventory, inspected the ships, dealt with the captains, and heard the rough talk of the crews. She listened to him bargain with merchants and berate them when he thought they were charging too much. She followed along when he took her to the countinghouse and showed her how to read the ledgers, or brought her to the brokers and taught her how to trade commodities. She paid attention when he repeated again and again that property was a trust to be taken care of and enlarged for future generations. She obeyed when he insisted that she keep her own accounts in order and later praised the experience. "There is nothing better than this sort of training," she said. A girl "acquires the habit of keeping track of every cent and gets the most value for every dollar she spends." Knowing how frugal and fond of money he was, she imitated her father's ways. Slowly, she flourished and felt she was gaining his approval.

She joined him as a regular for lunch at the Central Union co-op, where the floor was covered in sawdust and the air smelled of strong food. With little regard for her clothes, she plunked herself on one of the wooden barrels and munched on pickles and chunks of yellow cheese. While her father traded stories with the other men, who all owned shares in the store, the attractive young girl with intense blue eyes and red lips laughed along with them. Her long limbs and buxom figure drew their admiring glances.

At her father's house, when his eyesight began to fail, she read him the evening news from the *Boston Herald* and *New York Tribune*. When she asked questions, he took the time to explain, teaching her the meaning of stocks and bonds, bulls and bears, commodities and market fluctuations. With more to gain in New Bedford than at the school in Sandwich, at the age of fifteen, Hettie H. Robinson (as she spelled her name at the time) enrolled in the summer session at the local Quaker school.

The principal design of the Friends Academy was "to diffuse useful knowledge," "to guard the morals of the youth," and "to encourage piety and religion in their progress in literature." It was only recently that the Quaker students had won permission to read Shakespeare and Rousseau, but Erasmus Darwin's *Botanic Garden,* Locke's essays, and Gibbon's *Roman Empire* were all required, along with spelling, composition, penmanship, and calisthenics. For two years, Hetty joined the girls in her class as they sat through tedious lessons, took turns ringing the bell, swept the floors, and kept the fires kindled.

Despite the school's attempts, Hetty's interest in academics, as well as her terrible spelling, showed no sign of improvement. The language she heard on the docks rolled from her lips as easily as from a sailor's; what's more, her appearance was scruffy, and her clothes, approved by her father, were disheveled and shabby. In the judgment of the neat and resolute Sylvia, the Howland/Robinson family's only heir required some refinement. Hetty was reaching the age of marriage, and with the family fortune at stake, her aunt was concerned that she lacked the ability to attract the right kind of man. If Sylvia could not enjoy a better life herself, at least she could help her niece attain it.

Anna Cabot Lowell gave considerable thought to the education of girls. Religion and fulfillment of the soul, she said, deserved equal time with the scholarly pursuit of algebra, astronomy, Cicero, and Milton. But a young woman also had an obligation to learn how to run a household, nurture children, and engage in social intercourse. At the finishing school she ran for fashionable girls in Boston, Hetty's family paid twenty dollars per quarter to give her the chance to engage in her studies, develop her penmanship, practice the piano, and perfect her needlework. The school was given the chance to turn a rough mollusk into a cultured pearl.

In part it worked. From nine in the morning till two in the afternoon there were sessions in geography, English history, and biography, and discussions, too, about new novels. If they read *Moby-Dick,* Hetty could enlighten her classmates with her personal knowledge of whales and whaling ships. But when they studied *Uncle Tom's Cabin,* it was the tragedy of one particular girl that really brought home the plight of the slaves.

It took a long time before the girls stopped talking about their classmate who had gone home for her father's funeral in the South. Unbeknownst to her fellow students, the girl was a mulatto who passed for white; she had been sent north by her slave-owning father to live as a member of his family. After her father's death when she went back south, she assumed she would be accepted as a freed slave. But her father's brother thought otherwise: he claimed her as his legal inheritance. Devastated at the thought of being a slave, the girl committed suicide. It was a tragedy that tore at the hearts of her classmates.

Nonetheless, as adolescents do, the girls put aside their sadness and managed to amuse themselves. They took walks in the Boston Commons, just a few blocks from school, and paid visits to Faneuil Hall. They heard arias by the Swedish opera star Jenny Lind at the Boston Musical Hall and went to teas at the homes of friends. Hetty's brusque manner showed through in her reply to an invitation from the wife of her father's business associate. "Shall we have the pleasure of your company to tea this afternoon to meet some of your young friends," asked Lydia Swain, adding, "A happy New Year to you— and to your Aunt and Mother." Hetty dispatched her response with little grace: "I can not expect to accept your kind invitation on account of sickness. Mother and Aunt's regards," she wrote.

Along with the city's most proper youth, Hetty took classes at Lorenzo Papanti's Dance Studio, where the thin, glossy-wigged count, wearing patent-leather pumps, taught them how to move and how to comport themselves. Under his wary eye, the students stifled a giggle now and then and learned to dance. "Point your toe, Miss Robinson!" Papanti might call out, and if Miss Robinson did not point her toe properly, the fiery teacher would rap her foot with his fiddle bow. "Back straight, Mr. Cabot!" he might say to another, and if the student did not draw himself up with his back erect, Papanti would drum the bow on his spine.

Not only were the students taught to dance, they learned how to conduct themselves at parties and balls. The rules were strict: a gentleman must bow when asking a lady to dance; he must not ask the same girl to dance twice; he should not take a seat next to a young lady he did not know; if he walked someone home after a ball, he must not enter her house, but should call on her the following day.

As for the ladies, they must remember not to hold hands or fraternize with favored men; must not refuse to dance with any gentleman; must not dance more than once with the same partner. The worst, as one woman complained, was the rule for moving about the room: "A woman, old or young, may not stir from her seat to get supper, or avoid a draught, or change places for a better view, without being annexed to the arm of some member of the selecting sex for whom she must wait or whistle."

Hetty polished her etiquette, pointed her toes, and stiffened her spine. Dressed in her best frock, dancing shoes, and long white gloves, she held her partner lightly as they stepped across the ballroom floor in a polka, a waltz, or a quadrille. Over the months the studio's big mirrors reflected her progress from a stomping adolescent to a graceful young woman.

It showed when the effulgent New Bedford debutante first appeared in public in 1854. With a wreath of flowers in her curly hair, a black velvet ribbon around her neck, and filigreed gold balls dancing at her ears, she held her hooped petticoats and curtsied in a white muslin dress. Her twinkling eyes and rosy complexion, robust figure and quick retorts dazzled the eligible young men.

Hetty did little to encourage them. When a starry-eyed suitor came to the family hardware store where she sometimes worked, he cast an eager glance as she lifted her skirts to climb the stairs, hoping for a glimpse of her graceful ankles. But the stars in his eyes nearly turned to tears when he beheld the sight of her ragged stockings hanging about her calves.

She may have been unmoved by the smitten young man, but the choice of husbands was slim in New Bedford and their bank accounts were even slimmer, compared to those of Hetty's family. No daughter of Edward Robinson and no niece of Sylvia Howland would marry beneath herself. Her mother's cousin Henry Grinnell, Joseph's brother, had moved with his wife to a bigger city where the chances of meeting the right man were far greater. Arrangements were made, and with a deposit of $1,200 placed in a special bank account, her father took her down to the waterfront and wished her well. Giving her orders to embellish her wardrobe, he waved goodbye as she climbed aboard an overnight steamer and set off alone for New York.

Chapter 3

A City of Riches

Rich, hemmed thick all around with sail ships and steamships . . . crowded streets, high growths of iron . . . the houses of business of the ship-merchants and the money-brokers . . . the carts hauling goods, the manly race of drivers of horses. . . . City of hurried and sparkling waters! City of spires and masts! City nested in bays! My city!"

Hetty awoke in the morning to Walt Whitman's beloved city, "Mannahatta": a hustling, bustling whirlwind of carts, wagons, hansom cabs, hackney coaches, and horse-drawn omnibuses clattering and clopping on the cobblestones, a cacophony of sounds ricocheting against the iron and stone buildings crammed together on the lower Manhattan streets. Hammers rang against stones as workers constructed new buildings, and all around, old structures moaned under crumbling blows.

New York was celebrating a financial boom. New institutions were opening on every corner, filling the canyons of Wall Street with retail banks, commercial banks, insurance companies, and brokerage firms. Investors in mining, real estate, and transportation were flush with funds. Eager to spend their new wealth, they were tearing down old buildings as fast as they could and putting up new ones so frequently that *Harper's Magazine* complained the city was unrecognizable for anyone born forty years before. Walt Whitman called it a "rabid, feverish itching for change."

Newly rich couples filled extravagant mansions with fabulous furnishings and installed bathrooms with hot and cold running water on every floor. Those who earned $10,000 a year and wanted a place in society were expected to have a big new house, a country place, a carriage, and a box at the opera, and, of course, to play host to lavish parties and balls.

Welcomed at the boat pier on the Hudson River, Hetty settled herself and her bags in the carriage and rode across town. The city founders had "the novel plan of numbering the streets," noted Isabella Bird, an English traveler visiting at the time. The carriage rolled along the cobblestones, past the posh new Brevoort Hotel at Fifth Avenue and Ninth Street to the older part of town where the streets had names: past the well-paved avenue of Broadway, burgeoning with shops and theaters; past the stately Greek Revival houses of Colonnade Row that were home to Vanderbilts, Astors, and Delanos; past the Society Library on Astor Place where members like Herman Melville borrowed books; past the new Astor Library, free to the public, on Lafayette Place; and on to the Grinnells' Greek Revival townhouse at the corner of Bond Street and Lafayette.

The city's swells might be marching uptown to newer neighborhoods, but successful merchants like the Van Cortlandts, the Tredwells (proud descendants of John Alden and Priscilla Mullens), and the Henry Grinnells (his brother Moses had moved uptown) still maintained their homes downtown, just a few blocks away from Grace Church, where the upper crust still worshipped.

No one challenged the status of Henry Grinnell and his wife, Sarah Minturn Grinnell. Henry and his two brothers had left behind their Quaker restrictions and made their mark on the world. Joseph, the oldest, had prospered in New York in merchant shipping before he served in Congress and started Wamsutta Mills.

Their younger brother Moses arrived in the city at the age of fifteen to make his fortune in the family business, completed one term in Congress, presided over the Chamber of Commerce of New York, and served on the commission helping to create Central Park. Not only did he have one of the finest wine cellars in the city, it was said he knew every important and influential person in New York. His wife was the niece of the author Washington Irving.

Henry Grinnell, whose intimate friends included the Whig senators Henry Clay and Daniel Webster, joined his brother Moses in the family's prestigious merchant shipping firm, Grinnell and Minturn. Owners of the famous clipper ship *Flying Cloud,* they were the largest shippers and consignors of whale oil, and were business colleagues of Edward Robinson in New Bedford. Henry Grinnell, a passionate student of geography and generous patron of Arctic explorations, distinguished himself as founder and first president of the American Geographical Society. When Hetty arrived, the latest expedition with his sponsorship was under way, one that would commemorate him in a book and immortalize him on maps when the ship's crew named a piece of Alaska "Grinnell Land."

With her own mother and aunt unable to help her, and with social rules allotting her just three years to become affianced, Henry and Sarah Grinnell invited the girl for her debut season in New York. Sarah, from a prominent merchant shipping family and the mother of four, had recently steered her oldest daughter, Sarah Minturn, into a successful marriage celebrated with a wedding at home. Now she offered to take this young cousin under her wing. She and her married daughter would guide the girl through an endless sea of social calls, teas, parties, dances, and balls, and serve as her chaperone as they scouted for appropriate men. With their help, Hetty would sail through the rigid rounds with grace and dignity. But Hetty did not always follow the prevailing winds.

Early in the morning upper-crust ladies began their routine, a regime repeated around town from Greenwich Village to Gramercy Park. While husbands set off for their offices, stopping first to order the household food at the market in Tompkins Square, the women prepared for their day.

After breakfast in the downstairs family room and a leisurely look at the newspapers, instructions were given to the Irish maids. They were to scrub the floors and ovens in the kitchen; clean the coal ashes from the fireplace grates; trim the wicks and fill all the lamps with oil; polish the furniture and dust the ground-floor front parlor, back room, and study, and do the same for the upstairs bedrooms and sitting rooms; wash and iron the clothes; knead and bake the breads for the family and the cakes and sweets for visitors; prepare and cook dinner by 2 p.m., when the head of the house would join them, and ready a supper with high tea later on, or if company was expected, prepare the many courses for a formal dinner to be served at six o'clock.

Their directives noted, the ladies clambered upstairs, where the maids had prepared the hot water in the new tin tubs connected to the city's water supply. As they bathed they could hear the noises in the street below: "Glass put in! Glass put in!" an old man shouted, while a fishmonger blew on a tin horn. A few minutes later a voice might call out, "Pots and pans! Pots and pans! Mend your pots and pans!" and another, "Rags for sale!" "I buy old rags!" All day long men came down the street offering their services: One rang a bell to announce he was the knife grinder, another rang to say that he ground horseradish. One blew his whistle to let everyone know he had pigeons for sale, another shouted that he mended umbrellas. And throughout the day horse hoofs clopped, carts clacked, and drivers shouted at the traffic.

Above the fray, as the women slowly dressed, their maids pulled the laces tight on their corsets, held their hooped underskirts for them to step into, and gently lowered the ruffled dresses over their heads. Downstairs, swaddled in fur-trimmed shawls and fur muffs, with French bonnets and veils firmly tied, the ladies set off in the snapping cold.

Snuggled under their lap robes, they rode in the parade of carriages up Broadway, ducking when they heard the warning bells of the horse-drawn railway cars thundering down the avenue. At Tiffany's, Brooks Brothers, and Lord & Taylor, they dashed in to inspect the fancy goods and bargain over the prices. When one Englishwoman gasped at the price of a diamond wristlet and asked, "Who would purchase a trinket costing 5,000 pounds?" the salesman shrugged. "I guess some Southerner would buy it for his wife," he said.

At A. T. Stewart's marble palace, the city's most talked-about new shop, they marveled at the huge domed skylight and five-story circular court and joined the crowd of women excited to watch a fashion show. As they fingered soft fabrics from Europe or asked the cost of a flounce of lace, the handsome young salesman, one of dozens in the specialized departments around the store, would inform them that, in contrast to other shops, here the prices were fixed. No one seemed to mind; the cash registers jingled as customers spent more than $15,000 a day. Little did anyone know that one day A. T. Stewart's would borrow money from Hetty.

Outside, a promenade of ladies in French bonnets and rich silk dresses under their cloaks strolled by, more elegant than those seen in a week in Hyde Park, said an English visitor. Businessmen, more frantic to make money than businessmen anywhere else in the world, rushed past at a dizzying pace, slipping in the slush of mud on the cobblestone streets. Sidestepping men who carried sandwich-board signs on their backs, the crowd tried to avoid the flood of pamphlets and fliers pushed into their hands. In the shop windows, handwritten notices advertised goods, and posters shouted the arrival of new businesses and theatrical performances. Everywhere the noise of carts and horses and angry drivers shattered the air.

If downtown was crowded with shoppers, far uptown at the edge of the city, behind the Croton Reservoir at Fortieth Street and Fifth Avenue, the streets were packed with sightseers. The Crystal Palace, all glass and iron, beckoned visitors to reach its heights, its steam-powered elevator, invented by Mr. Otis, ready to loft them to the top for spectacular views of the city. At night, its mass of lights glowed like lanterns with Oriental elegance. In the daytime, guests gazed at the finest French tapestries and porcelains and English silver and earthen-ware, along with Italian, Dutch, and German treasures. A pale copy of the Crystal Palace in London, it nonetheless showed Americans the miracles of art, science, and mechanics. The huge display—"a modern wonder," said Whitman—gave millions of people a glimpse of the future.

After they lunched with husbands and children, society ladies were off in their carriages again on the obligatory round of calls. For a quick stop at one house, they held their long skirts and climbed the steep steps to the front door, nodded to the parlor maid who answered, and advancing no farther than the vestibule, dropped an engraved card on the silver tray, then left. But at the homes of friends or neighbors like the Tredwells, they presented their card and asked to see the lady of the house. A quick glimpse in the hall mirror to check their hair, and they were ushered into the front parlor. While they sat on the new French sofa waiting for their hostess to come down, they took in the furnishings of the room. Their eyes darted from the whale-oil lamps on the marble mantel over the fireplace to the bronze gas chandelier hanging from the high ceiling, to the square piano and the French carpet woven to look like Roman frescoes. A ten-minute chat with their friend, some good gossip, a critique of the nine-course dinner party they attended the night before, and they were off again in their carriages. A few blocks away they stopped for tea with a dowager, a chance for the young debutante to say a few clever words; a nod from their hostess could only help.

In the evenings, they attended theaters such as Wallack's on Broadway and chuckled at Lester Wallack, starring in the new English comedy *The Bachelor of Arts,* or they went for a more thought-provoking production at the National Theater, where *Uncle Tom's Cabin* was playing to packed houses, and every night the audience sobbed over Little Eva's plight. At the Broadway Tabernacle, Theodore Eisfeld conducted the Philharmonic Society, and at Metropolitan Hall or the Astor Opera House the sopranos sang while audience members pulled out their opera glasses and spied on one another.

The only thing New Yorkers enjoyed more than making money was dancing, and the most important events were the season's parties, dances, and balls. Hetty's cousin William, just three years older, might accompany her, but his mother or his sister always chaperoned, while their husbands sometimes stayed home.

As their carriages drew up to the townhouse and the men jumped down, the ladies alighted, climbing up the front stoop and following the rest of the women up the carpeted stairs to their hostess's bedroom. Adding their coats and capes to the pile on the bed, they removed their heavy boots, slipped on their dainty shoes, and turned their attention to the mirror. All around Hetty, small cliques of women who had grown up, gone to school, or summered together laughed and whispered knowingly as they smoothed their hair and pinched their cheeks to make them pink. A glance at Hetty showed them a tall young woman with blue eyes and peach complexion, dressed in a smart new gown. Handsome, yes. But an outsider, decidedly. Even the most attractive young woman might lose her confidence in their midst.

They smiled at their men, who waited outside the door and escorted them down. In the drawing room, exchanging pleasantries, everyone seemed to know everyone, except for the young girl from out of town. If dancing followed the supper, the ladies were asked for a waltz or a polka, but only the best were invited to do the quadrille.

It could be a long evening for a young woman from New Bedford, but the sparkling Hetty was often asked to dance.

Hostesses sent an endless stream of invitations for dances, costume parties, and masked balls, but without a doubt, the event of the year was given by Mrs. William Schermerhorn. The current rage was for fancy dress balls where costumes ranged from nuns and devils to Ivanhoes and harlequins. The craze was declared "insane and incoherent" by George Templeton Strong, the Wall Street lawyer on everyone's invitation list.

Mrs. Schermerhorn announced something different: a themed costume ball in the style of Louis XV. Important households fluttered with excitement as the women studied paintings of French palace life, men wondered what to do about their whiskers in the clean-shaven court, and everyone ordered their seamstresses in Paris to stitch up clothes like those worn in the mid-eighteenth century.

The night of the ball, a long line of hansom carriages with liveried coachmen drew up in front of the Schermerhorn mansion on Great Jones Street. Servants dressed in court costumes and white wigs welcomed the six hundred guests, the cream of the city's fashionable set. Astors, Aspinwalls, Brevoorts, Rhinelanders, and Knickerbockers gushed when they saw the dark, heavy interior transformed into a light and fanciful Versailles. The walls shimmered in their coats of wedding-cake white with gold trim, the crystal chandeliers glittered over graceful rococo furnishings, vases and baskets burst with elaborate flower arrangements, and gilded mirrors reflected the spectacularly costumed guests.

Merchants, lawyers, and real estate tycoons ordinarily seen in tall hats, high pointed shirt collars, shapeless black waistcoats, and black broadcloth frock coats—"a fearful sight," according to Walt Whitman—became Louis XV or his courtiers for the night. Their heads covered in powdered wigs nipped at the nape with velvet bows, they waltzed in with long panniered coats and frilly shirts, lace cravats and lace cuffs spilling out from under their embroidered coat sleeves. On their limbs they showed off silk stockings and satin breeches; on their hips some carried sheathed swords.

The rich businessmen's wives and daughters, transformed into aristocrats, dazzled with their diamonds and colored jewels. Hairdressers had worked for hours arranging their huge wigs, curled and powdered to perfection, and on their faces they had carefully painted beauty marks. Fluttering their fans, bending this way and that to show off their swelling breasts, they pirouetted in their broad panniers and ruffled satin gowns, each a perfect Madame Pompadour.

To make the occasion more memorable, the costumed musicians played the German cotillion, and guests arranged in small circles followed the intricate calls as they paired, flirted, parted, and paired with someone else. Two hours of the German cotillion: unheard of! Supper offered an extravagance of crystal and silver gleaming on crisp white damask: a banquet table laden with creamed soups, plump oysters, jellied fish, roasted meats, citrus sorbets, sweetmeats, rich cakes, and spun sugar confections. Everyone pronounced the Schermerhorn ball a triumph. It would be remembered for years to come.

While Mrs. Schermerhorn drew accolades for her party, one of the guests, her husband's cousin Caroline, was beginning to stir some interest of her own. Four years older than Hetty Robinson, Caroline Schermerhorn grew up just a few doors down from the Grinnells in a family of wealth and lineage. With a childhood that was the polar opposite of Hetty's, "Lina" enjoyed the role of family pet. The youngest of eight, she was fussed over as an infant by a slew of nurses and nannies, was schooled by a French tutor, spent weeks every year in Europe, and was introduced to society at a ball in her parents' stately home. Then, only a few months before Mrs. Schermerhorn's ball, at the age of twenty-four, the plain-faced and pudgy Lina married William Backhouse Astor Jr., heir to the vast fur and real estate fortune. Their posh wedding at Grace Church raised more than a few eyebrows. Did she do it for money? gossipers asked. And why did he marry her?

In a prenuptial agreement, it was later revealed that William received a trust fund from his parents with $185,000 in securities plus income from property at Fifth Avenue and Thirty-fourth Street, site of the future Empire State Building; the agreement stipulated that after his death, Caroline would receive $75,000 a year for life.

Descended from two of the earliest Dutch families in New York—a seventh-generation Van Cortland on her mother's side and fourth-generation Schermerhorn on her father's side—Lina knew the old Knickerbocker maxim "Live handsomely but not lavishly." But she felt otherwise. She was developing a taste for Parisian gowns by designers such as Worth, precious jewels with aristocratic provenance, a box at the opera, and parties on a lavish scale. Her husband could provide it all. And she could provide him with a pedigree.

William Astor grew up in a family obsessed with making money. His grandfather John Jacob Astor, a coarse-spoken man with crude manners, felt it was his mission in life to amass a fortune and pass it on to his heirs. Like Edward Mott Robinson, he lived to accumulate dollars and loved enlarging the pile. He expected his son William Backhouse to do the same.

In the course of his life, William Backhouse doubled his father's fortune. He developed rows of tenements and crammed the toiletless firetraps with hordes of the Irish, Jewish, and German immigrants flooding New York. He knew every piece of property he owned, was familiar with all the details in his leases, and had an aptitude for increasing the value of his real estate holdings. But as rich as he was, he held his money as tightly as a beggar clutching a tossed coin. He bought coal for his house in the middle of summer when prices were at their lowest, refused to ride in a carriage, and walked wherever he could. Waste was wicked; frugality was his watchword.

His son William joined the family business, married Caroline Schermerhorn, and would father several children and retreat from the New York world. He would seek investments in other cities and women in other ports. But he would provide his wife, Caroline, who had huge social ambitions, with the vast wealth to carry them out.

While Caroline thrived on New York's social whirl, Hetty sought escape from the city's commotion. While Caroline gushed with friends over the latest fashions, Hetty cocked an ear toward the men conversing on finance. While Caroline was intent on enhancing her position, Hetty was focused on expanding her fortune. The debutantes' world held little attraction for her: she may have enjoyed dancing, and she may have indulged in gossip, but she had no taste for frothy teas, no craving for fussy clothes, no liking for luxuries that money could buy. Hetty hungered for money itself.

Money served as a substitute for her family's love, a sweetener that satisfied her gnawing need for affection. She knew that money pleased her father; what she yearned for more than anything else was that her father be pleased with her. An astuteness for money might win his respect. Writing to him from her cousins' house, she told him she had had a gay time in New York, but she was tired of the round of parties and balls. Could she have his permission to return to New Bedford? She was soon on the steamer headed for Massachusetts.

"My father was as pleased to see me as I was to be back," she said later, though she admitted he was surprised that she cut her trip short. When he asked her why she still had money in her New York bank account, she told him that with the $1,200 he had given her, she had bought $200 worth of clothes. The rest, she proudly announced, she had invested in bonds that had already grown in value. "That investment turned out so well that I soon made others," she told an acquaintance. Her lack of interest in clothes may have dismayed her aunt, who enjoyed dressing up even with nowhere to go; she accused her niece of looking "like one of the orphans of some sailor lost at sea." Hetty may not have won her aunt's admiration, but by pursuing her father's interests she not only won his praise, she shared his pleasure in making money. She was not alone.

Chapter 4

===

America Booming

Money was on everyone's mind. Ever since President Thomas Jefferson's Louisiana Purchase doubled the size of the country in 1803, Easterners lusted after wealth in the remote new areas in the West. After the Mexican-American War in 1848, when the United States won control over Texas and the area that would comprise Arizona, California, Colorado, Nevada, Utah, New Mexico, and Wyoming, the desire for land increased.

After the first successful gold strikes in the Sierra foothills that year, tens of thousands more hankered to go out west. Factory men in New England, immigrants in New York, farmers in the South left their homes and families to seek their fortunes with picks and shovels. They may have left for paradise, but they went through hell to get there.

If the deepest reaches of the earth coursed with golden veins, the surface of the country was clotted with rugged routes. Many crammed into ships, determined to make their way west on the two-ocean, months-long journey that brought illness and queasy stomachs for long stretches on rough seas. Some went overland from the Midwest along the Oregon Trail in stagecoaches or covered wagons, bouncing along through parching droughts, drenching rain, blistering heat, and freezing snow.

A fortunate few took trains, the most efficient form of travel. With heated cars, upholstered seats with spring cushions, oil lamps for light, and even toilet rooms, trains made travel easier and lowered the cost and time of transporting goods and people. At the start of the gold rush, however, most rail lines ran only in the Northeast, and few lines existed west of Chicago; no tracks ran for longer than 250 miles; and no railroad crossed the continent.

From the 1840s, small rail lines reached north from New York to Maine and south from New York to Atlanta. Trains carried cotton grown in Georgia all the way to New Bedford, where the Wamsutta Mills turned out finished textiles that were transported back to New York. After its opening in 1851, the Erie Canal connected the Hudson River with Lake Erie and short rail lines linked New York with the Midwest; other lines joined Pennsylvania with Ohio, and Chicago with the Mississippi River. But no lines ran to the Pacific Ocean.

The only long-haul carriers that reached the Far West were sailing packets and steamer ships conveying goods, passengers, and the mail down one coast, across the Isthmus of Panama, and up the other side. But the ships that plied these seas took several months at best; at worst they were waylaid by weather and sank in storms. In the rush to open up the West, better transport was needed, and better transport required men to make it.

Thousands of workers were hired to mine the iron ore used to build new railroad tracks, and tens of thousands of workers were employed to construct them. New tracks required new towns where the lines met and workers and travelers could stay; new towns, such as Dallas, Denver, and Oklahoma City, needed people to settle them and goods and services to provide for the settlers.

Entrepreneurs willing to build the rail lines prodded the federal government to grant them land along which they could lay the tracks. But even though the land was free, they needed money for payrolls and equipment. Smart investors and shrewd speculators could see the future whizzing before them. Tempted by the possibility of huge returns from railroads and from the development of the land surrounding them into towns, mining centers, and manufacturing hubs, they poured money into New York banks. A flood of new funds arrived from Boston and New Bedford, from Chicago and St. Louis, and from London, Paris, and Frankfurt. Awash in capital, the banks loaned money at easy interest rates to railroad promoters, mining prospectors, land speculators, merchants, and farmers.

The nation was bursting with new inventions and new markets and hungry for better transportation. Technology such as the steam engine quickened the pace of manufacturing and railroads. Samuel Morse's new telegraph put cities in touch with one another and spurred a surge in communications. The discovery of metal ore in the West led to the invention of new tools and instruments like sewing machines and steam irons that were produced in the East. The newly improved cotton gin in the South meant more cotton for more goods that could be made better and faster in the North or exported overseas to England.

Factories sprouted everywhere: Pittsburgh, Pennsylvania, manufactured iron, glass, and textiles; Lowell, Massachusetts, made textiles and leather goods; New Haven, Connecticut, produced hardware, guns, and clocks; New York produced books, newspapers and magazines, chemicals, and clothing of all kinds. As a meeting point in the Midwest, Chicago grew at a furious rate, its rail lines stretching west and its population tripling, while New York became the country's manufacturing center, its financial core, and its transportation hub.

Even a war in Europe benefited the nation. Grain from the Midwest, already in demand in the East, found new markets across the ocean when the Crimean War broke out at the end of 1853. The conflict, which pitted Russia against the Ottomans, the British, and the French, caused the czar to cut off wheat exports and forced Europeans to turn to America for their grain. Trains carried wheat and corn from Chicago to New York, where dockworkers on the Hudson River piers hurled the foodstuffs onto steamer ships bound for Europe.

Packet ships continued to carry goods and people and mail to California, and when the ships returned from the West, they brought back stacks of gold bars. But new trains sped hundreds of thousands of travelers westward faster and cheaper, and hauled more manufactured goods out from the East and more grain and food supplies back from the Midwest. The country was growing by the hour, proving almost daily its divinely ordained Manifest Destiny.

Everyone wanted a piece of the prosperity pie. Eager clients could almost taste their earnings as they bought shares of everything from the Crystal Palace, even as its stock was plummeting from 175 to 53, to the Reading Railroad to Pacific mining ventures. "You can't lose," stock salesmen promised naive clients. Trading in railroad stocks zoomed. Canny manipulators devised new instruments that enabled them to purchase more shares with less cash. In April 1854, *Harper's Magazine* ridiculed the Wall Street operations of the firm of "Dry, Sly and Lye" and mocked its greedy customers who gambled on thin margin, bought puts and calls, and sold stocks short. It was no different from being at a roulette table, the editors said, not knowing how often future generations would repeat the scenario.

That same month Erie Railroad stocks started sliding. Soon after, investors were agog when the New Haven Railroad announced that its president, Robert Schuyler, a prominent member of New York society, had swindled the company of $2 million. More railroads slipped as confidence fell, and for a few months Wall Street, trading primarily in railroad stocks, ran gloomily off the track. But if speculators who had bought on margin were forced to sell their shares to cover their losses, shrewd investors like Commodore Vanderbilt and speculators like Jay Gould swooped up the stocks at low prices. Hetty Robinson would later do the same.

Railroads were falling, but a feverish rush for gold sent mining stocks soaring. Midwestern banks opened branches in New York so that customers could redeem their notes in the East. Five new bank buildings, commended for their graceful architecture, were under construction on Wall Street, and the total number of banks in the city was on its way to doubling. It seemed as though everyone was becoming rich.

For three years the boom continued. Banks encouraged spending and loaned generously at low interest. When customers reached their credit limit, instead of cutting off further loans, the bankers urged them to borrow more, and then sold the loans at discounted prices to other institutions. With easy money, merchants and manufacturers expanded their businesses. Consumers shopped at a furious pace, importing fancy French furnishings for their oversized mansions, cashmeres and furs for their elaborate wardrobes, truffles and caviar for their lavish dinners and opulent balls. The banks exported gold to pay for them.

The country was drunk on prosperity. The nation reveled. New York floated on bubbles of champagne. New Bedford tippled. In 1857 the city boasted a record number of ships in its whaling fleet, and local citizens thrived in its commerce. For those who sought new homes, the New Bedford Five Cents Savings Bank opened its doors to lend them low-cost money for mortgages. To decorate their new houses, a few bought paintings from local artist Albert Bierstadt.

Henry David Thoreau's Lyceum lecture "Getting a Living" drew a sizable crowd. The impoverished author of *Walden* wrote that he was "rich in sunny hours and summer days." He had no regret, he said, that he had not wasted his hours in a workshop or a classroom. He preferred truth to money. "Money is not required to buy one necessary [necessity] of the soul," said Thoreau. In the New England town where many like Edward Robinson equated wealth with virtue, the puzzled audience walked away scratching their heads. They found his words "decidedly peculiar," the local newspaper said.

Instead, the hardworking residents of New Bedford erected a new building for the Friends Academy, started new enterprises, and enlarged their existing businesses. One entrepreneur, Abraham Howland, experimenting with coal, discovered a way to distill the chunks of fossil so that drops of oil trickled out. It was a portent of things to come.

Like other firms, Isaac Howland Jr. and Company prospered, making Edward Mott Robinson and Sylvia Howland two of the richest people in town. Sylvia spent some of her time eyeing her investments and much of her time in the world of books. Her favorites included the abolitionist works of Harriet Beecher Stowe, the lyrical travel writing of Bayard Taylor, and the feminist volumes of Fredrika Bremer.

The Swedish author traveled for a year around America and wrote a forthright account of her impressions. She admired the country's education of women and the value its citizens placed on teachers. After meeting Quakers, she praised the "chaste and dew-like purity" of their women and applauded the antislavery position of the group. But she derided their suspicion of beauty and art and their fear of joy, and she noted that their numbers were dwindling. Attending a Friends meeting one hot day, she observed that not a single person was moved by the spirit inside them. After an hour of utter silence in the trying heat, the assembly finally broke up. "Peace be with them," she said.

Bremer spent time with friends in New York and complained about the crowds and the bustle and the boring dinners. "Is there anything in this world more wearisome, more dismal, more intolerable, more indigestible, more stupefying, more unbearable, anything calculated to kill both soul and body, than a great dinner in New York?" she asked.

Hetty Robinson gave her own account to her aunt. Her stories of endless dinners and chatty teas, costly clothing and overfurnished homes, relentless traffic and dizzying throngs fed the imagination of Sylvia, who might have enjoyed this life. How different the Grinnells' world was from the dull routine of the frail spinster whose companions were more and more the maids and nurses who looked after her. She was pleased her niece had spent time in New York and disappointed she had shortened her trip. Sylvia may have wanted to live her life through Hetty, but Hetty kept thwarting her dreams.

In New Bedford, Hetty shuttled between her father's house on Second Street and her aunt's house on Eighth Street and kept a room at both. Weekends and summers, she and Sylvia, one rumpled, the other crisp, rode in the carriage together on the two-hour trip to Round Hills. But tensions ran high between them. The young woman who had been sent to Quaker schools to learn plainness and thrift frowned on her aunt's indulgences. Hetty insisted on using simple linens for entertaining and complained when Sylvia wanted a butler instead of a servant girl for a dinner party; she criticized her aunt for hiring a fancy livery hack instead of keeping a one-horse carriage; she admonished the older woman for keeping too many in help.

Hetty's insolent behavior irritated Sylvia. Her sorry wardrobe had not improved, her temper tantrums had not ceased, and her air of defiance had not eased. She argued incessantly with the servants and ignored her aunt's advice. When Sylvia warned her away from a dangerous horse, Hetty took it upon herself to break him and rode the wild animal until he settled down. The agitated Sylvia, trembling from head to heels, had to be put to bed.

Under her father's sharp eye, however, she worked for her money and kept an accurate account of her spending. Once more she set off with him to the countinghouses and storerooms, the commodities traders and stockbrokers, and followed the intricacies of his dealings. He often reminded her that as the sole heir of her aunt, her mother, and himself, she would inherit the family's entire wealth. "If you can manage your brain," he told her, "you can manage your fortune." She knew from his frequent admonishments that it would be her responsibility to turn over the fortune undiminished to the next generation. His lessons taught her the value of money and the necessity of having it. "We have to have money to be happy," she said. But she carried the burden like a sack of gold bricks strapped to her back.

Chapter 5

Irrational Exuberance

"Are we a happy people?" asked *Harper's Magazine*. "The richest man has no definite idea of a fortune, and is more eager to double his million than . . . to turn his first dollar. His only sense of enjoyment," the editor said, "consists in making more." More happy people were making more dollars in New York.

And then the bubble burst. Toward the end of 1857, the news from the Ohio Life Insurance and Trust Company leaked the first bits of air. Unbeknownst to its Midwestern directors, the manager of its New York branch had embezzled millions of dollars. In addition, the bank had borrowed funds from other New York institutions in order to lend money to railroad builders and speculators in railroad stocks. But European demand for American grain had waned with the end of the Crimean War, and with bumper crops around the world, Midwestern farmers received lower prices and shipped fewer foodstuffs by railroad.

The overextended railroads had borrowed millions of dollars from Ohio Life and could not pay them back. When the insurance company revealed its $2 million loss from the embezzlement plus $5 million in losses on loans to railroad builders, stock speculators, and in its own trading accounts, the New York banks demanded the money owed them. In response, Ohio Life declared bankruptcy at its New York office and shut its doors.

Events spiraled downward.

Midwestern banks were forced to borrow more money from New

York. The farmers who withdrew their money from their accounts every summer to cover seasonal costs could not replace it in the fall; nor could they repay the merchants who had extended them credit. N. H. Wolfe, the oldest flour and grain company in New York, declared bankruptcy. The president of a Michigan railroad announced his resignation. Railroad stocks slid to half their prices of four years earlier.

Big bankers, worried that other clients were overextended, nervously called their customers for immediate repayment of matured loans. But Ohio Life was not the only one that had borrowed far beyond its means. Within weeks other banks and major Wall Street investors, ruined by bad loans, suspended operations or defaulted. Rumors raced through the city, growing more exaggerated at every telling. Crowds huddled in the canyons of Wall Street as panicked creditors, worried that their banks would not be able to pay them, withdrew their money. Although each bank issued its own version of paper money backed by gold, in reality the paper notes were not at par value with the metal. The public demanded the gold. With imports high and confidence low, the banks were forced to make their payments in gold, but their stores of specie, as metal coins were called, were shrinking.

Dark clouds hovered. "People look dubious and whisper darkly," one man wrote, noting that several stock operators suffered serious failures. A few clever men like Russell Sage, a future role model for Hetty, kept substantial amounts of cash on hand and used it to buy stocks at rock-bottom prices. John Pierpont Morgan told his son there was a good lesson to be learned from other people's greed and good bargains to be found in the aftermath. In future times, Hetty would always keep cash available and use it to buy when everyone else was selling. Much later, Warren Buffett would do the same. But most people watched their money wash away in the flood; it felt like the crash and depression that had taken place twenty years before. "Wall Street stocks panting and tumbling under a pressure that reminds one of the financial tragedies of 1837," wrote George T. Strong.

The situation grew worse. The English needed capital to fight a rebellion in India and raised their interest rates for depositors to attract funds. European investors, concerned about American banks and drawn to the higher rates in London, demanded their deposits in gold from the New York financial institutions. In the spring of 1857 the steamship *Central America* set sail from California with four hundred passengers and $1.6 million in gold bars for the New York banks. But a few months later, as the steamer rounded Cape Hatteras, a hurricane smashed across its hull. The passengers and the gold went down with the ship.

"Extra! Extra!" newsboys called out every day, as customers grabbed the latest edition of bad news. More banks in New York and other cities suspended business, seven railroads failed, including the Erie and the Reading, factories closed, and merchants around the country shut their doors. Bankers, worried about the solvency of their borrowers, raised their interest rates and refused to lend money to anyone who did not have rock-solid collateral: certified checks were required; stocks and bonds were dismissed as worthless.

In the past, merchants with accounts receivable could bring their due bills to their bankers, who would take off a percentage of the funds payable and give the rest to the merchant. But now, no matter how strong the creditor's reputation, banks refused to accept the receivables. Even the credit of reputable merchant princes like Henry Grinnell was questionable, because chances were they had been operating and gambling in stocks and railroad bonds. All those securities were unmarketable and useless.

Old-line conservatives mocked the newly minted millionaires who were agonizing over worthless securities and pleading vainly with the banks in a desperate fight to save their social status. If only they could hold on to their big mansions on Fifth Avenue, continue to entertain their boring friends at outrageously expensive dinners, and maintain their private boxes while they yawned through the opera, they begged. But their pleas did not budge the adamant directors and rigid cashiers.

A congressional banking oversight committee blamed the disaster partially on the lightning speed of the latest tool, the telegraph. What's more, information from the telegraph now raced across the country and around the world via the new railroads and better-equipped oceangoing steamships. The innovative methods of communication and transportation wiped out "distance and time," said an observer. Informed depositors worldwide, worried by what they read, rushed to the banks demanding the return of their money immediately in gold.

In October 1857, the banks announced they would no longer pay depositors in specie. They hoped the move would stop the drain on gold and force customers to accept paper money at par. The *New York Times* heaved a sigh of relief and accused the bankers of having created the crisis of confidence in the first place. Their reckless lending and risk taking were irresponsible. "Banks as business concerns must act upon the same principles and be governed by the same laws as individuals," the newspaper said. It would repeat those warnings a century and a half later.

As often happens in crises of confidence, people panicked and put away their wallets. George T. Strong observed "an epidemic of fear," blaming it more on crowd psychology than on financial reality. Prices for everything were coming down in the panic; all businesses were affected, and merchants suffered badly. Brooks Brothers, Lord & Taylor, dry goods stores, and small shops on every street declared drastic sales with prices well below cost. Construction came to a halt; unfinished buildings stood naked around the city.

With customers afraid to spend their money and goods piling up on the shelves, manufacturers were forced to close their businesses. Tens of thousands of people lost their jobs, and the salaries of many others were slashed. In New York, unemployment rose from 40,000 to 100,000. Men without jobs, but still with families to feed, took to the streets to protest. Major riots broke out. Robberies increased, gangs roamed the streets, and the city, already corrupt, became so dangerous that at night many gentlemen carried guns to protect themselves. "It was," said one banker, "the most violent and destructive financial panic ever experienced in the country."

The panic reverberated on an international scale as the crisis spread from Wall Street to Main Street and then to South America and to Germany, France, and England. A few years later the British statesman Benjamin Disraeli noted the problems brought about by "all the bubble, blunders and dishonesties of five years' European exuberance." The cause of it all, said the *Louisville Courier*, was Wall Street: "Their houses are dens of iniquity. Their aim is financial ruin. Their code of laws is that of the gambler, the sharper, the impostor, the cheat and the swindler." The bubbles continue to burst; the words continue to echo.

A few places remained untouched. California prospered with its gold mines. In the South, plantation owners profited as European orders for cotton increased and prices rose. The country's largest export, cotton was king. Southerners looked for more land to plant their crops and more slaves to work them. They turned their attention to the territories out west where they could also grow more sugar, rice, and tobacco. Textile manufacturers in New England and merchant shippers in New York, who exported the goods and benefited from the increased production, supported them. Some New York bankers even accepted receipts from slave purchases as collateral.

Southerners rejoiced at the Dred Scott Decision, in which the Supreme Court declared that slaves were property and could be legally transported either to the North or into the western states. That 1857 decision, along with the deep recession, shook the country to its foundations. Southerners clamored for slaves in Kentucky, Kansas, Mississippi, Louisiana, and other states, while Northerners argued against it. In Massachusetts, freed slaves and slaves who had escaped through the Underground Railroad convened in New Bedford to protest.

In that same city the flour mill expanded, and a new candle and oil company was established. The paper money issued by the Mechanics Bank featured a whale, and whaling reached its peak, with more ships, more capital, and more sailors than ever, making New Bedford the richest city per capita in the world. But at the end of 1857, as people switched to kerosene, the price of whale oil seeped down, and the New Bedford Bank went under. Edward Robinson, who made it a practice never to borrow, kept his business buoyant; he even won a bid for election to the town council.

Some of the time Hetty lived with her father as they followed their old routine. Days were spent down at the wharfs and countinghouses, where he watched his pennies with a miser's eye. Evenings Hetty read him the news. It was hard to ignore the papers' reports of the Illinois senatorial debates taking place in the summer of 1858 between the Democratic incumbent Stephen Douglas and the Republican upstart Abraham Lincoln. The Howlands, the Grinnells, and Robinson had long supported Lincoln, who, like the Quakers, saw slavery as a moral wrong.

From physical shackles to emotional chains, slavery comes in many forms. Abby Robinson, enslaved by her psyche, suffered bodily pain and mental anguish. Depressed, she lived for years as an invalid, but when the agony became unbearable, she escaped from Edward's house and entered her sister's world. Sometimes Hetty stayed with them too, in the room set aside for her over the kitchen, and heard the angry accusations hurled at her father by her mother and her aunt.

Tortured by fears of her husband, tormented by her own sense of failure, on February 21, 1860, at the age of fifty-one, Abby Howland Robinson died. The motherless woman had never known how to be a mother herself. Her death seemed to mean little to her daughter, who had nothing to mourn but the loss of love she never received. Abby's only way to express affection was through her money. Yet she died without a will; her entire estate of more than $100,000 went to her husband.

Hurt and angry and urged on by her aunt, Hetty appealed to her father for her share in the inheritance: the Howland fortune, which had gone from her great-grandfather Isaac Howland to her grandfather Gideon Howland to her mother, Abby Howland, should now go to her, the only direct living heir. But Edward insisted he knew how to invest the money and make it grow. Not only that, he had the responsibility to increase it until his death. Then, he reminded his daughter, he would turn the money over to her to do the same.

They took the case to the family's attorney, B. F. Thomas, in Boston for arbitration. But instead of the Solomonic decision Hetty hoped for, Edward was allowed to keep everything except for a house worth $8,000 that was given to her. Hetty was devastated. Alone and adrift, she sought solace with Sylvia.

Money may have ruled discussions in the Howland and Robinson households, but it was the demands of the South that inundated conversations around the rest of the country. Not only was cotton the nation's largest export, the South's slaves had a dollar value far greater than the money invested in railroads or manufacturing; slavery represented 80 percent of the country's gross national product.

Along with the continued use of slaves in the established areas and the expansion of slavery in the newer parts of the country, the Southerners had two more demands. In order to encourage the Europeans to purchase more cotton, the South was insisting on lower import duties to help the English and French sell their own goods in America; in addition, the South wanted to control the railroads going west. These were costly concessions for the North. But if the North would not accede to their wishes, the Southerners would not bend: they believed their strong economy would allow them to survive on their own. The southern Democrats were calling for a break with the Union. Northerners feared their own economy could not be sustained without them.

A few days after the death of Hetty's mother, the newspapers reported a remarkable speech by Abraham Lincoln. Invited by the Reverend Henry Ward Beecher to address an audience at Cooper Union, the new free college in New York, the odd-looking Westerner delivered a stinging attack on slavery. As he traveled through New England over the next few days, on his way to see his son at Exeter, he repeated his ideas again and again.

The tall and gangly "prairie orator," as he was called by the *Times,* spoke in simple words and held the Cooper Union audience in silent awe as he told them that, without question, slavery was evil. Yet it must be tolerated in the South, he conceded, because it had been granted by the fathers of the Constitution. Nonetheless, like George Washington, he was against the expansion of slavery into the West. And like Thomas Jefferson, he hoped that white labor would slowly replace it, putting the evil condition, he said, "on the course of ultimate extinction."

Lincoln appealed to his fellow Republicans for harmony and peace. He denounced the inflammatory actions of John Brown and his band of men who had seized the southern city of Harpers Ferry in an attempt to rally its slaves. The state of Virginia soon hanged Brown, but his mission reverberated around the country. Slavery was an issue that could not be shrugged off, Lincoln warned; we must care, and emancipation must come. "Let us have faith that right makes might," he said. "And in that faith, let us, to the end, dare to do our duty as we understand it." Some men worried his words meant war.

As Lincoln addressed the crowd at Cooper Union, the city was once again enjoying prosperity. Europe's increasing demand for cotton from the South meant that New York business had come back at a rapid pace; the most thriving business in New York was merchant shipping. More ships were steaming across the Atlantic carrying cotton to Europe, and more packets were sailing into New York carrying gold.

But boats sailed in and out of the East River harbor more frequently than New Bedford. As always, accidents occurred, like the loss of the steamer *Baltimore*, which sank in a collision, or the demise of the *Shooting Star*, a Howland & Company ship that ran aground outside Portsmouth. In addition, overzealous whaling had diminished the nearby supply and made the giant mammals harder to find, forcing vessels to travel farther and longer before they could harpoon their prey. What's more, costly whale oil was being replaced by kerosene, which now fueled many lamps in America and Europe.

Worst of all, explorers deep in a well in Pennsylvania discovered a greenish black substance oozing from the earth like a monster rising from the depths of the sea. The discovery of fossil oil in America made it clear to Edward Robinson that the need for whale oil was coming to an end. He was right: within six years Pennsylvania workers would be drilling three and a half million barrels of crude oil a year. A cold, hard look at the industry left him with little doubt the time had come to divest himself of his business. What's more, the death of his wife not only enriched him, it freed him to rethink his life.

As he made plans, he offered his daughter a change of pace. When the warm weather came she traveled by train to upstate New York. Above Albany, the smart resort of Saratoga served as a gathering place for frenzied Wall Street businessmen, prosperous New England industrialists, and southern plantation owners fluffed with cotton. Wives and daughters in tow, they drank in youth at the bubbling mineral waters of the Congress Spring, cheered the thoroughbreds at the racetrack, and paraded up and down the elm-shaded avenues. Evenings they dined in the hotel dining rooms and attended the informal hops at the Union House, where sharp-eyed mothers surveyed the room and saucy-eyed daughters smiled and hoped they would be asked to dance. In the summer of 1860, young, pretty Hetty Howland Robinson waltzed across the ballroom floor.

Throughout the days in Saratoga, on the wide porches of the grand United States Hotel men lazed side by side in rocking chairs, feet stretched out, straw hats pushed back, Havana cigars in hand, mint juleps at their side. Colleagues in business, northern "lords of the loom" expressed sympathy for the southern "lords of the lash" lounging next to them; they benefited together from the expansion of slavery. And when their sons and daughters married and their businesses merged, so much the better.

The presidential elections spun through the porches of Saratoga that summer. In May, "Honest Abe," the "man of the people," as Horace Greeley, publisher of the *Tribune,* called him, had won the Republican presidential nomination on the third ballot at the Chicago convention. The party platform pledged not to extend slavery and promised a protective tariff, free land for homesteaders, and a railroad to the Pacific Ocean. In August the Democratic opponent, Stephen Douglas, spent a week at Saratoga and was given a reception on the balcony of the United States Hotel. He may have shown more bluster than humor, but his wife charmed all the guests.

Although politics was on everyone's mind, for Hetty the highlight of the visit was not the coming election, in which women were not allowed to vote, but the dinner party to which she was invited. Former U.S. president Martin Van Buren, a Democrat, asked her to dine at his cottage on Saratoga Lake. For many years a photograph of Hetty, taken on her way to the dinner, rested on her rolltop desk. Visitors who saw it remarked on the striking young woman with the broad forehead, sharp nose, and keen blue eyes.

Her chaperone for the evening was Baroness Stoeckel, wife of the Russian ambassador, and among the distinguished guests were Van Buren's son John, a brilliant orator; Lord Althorp, the future Duke of Northumberland; the witty Lord Harvey; and Captain Tower, who had fought in the Crimean War with the Coldstream Guards. Eager to show off her wit, Hetty turned to one of the guests and, eyes twinkling, asked: "Do you know how you can see the masses rising?" No, replied the aristocrat. "Go west to the Mississippi and go aboard a high-pressure steam boat," she said. "You will see masses of people rising on deck."

Nothing could outdo the flurry of excitement that Hetty encountered when she returned to New York in the fall of 1860. The city shimmered with news that the Prince of Wales was coming to visit;

in his honor, a group of leading citizens was organizing a ball. The party committee—including Arthur Leary, Moses and Henry Grinnell, and a fellow member of the Union Club and the Geographical Society, John Cisco, the respected U.S. assistant treasurer at the Sub-Treasury in New York—had enormous amounts of work to do. Guest lists needed to be created, invitations engraved and sent out, and an evening planned down to the very last detail. Everyone clamored to be included. Ambitious mothers and young daughters spent hours daydreaming about the possibilities: the prince was only nineteen, but no more eligible bachelor existed than the heir to the British throne.

The day of his arrival the city was out in force: businesses closed, Wall Street was deserted, and hundreds of thousands of people thronged the streets. Huge banners welcomed "Victoria's Royal Son," as cannons blasted and bands kaboomed in the parade to Twenty-third Street. A short while later, the crowds went wild when the genial prince stood on his balcony at the Fifth Avenue Hotel and waved to the masses.

The next day, society men trimmed their mustaches and clipped the hairs of their side whiskers, while women spent hours twisting their curls and preparing their toilette for the ball. At 9 p.m. that evening of Friday, October 12, excited couples who had paid ten dollars apiece arrived at the Academy of Music on Irving Place. Men in white tie and tails and women in hoop skirts covered with satins, brocades, and a blaze of jewels gave "aren't we special" nods to acquaintances and breathless hellos to friends. Gusts of anticipation filled the gigantic hall as everyone waited for the royal guest to arrive.

Precisely at 10 p.m. the orchestra played "God Save the Queen," and led by an entourage of lords and dukes, the slight, small prince, dressed in military uniform and sashed with the Order of the Garter, stepped into the room. "The crest of the Prince of Wales blazed out in plumes of diamond like light over the floating folds of a vast tent of pink and white drapery," gushed the *Times*. For two hours, nearly three thousand of New York's finest citizens rushed like schoolgirls to meet him, and in the mad crush the wooden floor built specially for the occasion collapsed.

Never mind. No one was hurt. While the bands played furiously, the prince and his court were led upstairs to a long dais, where they were seated and served, and the prince sipped his favorite sherry and seltzer water. The guests rushed to follow. At a separate entrance and exit, guarded by such prominent men as John Jacob Astor, fifty people at a time were permitted to enter the room. A horseshoe table around the perimeter welcomed them with a profusion of flowers and food, and with liveried waiters elbow to elbow to serve them, they piled their plates with filet of beef, lobster salad, pâtés, truffles, and grouse, and filled their glasses with champagne.

At 2 a.m., the dance floor finally fixed, strains of a Strauss quadrille could be heard. As had been carefully planned, Mrs. Morgan, wife of the governor, wearing glowing diamonds and a cloud of crepe, was asked by the prince for the first dance. Eager females, young and old, waited their turn for a waltz or a polka, and finally the young woman from New Bedford was tapped.

Stunning in her low-cut white gown sashed with pink, her arms covered in long, white gloves, an ostrich feather fluttering in her hand, Hetty was introduced to the Prince of Wales. "And I am the Princess of Whales," she rejoined. "Ah," the charming prince replied, "I have heard that all of Neptune's daughters are beautiful. You are proof of that." And then he sailed her away on the dance floor.

"Nothing could ever have been more successful or better done," declared the social arbiter Ward McAllister after the ball was over. "Brilliant and beautiful," said the *Times*. Guests recalled the evening for their children and grandchildren. Hetty stashed her memories in a box.

Chapter 6

A Willful War

With 60 percent of the electoral college but less than 40 percent of the popular vote, in November 1860 Abraham Lincoln won the election for president of the United States. The following February on his way to Washington, he stopped in New York, where he was less than a favorite: he had won the state handily but lost the city badly. As he rode in his barouche to the Astor House hotel on Broadway, the large crowds inspected the length of him, head to toe in black.

Addressing a dinner group that night, the thin, gaunt Lincoln admitted he had not spoken publicly since his election. With a twinkle in his eye, he said: "I have been brought before you now and required to make a speech, when you all approve more than anything else of the fact that I have been silent." The crowd murmured in agreement.

The next morning at eight, dressed as always in his stovepipe hat and somber clothes, the president-elect arrived at the home of Moses Grinnell's daughter to breakfast with one hundred of New York's most prominent merchants. His lanky body and hard features surprised at least one of the guests, who called him "among the ugliest white men" he had ever seen.

But it was Lincoln's attitude that was on their minds. Soon after the elections, the state of South Carolina announced its secession from the Union. Lincoln's refusal to bow to the South's demands did not lose him the support of Moses Grinnell, but Henry Grinnell and others were concerned. As the correspondent for the London *Times* wrote about New York, "her conscience choked with cotton, her mouth kankered with gold," much of the city's finance depended on the South. If the rest of the South seceded, merchants said, New York business would be destroyed.

A few days later it was Lincoln who was nearly destroyed. On the way to Baltimore, a plot to derail his train was foiled by Pinkerton detectives who had infiltrated a group of potential assassins. After the president-elect changed from his dress suit into a traveling suit and donned a broad-brimmed hat, Pinkerton smuggled Lincoln into a one-car train and he continued in disguise to the capital.

By the time Lincoln took the oath of office on March 4, 1861, six more states had sworn to secede from the Union, and the Confederate States of America had seized Fort Sumter in South Carolina. Less than two months later, challenged by the North, they refused to remove their flag from the fort and brazenly fired at the Union garrison. The president arranged his long legs under his White House desk and signed a declaration of war.

"Extra! Extra!" "War has begun!" newsboys shouted on April 12. Looming over New York was the threat that the South would lower its import duties to half the northern tariffs, ship cotton to Europe, and open its harbors to household goods and war matériel. What would happen if southern cotton no longer flowed to New York? If southern loans were no longer paid to the city's banks? If southern orders for goods were no longer sent to New York?

With visions of ships rotting in the East River and grass growing in the streets, New York businessmen were roused from their neutral slumber. They could no longer afford to rest while another financial panic hit the city. Instead, they rallied to keep the Union intact. The economy rallied with them.

Factories hummed as the city toiled to supply the army with equipment. Brooks Brothers manufactured shoddy uniforms, Squibb and Pfizer produced medicines, Borden's condensed milk. Eagle produced pencils and steel nibs, Johnson's Foundry made munitions, Phelps Dodge made marine engines, Starr supplied revolvers and rifles, John Englis provided gunboats, others assembled ambulances, and Pulitzer, Hearst, and Greeley printed newspapers, all of which were shipped to the Union soldiers fighting in the South. What's more, the failure of European crops produced a demand for American grain five times the amount shipped in the years before.

The port bustled with activity as two-thirds of the country's exports and one-third of its imports were transported in and out. At the East River, swarms of people came to see the graceful clipper ships loading in their berths. At Piers 8, 9, and 10, the fleet of seventy ships owned by William T. Coleman & Company, one of the principal shipping merchants in New York, was laden with goods, sailing the seas between East and West. At the helm of the business, along with William T. Coleman, was Edward Mott Robinson. After selling most of his interest in his whaling fleet, in June 1860 he removed his Quaker brim and turned it in for a top hat, investing his money in the New York company. An advertisement in the newspapers announced he had become a partner in the prominent firm.

While New York rallied, New Bedford marshaled its residents. When the former governor of Massachusetts spoke on the steps of City Hall, the citizens united against the Confederates, and despite the Quakers' resistance to war, New Bedford gave its all. Rachel Grinnell helped organize the Ladies' Soldiers' Relief Society and asked her younger cousin Hetty to help collect drugs, cotton cloth and flannel shirts, wool mittens and socks, lemons, apples, jellies, coffee and tea, brandies and wine, and money for the troops.

As the women assembled the goods, 3,200 New Bedford men went off to fight, and the city's ships sailed out to sea. But two dozen vessels were blown up by the Confederates, and in the summer of 1861 thirty whaling barques were commandeered by the Union Navy to use for a blockade. While the townspeople stood at the wharfs and bade a teary farewell, the ships were loaded with stones and sent off to the southern seaports. When they reached Atlanta and Charleston, they were sunk in the harbor channels. The boats served as a barrier to prevent the South from shipping goods to Europe, and, as Edward Robinson predicted, they were a symbol of the end of whaling.

While New England soldiers fought in the South, Hetty Robinson struggled up north. As the sole heir to the Howland money, she had been caught for years between her father and her aunt in their tug-of-war over the family fortune. With Sylvia growing more frail, Hetty wanted to be sure that, upon her aunt's passing, she received her rightful due.

Sylvia's illness may have made her physically fragile, but as her health deteriorated and her dependence on others grew, her desire for power increased. She wielded her weakness like a witch waving a wand: banishing enemies here, bribing others with gold dust there. In her constant game of manipulation, she threatened to cut off those she could not control and paid off those she needed most.

Sylvia had given her niece a gift of $20,000 in stocks, but as Hetty knew, this was a minor sum for a woman whose wealth ran to many hundreds of thousands of dollars. In theory, all that money would go to her. But after her grandfather left her with nothing, after her mother died intestate, and after her father disputed her claims, Hetty had to protect her Howland inheritance. She had to make certain the money was hers. It wasn't just a question of finance: it was the only proof she had of her worth and the only sense she had of their love.

Her relationship with Sylvia was complex, even precarious: at times she was her aunt's closest companion, at other times her contentious prey. Traumatized by rejection, Hetty constantly tested Sylvia's love, but as much as Sylvia may have tried to give it, Hetty pushed for more. Her behavior confounded her aunt.

Although Sylvia saw herself as a surrogate mother with Hetty's best interests at heart, her patience ran short and her empathy was limited. She often criticized Hetty, complained about her to friends, and was wary of her ties to her father. Indeed, she rarely confided in the young woman and, to Hetty's distress, kept her private matters locked in a hair-covered trunk. She never gave Hetty access; only her housekeeper had a key.

Sylvia employed a staff that increased along with her frailty. Besides Fally Brownell, her housekeeper and cook, there was Fally's husband, Frederick, her handyman; Electa Montague, the nurse who had worked for Hetty's mother; Pardon Gray, now her full-time carriage driver; and Eliza, a night nurse. In addition, there was sometimes a relief nurse, a cook, and a chambermaid.

Hetty not only felt the size of the staff was excessive, she saw it as evidence of her aunt's lack of love for her. How could the woman spend so much money on household help and fritter away her inheritance? How could Sylvia employ people who competed with Hetty for her love? When Fally served her food, Hetty complained she gave her the toughest meat. When the caretakers fluttered over their charge, she feared they were after her aunt's checkbook. Like everyone in New Bedford, they were well aware of Sylvia's huge bank account.

When her aunt announced she was building a wing to accommodate them, Hetty called the addition wasteful. In a fit of temper she announced she was giving up her own space for the staff: she opened her closet and bureau drawers and pulled out her clothes, stripped the mattress off her bed, and carried them all to the attic. Her upstairs stay was short, but she thought she had made her point.

In the early fall of 1861, still smarting over the loss of her mother's money, and angry at her father, Hetty sat down with Sylvia at Round Hills to discuss their mutual wills. They concurred that in the unlikely event Hetty should die first, she would leave her fortune to whatever children she might have, with half of it going into a trust fund; if she had no offspring, she would leave nothing to her father but would bequeath it all to her aunt's favorite charity, the New Bedford Orphans' Home. With witnesses in attendance, Hetty signed the paper and sealed it in a yellow envelope. Sylvia ordered her maid to unlock her treasure chest and place the envelope inside.

Sylvia's own will, written earlier, stipulated that a quarter of her estate would go to friends and charities, and three-quarters would be left to Hetty; of that, half the money would be put in trust. Now Hetty insisted that almost all the money be left directly to her. After hours of arguing, as darkness fell her aunt agreed to the idea; once they had worked out the details, Hetty asked her to sign the paper. But as the light flickered in a whale oil lamp, Sylvia said no, claiming she was too weak to hold the pen.

"I can't. I'm not able," she cried, quivering in her chair while her maid stood by. "Then you never will be able," Hetty snapped. "You can do it now as well as ever." Sylvia refused and went to bed. The paper remained unsigned. Rebuffed, Hetty warned the maid, "I never set out for anything that I don't conquer."

For weeks she pleaded with her aunt, her bullying tone receding into begging. If the money did not go to her, she wailed, she might become "a poor, neglected orphan" and a "recipient of public charity." As absurd as it may have sounded to the servants who overheard her, for Hetty the fears were real. Injured by her mother's indifference, foiled by her father and his grip on her money, frustrated by her aunt's manipulations, she felt helpless and fearful of what might happen next. If the money went into a trust, she would have no control over it. Hadn't her father demanded that she maintain the family fortune? But what if the trustees cheated her? What if they did not invest it well? What if they lost it all? The father who rejected her for being a girl, who cast her off as an infant, and deceived her about her inheritance, could easily leave her destitute. Yet her only value as a person was her fortune. She simply had to inherit Sylvia's assets. In a family that equated righteousness with money, what was she worth without wealth?

It took months of coaxing and cajoling, but at last, in January 1862, Sylvia succumbed. Seated on a lounge chair in the front room over the parlor, her spine propped up with pillows, a book on her lap to lean on, in the presence of witnesses she slowly penned her signature on the will. Later, Hetty would say that she and her aunt had written a second piece of paper that her aunt had signed when they were alone. For now Hetty felt triumphant.

Nonetheless, the household stormed with suspicion. Hetty's arguments with the staff swirled through the rooms and reached a breaking point two months later, when she battled with Fally, the housekeeper. Once before they had fought so hard that Hetty had told the housekeeper: "Take your duds and leave." Fally refused.

This time Hetty was breakfasting with her aunt and Electa, the nurse, when she left the table and went upstairs where Fally was cleaning the chamber pots and filling pitchers with water. A sudden crash drew the attention of the women downstairs. In a fit of temper, Hetty had pushed the housekeeper, who tripped and fell down the steps. When Sylvia heard the story she turned rigid with rage. Sylvia threatened to call Thomas Mandell, trustee of the estate; terrified of losing everything, Hetty begged forgiveness while Fally was given a gift of $1,000 by Sylvia to keep her in the household. It was time for Hetty to join her father in New York.

New York was the essence of America's moneymaking ethos, the perfect setting for Edward Mott Robinson. As an English visitor of the time observed, "Americans speak of a man being worth so many thousands or millions. Nowhere is money sought so eagerly; nowhere is it so much valued; and in no civilized country does it bring so little to its possessor. The real work of America is to make money for the sake of making it. It is an end, not a means. The value of the dollar consists in the power to make dollars. It is an almost universal maxim. In politics and business and I am afraid in many other matters," said Thomas Low Nichols, "money is the great object . . . the habitual measure of all things."

From his offices at Pearl and Wall streets, Edward Robinson surveyed the flourishing city and saw the great potential for making more money. Gold was flowing in from California, oil was oozing in from Pennsylvania, grain was billowing in from the Midwest. Railroads were hauling record amounts of freight, and ships were loading more goods than ever in the New York harbor.

Robinson's firm, William T. Coleman & Company, earned its profits several ways. It shipped cargo to China, California, Boston, and New York; it served as a factor, advancing discounted money to merchants who shipped goods on Coleman's boats. Additionally, Coleman & Company often purchased entire consignments of wheat and other goods and traded commodities futures to protect themselves.

Edward Robinson was prospering from his large stake in the business and from other astute investments. Like other shrewd financiers, he used devalued greenbacks to buy government bonds that paid interest in gold. The 6 percent rate offered in metal currency, called specie, by the Treasury when it needed money for the Civil War effort was just the sort of return that made him smile. Indeed, on one of his frequent weekend trips to New Bedford, he told his lawyer, William Crapo, that he was doing so well he was even considering starting a private bank.

Edward wasn't the only one thriving in New York. Although the early scare from the South before the start of the war had sent the markets tumbling, the city's rich were now more numerous than ever, and once again they went on a spending spree. When Hetty came to stay with her father, the city glittered with the gold flashed by millionaires.

But even as New Yorkers celebrated prosperity, some watched

with sadness and pride as their sons signed up as volunteers for the war. When volunteers were no longer enough, Congress passed a conscription law that drew on the names of all eligible young men. Carnegies, Morgans, and others rich enough to pay $300 escaped compulsory service, but a few went willingly, with velvet camp stools and sandwiches packed by Delmonico's. Phalanxes of poorer men were marched off to fight for the Union.

The Emancipation Proclamation, declared two months earlier, in January 1863, affirmed that the war was as much about abolishing slavery as it was about keeping the Union intact. The draft that followed enraged the mostly Irish immigrants in New York. They felt forced to fight for Negroes, who, they feared, were coming north to take their jobs.

Thousands of men protested; mobs rioted in the streets, striking innocent people and beating up policemen, breaking into private homes, burning buildings, and wrecking businesses. Racing to the Negro Children's Orphan Asylum, started by Quaker women twenty years before, a horde of men attacked the orphans and engulfed the building in flames. For four days the insurgency smoldered and thickened the air. More than a thousand people were killed, countless buildings were destroyed, hundreds of orphans were hurt, and thousands of colored citizens were driven from their homes. It took federal troops, city police, and a group of prominent men including Edward's partner, William Coleman, to quell the rebellion.

Weeks later the draft became an orderly process and life returned to normal. Once again, sumptuous carriages drove through the nearly completed Central Park; sopranos and tenors sang *Don Giovanni* at the Academy of Music; smart crowds celebrated at Delmonico's. Hetty roomed on Twenty-second Street and socialized with her cousins the Grinnells and their friends Catherine Lorillard Wolfe, whose family made their fortune in tobacco, banking, and real estate, and Annie Leary, whose rich father sold fur hats to Astors and other members of the upper class. With her good looks, Mayflower lineage, and the promise of a fortune, Hetty had more than enough of the requirements for a young lady in society.

Known for her translucent skin and twinkling blue eyes, Hetty dressed in hoop skirts and rustling taffetas and showed off her wit in the homes of fashionable families. She attended concerts and operas and waltzed at balls with prominent bachelors. Beau Brummells such as Annie's brother, Arthur Leary, and William Gebhard, members of the exclusive Union Club, and Joseph Choate, a lawyer, filled in their names on her dance card. The striking Hetty was a "brilliant, light hearted and greatly admired young girl," said Edward Pierrepont, who saw her at many parties. The *New York World* called her "a belle of New York society, ardently sought by numerous lovers not only for her wealth but also for her beauty." But like her friends Kitty Wolfe, who had lost the love of her life, and Annie Leary, who had no inclination to marry, Hetty was in no rush to wed.

From time to time Hetty traveled on business with her father to Boston, or rode the train on her own to see friends and family in New Bedford. She lodged at her aunt's, where she expected to be welcomed. But the withering Sylvia was now under the influence of a physician who fed her doses of laudanum and forbade her to see her niece. Instead, Sylvia spent her time at Round Hills, carried around by her servants while strapped in a sedan chair created by the doctor, and Hetty stayed in town. Occasionally, she sent a note to the nurse Electa, whom she considered an ally, begging permission to visit her aunt and giving them news of friends and relatives. "Will you ask Aunt if I may come over there any time after Thursday for a day or so. I shall try to go to Saratoga if I am well enough—I want to see her about something and should like to leave very soon," she wrote. At the end she added, "Cousin Lydia Congdon sent her love. Mrs Loring is dead. Grand Mother [Ruth Howland] is about the same."

On one of these trips Hetty learned that her aunt was proceeding with the addition to the house. It wasn't building the wing itself that bothered her, she wrote to Electa; it was being betrayed: "I cared more about her not telling me," she said. "It will take me two years at least to get over the shock." She added that the news brought on her old headaches, such terrible headaches that she could not read or sew. "Help me if you do not want me to live alone as an invalid all my days," she begged, pleading permission again to visit her aunt at Round Hills. But her request was denied. A few weeks later she tried again, and again she was refused. Rejected and suspicious, she returned to New York.

A few months later after another visit, Electa wrote, with her poor grammar, to wish her a happy New Year from her aunt and the rest of the household. "Very glad hear of your safe arrival your Aunt is so very glad that you have got such nice rooms to[o]. . . . we can talk about you almost see you made comfortable it gives us great joy." Sylvia was pleased that her niece had a nice quilt to keep her warm and "nice, clean clothes" to wear in New York. "Write soon," Electa scrawled. But she did not invite Hetty to see her aunt.

After another New Bedford visit, Electa sent a note saying how Hetty had disappointed her aunt by forgetting to take a black cashmere shawl. "She wants you to wear it and look like a lady," she wrote. As always she said, "She sends her love to you." Then she added, "O this awful war. Oh how many are killed."

Neither the smoke of burning plantations nor the stench of soldiers' charred bodies sullied the New York air, but the sidewalks were choked with rumors. Wall Street shook with fear that England would side with the South; it calmed only when news arrived that the battle at Antietam had ended in a draw. That was enough to worry the British and keep them out.

To finance the war, Washington issued $150 million in paper currency printed with green ink and backed, not by gold, but by the good word of the government. Markets roiled and men's hearts raced as stories of battles sent stocks bouncing up and down. Defeat in Lexington and Lynchburg caused a lack of confidence in the Union, devaluing the paper money and pushing gold prices up; success in Fredericksburg, Gettysburg, and Vicksburg sent greenbacks up and gold prices reeling down.

As always, Hetty traipsed between New York and New England, making excursions by steamboat to Saratoga in summer and traveling to New Bedford all year long. In 1864 on a trip to Boston she entered the popular dining room of the elegant Parker House hotel, famous for its puffy rolls and chocolate cream pie. Spotting a family friend, she stopped to say hello to Solon Goodridge, whose business, like her father's, was in China trade. He introduced her to his luncheon companion, Mr. Edward Green, who also knew her father. Miss Robinson's good looks caught the eye of the stranger. Goodridge's grandson recalled the story: "Hetty walked into the hotel dining room and Mr. Green fell for her." He had recently returned from Asia and was living in New York at the Union Club. Perhaps he might see her sometime.

As the war turned for the North, New York enjoyed another flourish. At Tiffany's, customers demanded egg-sized pearls and diamonds. At A. T. Stewart's, they made a monstrous rush for thousand-dollar camel's-hair shawls. On Thirty-fourth Street opposite Caroline Astor's new mansion, Mr. Stewart paid $100,000 for a house that he razed and replaced with a million-dollar marble palazzo. Farther uptown the thriving abortionist Madame Restell was planning a gilded French palace. On Madison Square, the Wall Street speculator Leonard Jerome built a brick house with a mansard roof, paneled walnut stables, and a private theater that seated six hundred guests. All around the city, middle-aged boys were building sand castles of marble and brownstone and lining their walls with landscapes freshly painted by artists such as Frederick Church and Thomas Cole.

Whatever others spent, Edward Robinson remained true to himself, as cautious as ever with every penny. While showy men stuffed their homes with flamboyant furnishings from France, he equipped his rooms with brown furniture from his house in Massachusetts. While speculators wagered on puts and calls and gambled heavily on thin margin, he invested cautiously in stocks and bonds, purchased parcels of real estate, including land outside Chicago, and put money in mines out west.

Thrifty to the point of stinginess, he was not so different from the man of whom Mark Twain wrote: "he dried snow in his oven in order to sell it for salt." His frugality showed in his support for the Illinois-born Abraham Lincoln. With the presidential campaign picking up steam, the Republicans asked for Robinson's help, and he proudly pledged $500 for Lincoln's reelection. Then he turned to his partner William Coleman, a Democrat, and announced what he had done. He advised the man to pledge the same amount for Lincoln's opponent, McClellan. "I told them the Democrats would expect $500 from you, and I was going to pair off. So mind," he said to Coleman, "you stick to that arrangement. It will be all the same to both parties, and it won't cost either of us a cent."

"He was a good fellow in the main," Coleman later remarked. "But he exceeded any man I ever knew in ingenious expedients for saving a dollar."

As much as Edward worried over saving money, Hetty agonized over her inheritance. With Aunt Sylvia becoming more sickly, the physician, William Gordon, hovered over her more closely. He had moved out of his house, where he lived with his wife and daughters, and established himself with Sylvia at Round Hills. The longer he remained, dulling her pain with opium, the more she relied on him, not just for medical care, but for advice of every sort. His influence grew by the day.

News of Sylvia's ill health and other activities traveled fast through the town of New Bedford and reached as far as New York. A letter to Hetty informed her that her aunt, now under the constant care of the doctor, had secretly drawn up a new will. Distraught, Hetty suffered again from headaches and turned to her father, who wrote to Thomas Mandell, the estate's trustee: "I am indifferent myself," Edward told his former partner, "strange as that may seem to you." But Hetty was "much troubled about it—made sick." In a lengthy letter back, Mandell reassured his friend, venturing an opinion that "Hetty has no cause to fear . . . her aunt will leave to her all the property she will ever need."

It may not have been much of a surprise that her aunt was growing more feeble, but Hetty was shocked when, in early 1865, her strong and healthy father took ill. Serving as his nurse, a role she always played with pride, she held the thermometer and recorded his fever, kept track of his nourishment, and noted the times of his medication. At his request, she worked closely with him on his portfolio of stocks, bonds, and real estate and on his shipping business, which demanded extensive daily attention to commodities prices and futures trading, shipping rates, banking rates, worldwide credit, and politics. After years at his side, Hetty felt more than competent to analyze the news, assess the financial markets, and keep her father abreast of changes. Yet she worried over her father's will and hounded his assistant to make sure she would receive all his money.

Chapter 7

═══

A Will to Win

Hetty's calling card announced she would be at home on Thursdays at 19 West Twenty-sixth Street. There, in the brownstone she shared with her father, Mr. Edward "Ned" Green arrived like a burst of fresh air. Well over six feet tall and weighing over two hundred pounds, with blond hair and blue eyes, he had a robust personality and a generous bent. Fluent in several languages, Edward Henry Green was a businessman who had ventured far and wide, a conversationalist who amused his audience with fantastical anecdotes, a gourmand who feasted on life.

Born and brought up in Vermont, he had trained in business in Boston and lived abroad for twenty years, representing firms in the Far East. He had worked for Solon Goodridge in Hong Kong and was a partner with Russell Sturgis & Company, a major merchant firm in China and Manila. Trading in tea, silk, and opium in China, and in sugar in the Philippines, Russell Sturgis used William T. Coleman & Company to carry some of its cargo.

Edward Green's travels had taken him across the Pacific and tested his personal skills. On a voyage with a colleague from Hong Kong to Macao and Canton, he came face-to-face with pirates and major storms, the common dangers of Chinese waters. Caught in a typhoon, with their boat forced to anchor close to an island, they found themselves surrounded by seven pirate ships. As the two American men looked out from their boat, they could see the cold eyes of a dozen men, the ugliest ruffians they had ever encountered, staring straight at them. While his friend shivered nervously at the sight, Edward Green sat in front of the window, his legs stretched out on the table, making faces at the wretched-looking crew. "He was the coolest man I ever saw. Nothing moved him out of his imperturbable calm," his friend later recalled.

In Canton, the two men received so many invitations to dinner, they didn't know which to choose. Never perturbed, Edward Green solved the problem by walking in the alleyways behind the kitchens of their acquaintances' homes. He surveyed the duck, the quail, the pheasants, and fish laid out by the cooks and chose the house that had the most tempting food. "He had a great way of taking care of himself," said his friend. He also took care of his family, and sent magnanimous gifts to his mother.

After two decades of overseas adventure, EH Green, as he signed his name, accumulated a fortune. A millionaire at the age of forty-four, he had decided recently to come home. It was time to marry, have a family, and settle down. He had taken up residence at the fashionable Union Club and found New York, as he wrote to a friend, "rather a pleasant place for a stranger. Lots of balls, dinners, parties going on all the time."

His money, ensured by his bankers, his background, vouched for by Mr. Goodridge, and his affiliation with the Union Club, where Henry Grinnell and William Coleman were also members, struck the right chord. Although his religion was Episcopalian and his attitude was extravagant, his heritage as a New Englander and his reputation for hard work held him in good stead. He may have indulged in too much good food and wine, but he had a keen sense for business and a proper respect for wealth. In the eyes of Edward Robinson, he was a suitable beau for thirty-year-old Hetty.

With her father's encouragement, Edward courted her. At the parties and dinners they attended and in conversations everywhere, they could not escape the latest news of the war. When the Union captured Richmond and the Confederate army withdrew in April 1865, New York went wild in celebration. Even as the fighting sputtered on, the war that had torn the country apart, destroyed the lives of more than 600,000 people, and shredded the South to bits was coming to an end. The city cheered with a sea of flags, bursts of cannon fire, and hundred-gun salutes.

How quickly the joy disappeared. Only a few days later, the headlines shrieked, LINCOLN ASSASSINATED. The flags that had waved so brilliantly were now lowered to half mast. The crowds that had cheered so noisily were now eerily quiet. The city that glittered in gold was now shrouded in black crepe.

Death was descending, too, in the Robinson household. As he lay in bed growing weaker, Edward Robinson worried over his daughter's spinster state and the state of her finances. When her suitor asked permission for marriage, Hetty's father eagerly agreed. He had told his associates he did not believe Hetty was capable of taking care of her money herself. His daughter needed a clever man to advise her and he was satisfied that Edward Green could do the job. Along with his shrewdness and abilities, the man had plenty of money to support her, and, Edward Robinson felt sure, Hetty's fortune was not his aspiration. Just to be certain, he made a stipulation in his will that the couple would have to live on her husband's money.

Edward Green would have no claim to Hetty's inheritance, her father said. That would be hers alone: "separate and apart from any husband she married and free from the debts, control or interference of any such husband," he wrote. In addition, his advisers informed Hetty, while he was dictating his will at home in March 1865, that he was leaving his daughter an amount equal to Edward's, but placing the rest of his estate for her in the hands of trustees. Two months later, as Edward Robinson's health declined, the couple announced their engagement.

Ordinary fetes were forgotten as Hetty watched her once-vigorous father waste away. Their relationship had been as tangled as a sailor's knot: wounded by his early rejection of her as a female, she felt healed somewhat by his reliance on her in his illness. As he lay dying and delirious, he told her he had been poisoned and warned her that she might be next. On June 14, 1865, she bade him an ambivalent farewell. The sixty-five-year-old man who made the bulk of his money from the Howland whaling business was buried beside his wife and father-in-law in the fading light of New Bedford's fortunes.

Edward Mott Robinson died rich by any standard, worth almost $6 million, but Hetty was as tense as a harpooner taking aim as she listened to the reading of her father's will. He bequeathed to his daughter $1 million: $919,000 in cash plus ownership of a San Francisco waterfront warehouse. The rest was to be kept in trust. She would receive the income but would have no control of the principal. Upon her death, all of the principal would go to her children. Hetty was crushed, diminished by the sweep of a pen. The prior knowledge of her father's will did not prepare her for the lightning bolt of reality: her father was dead and most of her money would be managed by others. Once again she felt betrayed.

For years she had apprenticed at her father's side. For years she had shown her father how skillful she was at finance. For years she had proved she was as smart as any man. Yet, gone was the respect she thought she had earned. Gone was the confidence. Gone was the proof of love.

This time, at least, she had her fiancé to give her comfort; she had confidence in him and was content to take his advice. The following day she dispatched a letter to her father's associates announcing that any financial decisions would have to be made with the consent of Mr. Green.

> Gentlemen:
>   I have to request that you will answer any questions that Mr.
> E. H. Green may ask you on all matters about my father's
> business affairs. I wish you gentlemen to consult with Mr. Green
> on all matters of importance where advice is required.
>   Hetty H. Robinson.

Years later, they would show the note as evidence that she was crazy.

Grieving over the loss of her father, angry at her lack of control over the money, and enraged over his lack of confidence in her, Hetty was taken aback when, less than three weeks later, on Sunday, July 2, she received a summons to come to New Bedford. Aunt Sylvia was dying. Stunned by the news of the double deaths, and facing a battle over another will, she girded herself and made the trip once more.

The family and friends assembled at the Howland house on Eighth Street hardly welcomed Hetty. The physician William Gordon transfixed her with a stare and said, "Really, Miss Robinson, I am very sorry to see you looking so miserable. At best, you cannot hold out longer than a year."

Standing alone in the parlor after the funeral, she noticed a painting that now belonged to her. *The Hunt for an Honest Man,* an eighteenth-century painting of Diogenes attributed to the Italian artist Guido Reni, was one of her favorite pictures. But someone else had already claimed it and tagged it with their name.

Hours later, silent, swathed in black, Hetty listened as Sylvia's will was read aloud. Her aunt was the richest woman in New Bedford, and she was the only direct heir to the family fortune. Now she learned that Sylvia Ann Howland had assets of over $2 million that would be distributed around the town. Among those included were several widows and friends to whom she left $10,000 each; her employees Eliza and Fally, to whom she gave $3,000 each, and Electa, $5,000. Others were given trusts of $10,000 each. The city of New Bedford benefited in several ways: the Orphans' Home was given $20,000; the not-yet-completed National Sailors' Home received $20,000; the poor, aged, and infirm women of the city were to share in a trust of $50,000. Sylvia left $100,000 to the town so it could bring in water and increase its manufacturing; another $100,000 was to be shared between "liberal education," assumed by town officials to mean access to literature, science, and art, and the public library.

To specific individuals she left the following: to Thomas Mandell, the executor of her will, $200,000; to the three trustees of her will, including Dr. William Gordon, $50,000 each, plus yearly fees for overseeing the estate. In addition, to pacify Edward Robinson she left him $100,000. But in a codicil she revoked the gift to him, thanked Dr. Gordon for his professional and other services, and left him another $50,000, plus $10,000 to his wife and $5,000 to his daughters.

The rest, $1 million, would go to Hetty. But the money would be in trust, not cash; Hetty would receive the income on the investments. The man who would be in charge of the investments was Dr. Gordon. Furthermore, upon her death, the money would not go to Hetty's children but would revert to the Howland family. The will was signed by Sylvia, witnessed by three people, including a friend of William Gordon's, and dated September 1863, a year and a half after the agreement Hetty and Sylvia had written. The codicil, conceived soon after Edward Robinson wrote to Thomas Mandell in 1864, was drawn up by Judge John Williams, the father-in-law of Dr. Gordon.

Devastated, Hetty rested near the piano in the parlor. Close by, she heard two distant relatives snicker, "When Hetty dies we will have a whole greenhouse built onto our house."

As soon as the house was cleared of guests, she called for Fally, the housekeeper, and demanded the key to her aunt's private trunk. Rifling through the jewels, the clothes, and the papers, she found two envelopes, one yellow, one white, and pulled them out. Inside the yellow one, she found a copy of her own will; in the other was the will written by Sylvia in 1862. Downstairs, she showed Edward the copy of Aunt Sylvia's will with a second page attached.

Next, she met with her family's attorney, William Crapo, and raged like the child he had heard years ago in the dentist's chair. It was Dr. Gordon, she pointed out, who had drugged her aunt with laudanum and then helped her draw up the deceitful will. Indeed, Hetty would soon discover that William Gordon had actually dictated the codicil.

The money Hetty had been told she had to manage was now being managed by others. Her very self-worth was at stake. Over the course of several weeks she approached members of Sylvia's staff and tried to persuade them to contest the will. She traveled to the town of Taunton to see the probate judge and, in an act of desperation, tried to bribe him to cancel the will. On all accounts, she lost. Like the great Leviathan, the will would not be harpooned.

Wherever she went, ladies whispered, children pointed, men stared. She was the rich heiress trying to steal New Bedford's newfound wealth. Gossips snickered and the town's skunks sprayed her path with ugly rumors. Shopkeepers charged her more, or so it seemed; lawyers' fees kept mounting; newspapers shouted her name in large print. Shaken by the deaths and the turn of events, and recalling her father's warning, she worried that someone would try to kill her.

Edward was back in New York and she was afraid to be alone in the house. She offered a floor to a friend and his wife, who accepted and stayed there. Others came to visit, but at night she climbed the stairs to the fourth-floor attic and, like a frightened animal searching for safety, she crawled under a bed. "For days I did not leave my room and lived on crackers and raw eggs," she said. "All the time those schemers were trying to get my money."

In November, after a trial that made headlines from Boston to Chicago, the will was approved in probate court in New Bedford. One of her father's sayings rang in her ears: "The poor can't sue, and if the rich won't, who is to bring rogues to justice?" One month later, in December 1865, with William Crapo as her leading lawyer and Edward Green at her side, Hetty brought her case against the executors and trustees to the Supreme Court of Massachusetts.

"Strange how these millionaire families quarrel among themselves about money," wrote George Templeton Strong. "Brother alienated from brother, sisters at daggers down with sisters—and all about property, of which everyone of them has more than enough." He was referring to his clients, the Astors, whose family feuds still continue today. But they were not the first family to find themselves in court, nor would they would be the last. From the continuing saga of the Astor heirs to Henry Ford, who sued his family over his trust fund, to four generations of Pritzkers skirmishing over the family estate, to Curtis Nelson combating his mother and Sumner Redstone's daughter suing her father, relatives have fought bitter public battles for control of their family fortunes.

Unlike most of the others, Hetty's turned into a landmark case. Her suit against the trustees claimed that she was the lawful heir and that her aunt had always wanted her to inherit the money. In fact, Hetty learned, Sylvia had even told her own lawyer that she did not want to write a new will without notifying her niece. It was the deceitful Dr. Gordon, Hetty believed, who had dulled her aunt's mind and persuaded her to draw up a will against her own wishes. The proof was in the letter, clearly dictated by Hetty, that she had kept attached to Sylvia's will:

> Be it remembered that I, Sylvia Ann Howland, of New Bedford in County of Bedford, do hereby make, publish and declare this the second page of this will and testament made on the eleventh of January in manner following, to wit: Hereby revoking all wills made before or after this one—I give this will to my niece

to shew if there appears a will made without notifying her, and
without returning her will to her through Thomas Mandell as
I have promised to do. I implore the judge to decide in favor of
this will, as nothing would induce me to make a will unfavorable
to my niece, but being ill and afraid if any of my care-takers
insisted on my making a will to refuse, as they might leave or
be angry, and knowing my niece had this will to shew—my
niece fearing also after she went away—I hearing but one side,
might feel hurt at what they might say of her, as they tried to
make trouble by not telling the truth to me, when she was here
even herself. I give this will to my niece to shew if absolutely
necessary, to have it, to appear against another will found
after my death. I wish her to shew this will, made when I am
in good health for me, and my old torn will made on the fourth
of March, in the year of our Lord one thousand eight hundred
and fifty, to show also as proof that it has been my lifetime wish
for her to have my property. I therefore give my property to my
niece as freely as my father gave it to me. I have promised him
once, and my sister a number of times, to give it all to her, all
excepting about one hundred thousand dollars in presents to my
friends and relations.

Sylvia Ann Howland

The problem was the signature. It was identical to the one on the will.

Nearly everyone associated with Sylvia Howland and Hetty Robinson was asked to give a deposition, and their recollections, along with the testimony of the trial, filled a thousand pages of transcripts. Accusations flew back and forth, as Hetty charged the household staff with being covetous and conspiratorial, and they attacked her for being hostile and cruel. But the defendants' challenge turned the case around. The question they asked was: Who actually signed the letter? They claimed it was forged.

Sylvia's signature on the second page was identical with the one on the will. In order to prove that this was impossible, the trustees' three lawyers brought in major experts. To prove that it was entirely possible, Hetty's seven attorneys brought in authorities of equal weight: doctors, lawyers, bankers, surveyors, engravers, and experts in penmanship. The courtroom became a platform for speeches of excruciating length, and a class in mathematical proportions.

When the penmanship expert Mr. Crossman testified on Hetty's behalf, he said that after many months of painstaking research, he was completely convinced that the signature of Sylvia Ann Howland was genuine. But when the trustees' witness, Mr. Southworth, took the stand, he said that after many months of painstaking evidence, he was completely convinced that the signature was forged.

At the request of Hetty's lawyers, the noted Harvard naturalist Louis Agassiz, chairman of the Department of Natural History and founder of a Harvard museum, was one of the experts to testify. He had examined the signature with his "naked eye," "with spectacles," and with low- and high-powered microscopes, he said, and there were no indications it had been traced.

Again, at the request of her counsel, the celebrated Harvard lawyer and doctor Oliver Wendell Holmes was called upon. Professor of anatomy and physiology, poet, philosopher, and renowned figure in the arts, he had studied the signature with compound microscopes and declared it definitely had not been traced. The third person they asked to testify, John Quincy Adams, vouched that his grandfather, the sixth American president, had penned his name many times and often the signatures were identical.

In response, the defendants produced numerous witnesses who swore that the signature was a forgery. Of all their experts, the most elaborate testimony came from Benjamin Peirce, the Harvard mathematician, and his son, Charles, who spat out numbers like a whale spouting water. After numerous hours of statistical exploration, they had concluded that such a coincidence could have happened "once in 2,666 millions of millions of millions of times," he declared. "This number far transcends human experience. So vast an improbability is practically an impossibility." Without doubt, both Peirces concluded, the signature was forged.

As the seemingly endless lawsuit continued, trailing headlines in its wake, Hetty and Edward traveled back and forth to Massachusetts until, finally, they settled in New York. Although Edward was still connected to Russell Sturgis & Company, they spent time together on her investments.

The outlook for the country was confusing. With the Civil War now ended, some investors believed the country's future looked rosy. Miners were uncovering vast deposits of copper, gold, and silver in the West, while huge numbers of people were taking advantage of the Homestead Act and settling the new land. In the East manufacturing was booming, more railroad tracks were being laid, and the transcontinental railroad would soon be hauling freight between the two coasts. It was a buoyant scene.

But as with the canvas of an artist who has changed his mind, a reverse image could be seen on the other side. The devastation of the South, the high debt caused by the war, and the disarray of the Union created a stormy picture. Many people viewed the country's economy as doubtful. Seeing chaos around the corner, they worried about the stability of the government and refused to pay face value for its greenbacks. Instead, they rushed to gold.

The rules of the marketplace state that for every seller there must be a buyer. The more the public discounted paper money, pushing it down as low as fifty cents on the dollar, the more Hetty bought. This was the start of the contrary investing she followed for the rest of her life: buying when everyone else was selling; selling when everyone else was buying. "I buy when things are low and nobody wants them. I keep them until they go up and people are crazy to get them. That is, I believe, the secret of all successful business," she said.

Her philosophy reverberates today in the transactions of Warren Buffett. After a tumultuous period in the stock market, he told his shareholders in 2010: "We've put a lot of money to work during the chaos of the last two years. It's been an ideal period for investors: a climate of fear is their best friend."

The American government was also finding bargains, paying $7 million to Russia for the vast and vacant territory of Alaska. The deal was arranged by the Russian ambassador, Baron Stoeckel, whose wife had chaperoned Hetty in Saratoga. "What can the country gain by ownership of that desolate, dreary, starved region?" asked George T. Strong. But even if, as he suggested, "the disquisition of territories endears administrations to the people," the government refused the offer from Spain to purchase Cuba and Puerto Rico for $150 million.

The appeal of America reached well beyond its shores. To those who were optimistic, huge opportunities could be seen in western mining, eastern manufacturing, and the prospect of railroads crisscrossing the country. In 1866, Edward Green traveled abroad to explore the possibility of attracting European investors seeking a place to put their money.

Hetty was having doubts about the forthcoming marriage. Edward's travels, the interminable court case, apprehension over matrimony, the clash of their strong personalities, all undoubtedly contributed to tension in their relationship. But a rare and newly discovered note that Hetty sent in 1866 may reveal more. On January 19, 1866, she wrote to the treasurer of the Boston & Providence Railroad: "Please pay Mr. E. H. Green any dividend now due on my stock in your road. Hetty H. Robinson." Edward was rich, but he had a reputation as a speculator and a gambler. Did he need money? Had he asked his fiancée for a loan? And did he do this more than once? The friction was so great that they broke their engagement several times. And this foretold troubles to come.

But Edward was the one person who had stood by her side through the deaths, the funerals, and the lawsuits. He was the one person whom she could count on for moral support. He was the one man her father felt would provide for her and their future family and would advise her well on financial pursuits. And he was the one man she cared for. After a round of lovers' quarrels and heated feuds, they settled their disagreements, and on Thursday, July 11, 1867, with the court case still hanging over them, they married.

The wedding took place at the home of Henry and Sarah Grinnell. As Hetty's guests rode in their carriages toward Bond Street, they saw shabby buildings and boardinghouses that had grown like patches of weed around what had been one of the most elegant blocks in New York. But like her cousin Henry, whose simple Quaker beliefs betrayed his high-toned Episcopal ties, Hetty cared not a whit for society's whims and its promenade uptown. The solid brick house where she had first been introduced as a debutante was the perfect place to celebrate her marriage.

Dressed in a Victorian gown, thirty-four-year-old Hetty wore a hooped skirt and a fitted, boned top that showed off her soft white shoulders; two pink roses and a profusion of curls set off her dark blond hair. Seen in a photograph, she looked "astonishingly beautiful," said a reporter later on. Edward, thirteen years older, wore his shock of blond hair parted in the middle and waved back, his thick mustache curled nattily. His large frame was draped in a well-cut suit, a red rose pinned on his lapel. They made a stunning couple.

Hetty invited Annie Leary to be her bridesmaid, and among the other guests were the children of Henry and Sarah Grinnell, her cousin Moses Grinnell and his family, and her friend Catherine Lorillard Wolfe. Edward's sister Henrianna and her husband, Reverend John Jay Elmendorf, who had established an Episcopal church and choir on Broadway and Thirty-fourth Street, no doubt attended, and so, possibly, did Edward's mother, who resided in Bellows Falls.

In the parlor, the wedding party looked on as the minister stood before the couple and asked for their vows. The bride and groom declared "I do," swearing to walk together down life's path. But Hetty had already set a course for her own life: her aunt had been the richest woman in New Bedford; now she was on the way to becoming the richest woman in America.

Chapter 8

═══

A New Life

It took several months to put their papers in order and make the proper arrangements, but in October 1867, with newspaper headlines still screaming about the Howland Will Case, Mr. and Mrs. Edward H. Green packed their trunks, ferried to Jersey City, and boarded the steamship *Russia*. Its maiden voyage just behind her, the sleek boat was the latest addition to Cunard's fleet. One of the fastest liners of the day, and one of the most graceful ships at sea, it carried mail back and forth across the Atlantic, brought cotton, cheese, grains, and leather to Europe, and yarn, textiles, and "articles de Paris" to America. The proud *Russia* steamed across the ocean with its figurehead preening from its bow and its red smokestack gleaming among its three white masts.

With the reliable Captain T. Cook at the helm, the daily regime began as the passengers awoke each morning to find their shoes polished and waiting at their door and their stewards waiting, at the call of a bell, to help them dress. They found breakfast ready in the huge dining room and stewards in blue uniforms ready to serve them generous portions of baked ham, Irish stew, mutton chops, broiled salmon, smoked salmon, cold tongue, veal cutlets, cooked eggs, tea, coffee, chocolate, hot rolls, and toast offered at the morning meal.

After they changed for their promenades, they held tight on the polished rails as the North Sea waves thrashed against the hull and the ship held against the roiling sea. Then, with blankets wrapped around them, they reclined on wooden chaises and breathed in the salty air.

Lulled by the maritime monotony, they sat with books borrowed from the ship's library, covers unopened or pages unread, while their main activities consisted of idle gossip or a fleeting gaze at a flying porpoise or a giant whale.

Later, attired in their dinner clothes, the newly married Mr. and Mrs. Green, the merchant shippers the Aspinwalls, the Basses, and other members of society in the first-class saloon toasted one another with Heidsieck or with Wachter's extra cuvée, the champagne preferred by the Queen Mother and the Prince of Wales. Attended by a surfeit of dining room stewards, their hunger increased by the bracing air, they shunned the foul-smelling water, chose from a menu that featured turtle soup and filet de boeuf, and washed down their food with a bevy of good red wines. Later, they played conundrums, charades, or chess, held spelling bees or history contests.

After tea in the main saloon, the men wandered into the paneled smoking room, where they played cards and puffed on pipes and cigars, while the women edged onto tufted chairs in the ladies' cabin and caught up on the latest shipboard romances. At the end of the exhausting day, they bid one another good night and, retreating to their staterooms, where the stewardesses had placed oranges and other goodies under their pillows, they tucked themselves under the eiderdown and let the waves rock them to sleep.

Two days out everything changed as the ocean opened up, the waves grew higher, the wind harder, the fog deeper, and the ship bounced like a toy tossed on the high seas. Fewer and fewer passengers appeared in the dining saloon and more and more the talk turned to remedies for *mal de mer*: everything from mustard plaster to pickles mixed with potatoes was suggested, but none of it worked. Instead, as Harriet Beecher Stowe described it, "You lie disconsolate in your berth, only desiring to be let alone to die."

And then, in nearly record time, little over a week, they made landfall at Liverpool. Their stay may not have been as extensive as the grand tour, but it lasted far longer than the typical honeymoon on the Continent; for the next seven years the Greens made their home in England.

Arriving in London, they found the city still in a swirl over the visit of the sultan of Turkey. Abdülaziz was the first sultan from Constantinople to make a peaceful visit to the West. His richly embroidered clothes, exotic harem, and intriguing eunuchs dazzled the British, who welcomed him with a festoon of flowers and flags, brilliant dinners, and a grand ball that drew fifteen thousand guests. The sultan reigned over one of the largest empires in the world, reaching from the Danube to the Persian Gulf.

It was the British Empire, however, that stretched around the globe. Its merchant ships sailed the high seas, bringing its businessmen to India and Australia, Canada and the United States, procuring the raw materials to manufacture at home and selling them back to the rest of the world, all at considerable profit. As the British navy ruled the seas, so Queen Victoria ruled the parlors, from royalty to peasantry. Save for a group of suffragists who fought for their rights from an office on Langham Place, women's lives were dominated by domestic skills and procreation, while the men strove to enrich the empire.

The Prince of Wales symbolized the glory of that empire, and when he snipped the ribbon on the new Langham Hotel, he opened the way for Americans to experience London at its most opulent. This was the place where Edward and Hetty resided. True to Edward's taste and paid for from his pocket, the Langham was the largest and most luxurious hotel in the city, with an elaborate ballroom with gilded columns and chandeliers, its own artesian well, hot and cold running water, and a bathroom in each bedroom.

As Hetty and Edward walked across the thick Oriental carpets and stepped into the elevator that lifted them to their floor, they were in the company of the rich, the titled, and the celebrated. In the course of the Greens' stay, distinguished poets and writers such as Samuel Clemens, William Cullen Bryant, and Henry Wadsworth Longfellow, along with the artist Albert Bierstadt, the entrepreneur Andrew Carnegie, and the explorer Sir Henry Stanley, could be seen at one time or another reading the *Times,* snoozing by the fire, or sipping a brandy in the lounge.

Once they settled in at the hotel on fashionable Portland Place, Edward attended to business in the City: at one end stood the Bank of England, stretched across Threadneedle Street, a Temple of Fortune for the here and now; at the other end rose St. Paul's Cathedral, a Temple of Fortune for the hereafter. The portly Mr. Green weaved his way through the narrow sidewalks of the world's financial capital, passing the speculators and financiers, the nail-chewing clerks, plump promoters, and dapper entrepreneurs who all hoped for blessings at both ends.

Based in his office in Gresham House on Old Broad Street, Edward represented his firm, Russell Sturgis & Company, on the board of a California bank. Like the financial houses of Jay Cooke and the Morgans, or the Seligmans and the newly established Kuhn Loeb, which had links to the rich but insular Jewish communities, the London and San Francisco Bank sought European money to invest in the United States. Founded by Milton Latham, a former governor and senator from California, the L&SF Bank's aim, in particular, was to entice British investment to the state. Along with Edward Green, the small board of directors included Junius S. Morgan, father of J. P. Morgan; two bankers, Henry Bischoffsheim, a prominent German investor, and Baron Herman Stern, nephew of N. M. Rothschild, who gave them access to Jewish financiers they ordinarily could not reach; and a handful of other distinguished men. They were "impressed with the promising prospects of California and its immense agricultural and mining resources," said the *Times* of London. They were also impressed with railroads and their impact on America.

During the Civil War, railroads were vital for transportation. With southern lines and waterways cut off, the Union government encouraged the consolidation of existing northern routes, enabling soldiers to travel to the battlefronts and facilitating the shipment of food from the Midwest to the East. But while the railroads were heavily utilized, most work on them had come to a halt. Promoters abandoned plans for new track and cars, and the existing equipment was overused and abused, hauling hordes of soldiers and tons of supplies, including mules, horses, guns, and gunpowder, to battle points and beyond. Some lines, like the Louisville and Nashville, profited from the transport; others were ruined, run into the ground.

By the end of the war, optimistic entrepreneurs focused on the railroads once again, knowing they were the fastest and cheapest way to ship the greatest amount of goods, bringing fresh meat and fresh grains back to the East, and bringing newly manufactured goods and a fresh supply of immigrants to farm the new land in the West.

Improved railroads would lead to increased production of iron, steel, coal, and cotton. They could fuel factories and provide jobs, enrich the earnings of average men, allow families to purchase houses, and enhance everyone's lives.

The engineer John Roebling, who went on to build the Brooklyn Bridge, called railroads "a magic wand that could open slumbering resources and long hidden treasures of the earth; convert stone, and iron into gold." The railroads were the great locomotive leading America's future. For Walt Whitman they were the "modern engine of motion and power/pulse of the continent." But financiers were needed to fuel that engine, to supply fresh money to replace the broken rails and rolling stock, and to begin the vital work on a line that linked the entire country east to west. "As yet, no portion of the world except a few narrow stretches of western Europe had ever been tolerably provided with the essentials of comfort and convenience," said Henry Adams. "To fit out an entire continent with roads and the decencies of life would exhaust the credit of the entire planet."

The U.S. government provided vast amounts of tax-free land around the tracks in the West and gave rights to the minerals in the ground; but in order to finance the projects, the railroad builders borrowed money, using the land as collateral. American bankers eagerly loaned them the money for construction, and then, to soften their own risk and increase their profits, they issued bonds. Seeking money for the bonds in London, Paris, and Frankfurt, they were welcomed with open arms. The Bank of England was paying interest rates of 3 to 6 percent, while the Americans were offering as much as 18 percent to lenders. Pleased to find such an attractive place for their funds, the Europeans quadrupled their investments to over $200 million in railroads and $1 billion in American stocks and bonds.

While Edward engaged in business for the bank, Hetty had her own business to attend to, concentrating on investing the interest from her father's trust fund. Like Andrew Carnegie, who cried, "Eureka! Here's the goose that lays the golden egg" when he discovered the power of dividends, Hetty had already learned the magic of compound interest. As a child she used her allowance to earn interest in the savings bank and saw it grow. Now she used her money to earn a high yield, paid in gold, on Civil War bonds. Even better, she could reinvest those dividends to earn more. And all the time she was compounding her return.

Abigail Adams, who had bought "State Notes" after the Revolutionary War when there was little confidence in the new government, found out the value of depreciated bonds. Against the objections of her husband, John, who put his money in land, Abigail used her pin money to buy the bonds, which increased far more in value than her husband's real estate. With Edward's knowledge of railroads and banking, with American industry booming, and with inflation soaring, Hetty increased her share of railroad stocks and U.S. Treasury bonds. The bonds would prove to be an outstanding investment.

"I started out by buying government bonds and Rock Island stock," Hetty said, describing her first year in London. Using the gold she received as interest, she bought the bonds at a discount and earned a solid dividend. Bonds yielding 6 percent that had sold in 1866 for a market price of $75 in gold were selling in 1868 for $82 in gold, and in 1869 for $90. "In one day of that year I added a clean $200,000 to my bank account. That's the most I ever made in one day," she boasted. By the end of a year in London, her profits reached $1.25 million.

The opportunities were enormous for those with the stomach to take the risks. "Never borrow," Hetty's father told her, and she obeyed. But men like Edward Green and J. P. Morgan speculated, borrowing money at low rates in London and using the funds to buy U.S. railroad bonds yielding higher rates, and then reselling them in Europe. Some traders were buying gold in London, packing it up, and shipping it to the United States, where operators like Jay Gould, eager to corner the market, were offering ninety-day notes at huge discounts in exchange for the gold. Gould and the others were cornering the market, buying all the available gold, pushing up the price, and forcing anyone who wanted to purchase gold to go to them. The American government broke the corner by putting more gold on the market, and many traders who had paid soaring prices for the gold lost their fortunes.

Opportunists in London were also buying greenbacks from local merchants: English businessmen were paid in paper money by American customers but could not exchange the greenbacks for a decent rate at the British banks. Promissory notes, cosigned by prestigious bankers, were being sold at discounts as high as 60 percent. Marcus Goldman, an immigrant from Germany, set up an office on Pine Street to buy and sell this commercial paper. Later he would team with his son-in-law Samuel Sachs, forming the company Goldman Sachs, to raise capital for American companies. When the American government agreed to pay par value for greenbacks, making the paper money almost equal to gold, arbitrageurs like Goldman and the Lazard Brothers, based in California and London, made a fortune.

Only a small group of investors had access to as much information as Hetty did on the railroads and their maze of lines. Her transatlantic connections, her insistent research, her in-depth questioning, and her constant reading helped her decipher the complicated financial code and decide which rails to invest in and which to avoid. Some roads were expanding, increasing their lines across lucrative territory; others were laying useless track. The Louisville and Nashville, one of the few to survive the Civil War, was growing from a local line to an interstate road. The Union Pacific was building its transcontinental route, and the London and San Francisco Bank was offering the bonds to finance it at 7 percent interest. The completion of the route, announced in May 1869, was "a most important event, national and international," noted one observer. Americans celebrated not just the success of the venture, but the triumph of connecting the country: in Washington, officials fired cannons, in New York and Boston, church bells rang, and in Philadelphia, the city fathers clanged the Liberty Bell.

Along with J. P. Morgan, Andrew Carnegie, and Commodore Vanderbilt, Hetty had amassed a substantial stake in the railroads. Correspondence in Hetty's handwriting that has recently been found suggests the extent of her transactions from London. Hetty was buying railroads like a giddy girl buying gumdrops. In a letter from Paris dated February 16, 1868, and sent to the firm of S. F. Goodridge at 81 Pine Street in New York, she ordered the delivery of eighty-eight shares of Western Railroad and thirty-four shares of Boston and Worcester Rail Road to John J. Cisco's bank. Four months later from London she ordered the delivery to Cisco of 1,250 shares of the "Pittsburg Fort Wayne & Chicago Railroad and 700 shares of Reading Railroad which you now hold belonging to me." In October 1868 she ordered $13,000 worth of Chicago and Rock Island Rail Road bonds delivered to Cisco. In January 1869 she wrote to Goodridge: "Please deliver to the order of Mr. John J. Cisco & Son one thousand three hundred and seventy shares of the Rock Island & Pacific Rail Road belonging to me . . . Hetty Howland Robinson Green." The following month she ordered Goodridge to deliver to Cisco more than five hundred shares divided among eight different railroads, including the Boston & Maine; Boston & Providence; Vermont & Canadian; and the Philadelphia, Wilmington & Baltimore (the predecessor to Amtrak). Hetty was no frivolous young wife wandering aimlessly through her inheritance; she was a brisk investor plowing her money into America's future.

Active in finance, Hetty was also flourishing on the personal front. She and Edward traveled across the continent and visited friends in the English countryside. At their London hotel, they could enjoy elegant meals in the brocaded dining room, or read in the palm-fringed lounge, or relax in their lavish suite. On August 22, 1868, in her bed at the Langham, she gave birth to a son, Edward Howland Robinson Green. Her mandate was to protect the family fortune and keep it intact for the next generation. Her son's birth ensured her an heir; she would make certain he inherited her wealth. Hetty's wish for Ned, his nickname for life, was that he be the richest man in the nation. She would do everything in her power to make that wish come true. But even before Ned was two months old, Hetty received news that posed an obstacle to her goal.

Hetty's Massachusetts lawsuit against the trustees of her aunt's estate was founded on the idea that she and Sylvia had made a contract to draw up mutual wills. The trustees had countered with charges that Sylvia's signature on the will was fake. In the end the judge ignored both sides and surprised them all when he declared a mistrial based on a technicality.

The state's law restricts the right of a witness to testify for him- or herself in an action involving a contract when one of the other parties is dead. With Sylvia no longer alive, Hetty could not testify on her own behalf. But without her testimony, the court declared there was not enough evidence to justify her claim. Nonetheless, the judge predicted, the case would serve as an example for establishing rules of evidence in other forgery cases. Indeed, the Howland Will Case, the first proceeding to use statistical evidence, continues to be read and discussed in legal textbooks and lawsuits.

Hetty's case was dismissed, but she was unwilling to accept the decision and filed an appeal. A few weeks later the two sides compromised. Hetty agreed that the parties would receive what they were bequeathed plus 6 percent interest annually from the date of Sylvia's death. Upon Hetty's death, the money would revert to the estate and be distributed to all her grandfather Gideon Howland's heirs. She insisted, however, that the taxes on the money be paid from the principal, not from the income, and resolution of the case was delayed again.

On January 7, 1871, Hetty gave birth to a daughter: Hetty Sylvia Ann Howland Green. To those who thought it strange she had named her child after the woman whose will she had allegedly forged, Hetty insisted it was proof of her innocence. "Why do you suppose I'd have named my daughter Sylvia Ann Howland if I had forged my aunt's name?" she snapped. "I'd have had a living picture of forgery before me all these years." Her daughter would be less an image of her aunt Sylvia, more a reminder of her mother, Abby: overshadowed by the rest of her family, the girl clung to her family's side, hesitant to speak, fearful of making friends.

With the birth of Sylvia, Mama and Papa, as they affectionately called each other, moved their residence from the Langham Hotel near Portland Place to a private house off Fitzroy Square, not far from the British Museum. The census that year listed the four Greens and their eighteen-year-old servant, Elizabeth Williams, as living at 33 Charlotte Street, noting that Edward's business was "East India merchant." But he was far more than that. He was an affable member of London's clubs, a speculator in the financial markets, and a prospering director of three banks that now included the German Bank of London and the London Banking Association, whose interlocking directorates boasted some of the world's most influential financiers.

Edward's business took him to the Continent, where the London and San Francisco Bank had agents in Paris, Amsterdam, Antwerp, Berlin, and Frankfurt. Hetty sometimes joined him, crossing the channel through the narrow Dover Strait, watching the white cliffs fade away as the boat hurtled toward the French coast. In Calais they boarded a train for Paris, Holland, or Germany, where Edward marketed his railroad bonds and together they attended concerts and visited galleries. Later Hetty told a reporter: "I have seen art as it is in Paris, in London, in Munich, in Holland, and there is real art there, as you no doubt know." There was real art in America too, she added.

Of all the experiences she had, there was one in particular that she liked to relive. Edward's colleague Milton Latham, the head of the London and San Francisco Bank in California, was building a home for his new bride. The million-dollar house on Nob Hill was being furnished by the well-known Herter Brothers in the Second Empire style, and Latham wanted five thousand yards of curtain lace to cover the windows in the fifty-room mansion. He asked Hetty to purchase the lace for him in Paris.

Staying at the Hotel du Louvre, in the shadow of the museum and the Palais Royal, Hetty had samples brought to the room and proceeded to order the delicate fabric. As always, she was wary of the shopkeeper. To make sure she received exactly what she wanted, she laid the piece of duchesse lace across a cushion and worked for hours pushing pins inside the cutouts to retrace the pattern. A few days later her order arrived, and just as she suspected, the fine lace had been replaced with a coarser one. Take it back, she told the owner, who informed her she knew nothing about lace. "I may know nothing about lace but this is twice as rough," she said. When the shop owner threatened to sue, the Quaker lady produced the pin cushion and the pattern she had laid out. "I'll sue you," she said (another pattern she would follow for life). With that, the shop owner produced the delicate lace she demanded. Hetty enjoyed almost nothing as much as outwitting a man, especially when the man was trying to outwit her.

Back in England, she and Edward enjoyed the company of W. Wetmore Cryder and his wife, and chose him to be godfather to their newborn daughter. Cryder, who came from a family of merchant shippers involved in the opium trade in the Far East, was now a colleague of Edward's. The two men planned a shipping company that would run a line of steamers from China and Japan to a U.S port on the Pacific that would connect with American railway lines, but the business venture never took off.

The Greens sojourned in the country and at the seaside and spent time in Sussex with Hetty's cousin Sylvia Grinnell. The daughter of

Henry and Sarah Grinnell, she was married in England in 1871 to Captain William Fitz-Herbert Ruxton, a British navy man. Hetty and Edward most likely attended her wedding and Sylvia Ruxton served as godmother to the Greens' daughter, Sylvia.

They visited their friends Robert Rodger, a British barrister who carried the titles Lord of the Manor of Hadlow and Peckham and High Sheriff of Kent, and his wife, Sophia, who was godmother to Ned. There was not only space for the children to poke around Hadlow Castle, the Rodgers' huge Gothic home in Kent, there was more than enough room to accommodate the Greens and their maid. The philosopher Edmund Burke, an eighteenth-century visitor, found the apartments "lofty and spacious"; few guests could ignore the eleven bedrooms or the 120-foot corridor illuminated by stained-glass windows, the sculpture court lined with ancient Greek statues, and the awesome tower inspired by Burke's *Sublime*. And as if staying in a castle were not enough, her friends arranged something even better: with an engraved invitation in hand, Hetty dredged up her debutante days and practiced her curtsy before she was presented to Queen Victoria.

In town, she enjoyed more pedestrian pleasures, taking the children on strolls to Regent's Park, to the zoo, or along the city's leafy streets. On a long walk from their house to Knightsbridge, Hetty noticed a delivery man suddenly fall from his cart. A crowd quickly gathered around and stared as the man lay bleeding, but no one did anything to help. Hetty, dressed as usual in plain, outdated clothes, told the children to stay near a tree while she rushed to the wounded man's side. Years of caring for her mother, father, and aunt had taught her skills in nursing, and she quickly ordered an onlooker to run for a doctor, told another to bring some water, and cleaned the man's cuts with her handkerchief.

As she returned to her children, a footman approached and asked that she follow him to his marchioness's house. There, the lady complimented the rumpled Hetty, explained that she volunteered at a charity hospital, and offered her a job as superintendent. When Hetty politely declined, the footman followed her home. Later, he returned with an apologetic note. The marchioness did not realize who she was; would she please accept the tickets to the bazaars and entertainments enclosed in the envelope? Hetty returned them all and later called on the woman, thanking her for the compliment of a job offer. She told the story often: more than an accolade, it was recognition of Hetty as a worthy human being.

If Hetty enjoyed her anonymity in England, another woman exulted in fame in America. Victoria Woodhull, a spiritualist from the Midwest, and her sister Tennessee, also a clairvoyant, had wooed and won the support of Cornelius Vanderbilt. Grateful for Victoria's advice on stocks, which she had given him while she was in a trance, the railroad king agreed to set them up with a brokerage firm on Wall Street. The women caused a stir. Wearing cropped hair, men's jackets, ruffled bibs, and bowties, with skirts that barely skimmed their ankles, they posed for photographers and quipped with reporters.

Their knack for publicity brought waves of curious men who pressed their noses against the windows and plenty of eager women willing to gamble their money with others of their gender. In the capacious back office, set aside for females and comfortably furnished with sofas and fancy glass, the sisters served strawberries covered in chocolate and toasted their clients with champagne. On the other side of the wall, their male employees carried out the business.

With a quick fortune in their pockets, the sisters soon began publishing *Woodhull and Claflin's Weekly,* condoning free love and calling for women's rights. Victoria even announced she was running for president of the United States. They held the public's attention with the first English edition of Karl Marx's *Communist Manifesto,* and caused a huge scandal when they reported the adulterous affair of the Reverend Henry Beecher with a married woman in his congregation.

Hetty Green had little interest in the suffragist movement or in the machinations of the sisters Woodhull. She was much more concerned with the alarming reports that arrived in the autumn of 1871. Telegraph wires across the United States and cables across the new transatlantic lines clattered out news that a fire was blazing across Chicago, devouring most of the city. Flames raced through the downtown, engulfing its wooden streets, wooden houses, banks and commercial buildings, its wooden hotels and churches, its wharves and grain elevators, destroying an area four miles long and one mile wide and leaving 150,000 people homeless.

Chicago had pulsed with the rhythm of trains and the surge of goods carried through its stations. The Midwestern hub for transportation and agriculture, it had helped fuel New York's and the nation's economy. Chicago's businessmen not only came to New York and stayed in its hotels, attended its theaters, dined in its restaurants, and had their shoes shined by its bootblacks, they borrowed their money, directly or indirectly, from New York banks and bought their insurance from New York firms. Now as they forfeited their bank loans and claimed their insurance losses, their impact was felt far and wide. The stock market tumbled, a few small New York banks immediately closed their doors, and the reputable Manhattan Insurance Company announced its end.

Stunned by the news of the fire, Americans living in London gathered at the Langham Hotel to raise money for the victims. Hetty had more than a passing interest: her holdings included land around Chicago that she had inherited from her father as well as ownership in the Rock Island Railroad, the Chicago-based line that stretched across the Midwest. As fear of a financial panic roiled across the ocean, Edward went off to assess the damage in Chicago. Sailing on the SS *Scotia*, the largest ship in Cunard's fleet, on October 19, 1871, he arrived in New York.

Despite the fire in Chicago, prosperity graced the city. Like London, New York was flush with money. The city was flooded with an endless stream of funds from Europe, ready credit from the banks for mortgages, 10 percent margin accounts on Wall Street, junk bonds and other newly devised railroad debentures, and other instruments for trading stocks, such as puts and calls—the option to sell (puts) or buy (calls) a stock at a specified price—used by the financier Russell Sage. The abundance of money had encouraged a 500 percent increase in railroad building since the end of the Civil War, gaining land grants for the builders but allowing tracks to be laid that sometimes went aimlessly from point to point. Along with the railroad boom came massive real estate speculation and a rash of consumer spending across the country.

"Everybody seemed to be making money," said one writer, adding, "nobody suspected he was living in a fool's paradise." Even Chicago was quickly climbing back on its feet, with orders in place for steel and iron to erect buildings that would make it the most modern city in the country. In New York, where as fast as the stock market dropped, it bounced back, elegant patrons dined on oysters and champagne at Delmonico's new restaurant, formerly the home of Moses Grinnell, and exuberant shoppers crowded A. T. Stewart's and the new Tiffany's at Fifteenth Street and Broadway. While Edward took part in the Christmas rush, Hetty spent Christmas and New Year's alone with their children in England. By mid-January 1872, after their baby's first birthday, Edward was back in London. He and Hetty were together again with Ned and Sylvie, as she was now called.

Edward had hardly unlocked his trunks when his attention was turned again. Over the past few years, the Wall Street speculator Jay Gould and his cohorts had cornered the market on gold, captured control of the Erie Railroad, enriched themselves with its assets, and flooded the market with illegal stock. The Erie Ring, as they were called, had managed to bribe corrupt politicians and remain in control, but by March 1872 public outrage had swept away Boss Tweed and the ring was broken.

When the scurrilous Gould and his band of thieves were forced off the Erie board, European investors, who owned the majority of the railroad's stock, turned to a small group of bankers to represent their interests. They appointed Henry Bischoffsheim and E. H. Green to a committee of five, "all being persons of unquestionable influence and position in the best City circles," said the London *Times*, noting it was the sole topic of conversation on the stock exchange. That summer, adding to his prestige, Edward was made a director of both the Erie Railroad and the Great Western of Canada Railway.

To ensure the company's "proper direction," the new group, along with Junius Morgan, bought 100,000 shares of Erie, promising to hold them until a new board was elected. Although they tried to rescue the Erie and put it back on track, another railroad scandal soon rocked the American public. At the beginning of 1873 the newspapers reported that the builders of the Union Pacific had created a company called the Crédit Mobilier that had siphoned off all the railroad's profits and paid them to members of Congress in exchange for more government funds.

Americans were appalled at the sleaziness of their leaders: from the federal government to local cities and states, corruption greased the pockets of almost everyone in power. In London, bankers faced other problems. Central European banks and London financial institutions had made money readily available for speculation in railroads and real estate. Developers in Paris, Berlin, and Vienna were furiously erecting elaborate public buildings and private homes in the beaux arts style, even using the promise of future houses as collateral on new mortgages.

The rampant rush to buy more land at low interest rates sent property prices soaring. Yet even as the costs rose, real estate opportunists continued to borrow until they reached a point where buyers could not afford the land. The speculators were unable to pay back the interest on their loans. When the worthless mortgages caused a few European banks to collapse in the spring of 1873, the British institutions, wary of more shaky mortgages held by the rest of the banks, raised their lending rates. The bubble burst on the Continent.

Moody's magazine observed a few years later: "The world as a whole was money mad. . . . All the great European cities seem to have had booms at this time. Vienna and Berlin were the most frenzied. The prices of sites went to purely fictitious figures, and the phenomenon was prevalent of the speculator who bought property, mostly on credit which he did not expect to use, with the expectation of forestalling the deferred payments by a sale at an advance." The editors continued, "At the same time, Europe was pouring the oil of its money on the flames of American speculation. Railways spanned the continent and gridironed the states.

"Suddenly something snapped, and the machinery stopped. A Vienna banking house broke under the weight of too heavy a load of Missouri, Kansas & Texas securities, followed by another carrying too much Canada Southern. The financial organism winced like a leviathan with a harpoon in his vitals." As the spasms spread from stock exchanges to banks, and from banks to investors, from Istanbul to Stockholm and from Edinburgh to Alexandria, the world crouched in pain. The wounds had come from speculation, but, said *Moody's*, "No war ever made more misery."

British investors had been funding American railroads at a furious rate. Europeans held 80 percent of the American bonds, but with their heavy losses and money now scarce, they could no longer support the debentures. Other recent events were sending the markets spiraling downward. The Chicago fire, followed one month later by a major fire in Boston that destroyed sixty-five acres of downtown property at a loss of $100 million, had burned the insurance companies and banks and caused them to hold back on new loans.

The scarcity of funds triggered disaster: merchants defaulted because they could not find money to run their businesses; farmers went bankrupt because they could not borrow to plant their crops; railroads lost income because of the smaller shipments of food. The railroads were already suffering from the Erie Ring outrage with its worthless stock and corrupt activities in Washington; the Union Pacific scandal, which, like the Erie, uncovered stolen profits and bribed politicians; and a general loss of confidence in railroad management.

For weeks the stock market had been quiet in New York. When the New York Warehouse and Securities Co., which had backed the Missouri, Kansas & Texas Railroad, closed its doors on September 8, Wall Street men drew in their breath and sighed, hoping this was an isolated case.

Then the mood changed precipitously. Ten days later the Northern Pacific Railroad, which had been running at a loss and spending money to lay track faster than it was acquiring funds, announced on September 18, 1873, that it could no longer afford to pay bondholders its 8½ percent dividend. The railroad folded in default. The highly reputable banking house of Jay Cooke & Company, which earlier had raised hundreds of millions of dollars in bond sales to finance the Civil War, had loaned money to the Northern Pacific. Now the railroad was unable to pay its debts to Jay Cooke, and the prominent firm was forced to close.

The news hit the Stock Exchange like a hurricane: some brokers let out screams of alarm while others stood frozen in fear. And then, as suddenly as they had stopped, men started running to notify their Wall Street houses of the failure. "The brokers surged out of the Exchange, stumbling pell mell over one another in general confusion and reached their offices in race horse time," reported the *Times*.

Brokers had no time to deliberate: the bears were selling, few were buying, and prices were declining rapidly. On Wall Street that morning crowds stood buzzing in the frantic unrest. Two other major banks, including the highly prestigious Fisk and Hatch, with investments in the Central Pacific Railroad and the Chesapeake and Ohio Railroad, sank in the sea of default. No one could find the lifejackets to save the drowning banks.

Two days later, with panic growing on Wall Street, the storm turned into a tidal wave. Twenty brokerage firms shuttered their doors. Hordes of people rushed to withdraw their funds from the banks. At noon, when it was clear that no one was willing to buy at almost any price, the Stock Exchange closed its doors and kept them closed for ten days. A feverish mob filled Broad Street. When the eminent banking house of Henry Clews and Company closed, a shroud of gloom hung over the street. On the first day of the panic Western Union stock dropped ten points in ten minutes. Within two weeks the stock of the Rock Island Railroad had plunged from 108 to 86 and Union Pacific dropped from a high of 39 to a low of 14.

"Sunday, September 21, 1873 will be memorable in our history," declared a diarist. With the nation on the verge of financial ruin, men who usually crammed into church for Sunday prayers instead jammed the Fifth Avenue Hotel to plead for help from the president. Ulysses Grant had come there to meet with New York's leading businessmen. The bankers, including Cornelius Vanderbilt and Henry Clews, who met with Grant and his Treasury secretary, William Richardson, begged them to ease the money supply. Instead, the U.S. government bought up $13 million in bonds. It was only a temporary plug.

The bankers agreed to form a clearinghouse committee and pool their cash. But the storm that washed through New York was racing across the country as fast as cholera. More farmers could not get the cash they needed to ship their wheat and corn. More railroads continued to fail and more factories were forced to close. Thousands of people lost their jobs.

The panic took its toll on almost everyone. It terrorized men who looked as though they had aged ten years in one day. Brokers, vigorous the day before, were walking with their backs bent from the blows of the market. Bankers, so confident yesterday, were leaning on canes, unsteady on their feet today. "Energetic businessmen toddle around as if they had just risen from a bed of sickness," said George T. Strong.

"Paralysis, apoplexy and worse were all created by the panic in the street."

The *New York Times,* covering a congressional hearing a few years later, reported that in every case financial crises followed a period of rampant and extravagant speculation. "The panic of 1873 was preceded by an era of gigantic railroad and real estate speculations which were the principal causes of the panic. . . . [T]he speculation in land was enormous all over the country. Prices in real estate were multiplied beyond all precedent. . . . The obligations incurred in building the railroads and in this rail estate speculation were too enormous to be sustained and when the time came to settle up, people suddenly found themselves unable to resolve their obligations and became insolvent."

Across the panorama of history, the same potent forces that have driven men to war and devastation have also driven them to financial destruction. The markets may change, the methods may be revamped, but as long as human beings are propelled by greed and ego, they are doomed to repeat the mistakes of the past.

It had been a good seven years in London for the Greens. But stock prices were falling across the board, banks were failing, and the lucrative market for money in London had dried up. Many speculators were losing fortunes and Edward was no exception. The future in Europe looked grim. It was time for Mr. and Mrs. Green to go home.

Chapter 9

Return to America

Hetty and Edward Green, their children in tow, sailed on the *Russia* in early October 1873. The same Cunard ship that swept them off to London on their honeymoon was now steaming them back to New York. The city had burgeoned in the boom years. Ten-story buildings stood tall on the horizon, and Central Park stretched north as far as Eightieth Street. Expensive brownstone houses replaced the shanties that had sheltered impoverished German and Irish immigrants along Fifth Avenue up to the park, and apartment houses, much bigger than the omnipresent boardinghouses where many people lived, appeared for the first time. Real estate prices were still climbing, and when the directors of Trinity Church considered moving uptown, the lots they looked at near Central Park cost almost $400,000.

Scribner's had opened the largest bookstore in the world, the spires of St. Patrick's majestically touched the sky, and Temple Emanuel, its walls inlaid with mosaics in the Egyptian style, offered services for German Reform Jews. The Metropolitan Museum of Art opened on Fourteenth Street with an array of treasures, including a show of ancient Cypriot pots and an exhibition of Dutch and Flemish paintings scooped up in Europe by its millionaire trustees. The new Museum of Natural History beckoned visitors with its fossils, flora, and fauna.

The exuberant spending that had once more infected New Yorkers was no different from the unfettered expansion fed by industrial entrepreneurs, railroad promoters, and real estate speculators in the

Midwest and the West. But by the autumn of 1873, when Hetty and Edward arrived, the financial panic had pricked the bubble of hope and flattened the country into despair.

New York jittered as stocks bounced up and down and gold prices continued to drop. More firms in the city declared bankruptcy, and businesses and farms around the country continued to go into default. A&W Sprague of Rhode Island, one of the most important textile manufacturers in the country, declared bankruptcy, Utica Mills announced it was running on two-thirds time, and Wamsutta Mills in New Bedford decreed a four-day workweek. Companies across the land were chopping their costs by laying off workers, cutting back on their hours, or reducing their wages.

On Wall Street men in frock coats, floppy ties, and silk hats, stunned by their losses, moved in a daze. Only a few months before, they had walked briskly, the bands of their stovepipes bulging with commercial paper; now they held on to their tall hats and worried over their jobs. Even lawyers suddenly found themselves unemployed. Shortly after Hetty arrived, she donned her dark dress and cloak, crammed her bag with stocks and bonds, and rode downtown to see her banker. Her appearance might have astonished J. P. Morgan, who refused to allow women into his offices, but she was not the first woman to arrive on the street. Fur-cloaked wives of famous businessmen, frumpy spinster teachers, and décolleté madams of bordellos were sometimes seen climbing down from their carriages or stepping off the horse-drawn omnibus, eager to throw the dice in the Wall Street game of roulette. But none had the keen eye, the shrewd head, or the courage of Mrs. Edward Green.

Head down, eyes peeled on her reticule, Hetty made her way along the route of America's riches: past the Custom House, past the respected Brown Brothers' offices, past the granite building of August Belmont, who represented the Rothschilds in the United States, past the shuttered doors of Jay Cooke and the darkened entrance of Fisk and Hatch. At 59 Wall Street she entered the offices of John J. Cisco, the conservative banker and friend of her father's who served on the board of Trinity Church alongside George Templeton Strong. She had known Cisco for twenty years, first as her father's banker, and then, after Edward Robinson's death, as banker for both her husband and herself.

Cisco led her past the glass divider that separated the public from his private office and welcomed her as she handed him her pile of certificates to stash in the vaults and her wad of cash to deposit. But Hetty had more on her mind. Cisco made his services available for her business on Wall Street, and at this time when stocks were being abandoned, Hetty wanted to trade. "I believe in getting in at the bottom and out at the top," she often said. "I like to buy railroad stock or mortgage bonds. When I see a good thing going cheap because nobody wants it, I buy a lot of it and tuck it away." For Hetty, the decline in the market offered an opportunity for the future.

"It takes a clear, cool head, a large amount of brains, and unfaltering nerve to thread one's way through the intricacies of the business of finance," said a journalist at the time. Hetty was a fearless pit bull charging into a sloth of frantic bears. True, she had a pile of cash when others were scouring for pennies, but she also had a deft mind and the colossal courage to push against the crowd.

It was far easier to lose money than it was to make it. Even Commodore Vanderbilt had been badly hurt on September 18, 1873, the day of the crash. Most of his railroad stocks had plummeted and some of the firms he did business with were forced to close. Vanderbilt bought his stocks for cash and was able to wait out the market. But his followers, who risked their money on 10 percent margin, were racing to cover their losses. When a friend complained, he replied, "If you had bought a hundred shares instead of a thousand, you could have held on. Never be in too great a hurry to get rich." Like Hetty, he bought his railroads for the long haul.

It was said that word of Hetty's arrival sent brokers scurrying to watch. She may have been out of the country for seven years, but the extent of her wealth was well known. When news seeped out that Cisco's traders on the floor of the Stock Exchange were waving their hands to buy, it sent a rush of hope through Wall Street. The positive mood continued, and by December spirits were higher even though incomes stayed low. George T. Strong wailed about his bills but still partook in the Christmas rush, joining the shoppers jammed into Tiffany's and complaining about the fleet of carriages in front of A. T. Stewart's, tying up traffic on Broadway. Others bought at Lord & Taylor's, where the *Times* reported the store had taken advantage of low costs during the crisis and was able to offer its customers a tempting array of goods at reasonable prices. Ladies' sealskin jackets, gentlemen's furnishings, and a sprawling display of children's toys, including "automatic" Negro plantation dancers, music boxes, and monkeys playing the harp, made for compelling shopping.

As prices declined and imports decreased, new opportunities opened up for innovative entrepreneurs. With lower wages to pay and lower prices for raw materials, American industry prospered. Yet, in a paradox that presaged future recessions, unemployment increased and businesses continued to decline. More than five thousand companies closed their doors in 1873 and more than six thousand in 1874; within one year, three million people lost their jobs, and the recession continued for ten more years.

While government officials and Congress argued over whether to allow deflation or encourage inflation, farmers and even small businessmen resorted to methods of barter. In 1874, a conservative Congress passed a bill to devalue the dollar by printing more money. The following year, after the economy failed to improve, Congress legislated to strengthen the system by backing U.S. dollars with gold. Those like Hetty, who had held on to their discounted greenbacks bought after the Civil War, were now flush with wealth.

Dogged in their pursuit of fortune and determined to flaunt their wealth in goods, the rich kept buying. But as much as they bought, it did not satisfy their craving for more. Although they had achieved social status at home, their grand tours and travels to Europe gave them a taste for titles, and they longed for aristocratic approval abroad. But money had its limits: the upper crust of New York was no match for the nobility of the Continent. To set themselves apart from the masses of newly rich Americans, a small group of New York men, led by an ambitious Southerner, Ward McAllister, organized themselves into an exclusive club called the Patriarchs. An invitation to one of their evenings, which included such patricians as John Jacob Astor III, William Astor, William C. Schermerhorn, and Arthur Leary, tapped the recipient into the circle of New York knights; marrying off one's daughter to a titled European earned him a crown.

The Wall Street speculator and racetrack owner Leonard Jerome won new standing when his daughter married the cash-poor Duke of Marlborough. The wedding of Randolph Churchill and Jennie Jerome was the perfect melding of money and title. The noble and landed Churchill was too poor to maintain his family homes, while Jerome had the funds to help him out. When less than nine months after they married, Jennie bore him a son, Winston, nasty gossipers shrank back; they dared not deface the name of the aristocratic Churchill's new wife. Rich New Yorkers were soon seeking titled men for their daughters to wed, and the writer Henry James had fertile soil in which to plant his stories.

While Jennie Jerome basked in the spotlight, most of the nation slogged through the recession and tens of thousands of men sought work out west. Hetty adjusted to life back in America, but in 1874 she suffered the loss of her cousin Henry Grinnell. In the scorching heat of the summer, his brothers Moses and Joseph and their families, business associates, a group of Friends, and officials of the American Geographical Society gathered for the quiet funeral that revealed his Quaker roots. The ceremony at Episcopal Trinity Church in New York displayed no flowers and offered no music, but attendees praised its dignified style.

The temperature rose as Edward and Hetty made their way with their children to the Grand Central Station on Forty-second Street. "Grand Central Depot of New York eclipses anything of the kind that the world has ever seen," declared the *New York Herald*. The intricate truss work that spanned the infinite roof, the acres of glass set between the iron sashes, the barbershops, hairdressing salons, toilets for ladies and gentlemen, restaurants for ladies, dining rooms that rivaled the best restaurants in the quality of the food and service, the waiting rooms and plush drawing rooms all made it a cathedral to railroads.

Setting off on the seven-hour train ride to New England, young Ned and Sylvie could see the ferries that crisscrossed the bustling East River between Brooklyn and New York, busy with steamers carrying cargo and people south and north. As the train chugged along, the gray thoroughfares of the city gave way to rolling green hills reminiscent of the English countryside. Low stone walls hugged the soft fields, cows and sheep munched in the meadows, white clapboard houses and Congregational churches stood crisply as the railroad made its way past New Haven and Hartford and up the fertile Connecticut River Valley to Vermont. No wonder they called it New England!

Edward Henry Green had left Vermont at the age of twenty to make his way in the world. With his broad build and strapping height he stepped through the narrow frame of Bellows Falls and went to Boston in search of daring adventure; from there he sailed off to find the exotic riches of the Far East. But as big and bold as his life became, a piece of his heart remained in Bellows Falls.

The town thrived on its pulp and paper mills, which drove rafts of logs down the river, providing newsprint for the *Boston Herald* and *Baltimore American*; it prospered from factories that produced machinery for sheep and dairy farms. As one of the main connecting points for trains steaming to Massachusetts, New Hampshire, and New York, Bellows Falls hosted a multitude of travelers at good hotels like the Island House, where rich Southerners vacationed before the Civil War, and the Towns Hotel, which served them hefty drinks and hearty meals in its basement tavern.

This was the place that had three streets—Henry, Atkinson, and Green—named after Edward's family; where Edward's great-grandfather, and now he, owned the first covered toll bridge across the Connecticut River and collected the fares from carriages traveling between New Hampshire and Vermont; where his father, Henry Atkinson Green, had owned Hill and Green's, the general store at the center of Union Street on the Square and where Henry helped found the Bellows Falls Bank; and where Edward's widowed mother, Anna Tucker Green, now resided, regaling her friends with stories of her millionaire son.

For years the people of Bellows Falls had heard the tales of Edward Henry Green and his worldwide travels. They knew of his huge success, took pleasure in seeing him on his occasional visits home, enjoyed his gifts and his gab. They smiled at his bulldog and his bulging wardrobe of more than thirty suits and were bemused by his Japanese valet, who brushed and pressed all his clothes. They knew of his generosity toward his parents: they heard about the munificent sums he mailed them, which his father sometimes refused because they were too much; they saw the sable furs he gave his mother and the minks he gave his sister; they visited the small, sweet house on Henry Street that he bought for the widowed Anna, and admired the objects he had sent from the East to furnish it, like the blue and white Canton china and the work stand with dragon feet, festooned with gold.

For the past seven years they had heard from the elder Mrs. Green about her son's millionaire wife. They had read the newspaper accounts of Hetty Robinson and the Howland Will Case. Now when Henry's mother told them her son was coming home with her famous daughter-in-law and grandchildren, they shivered with excitement. Merchants envisioned their most expensive goods flying off the shelves and into the basket of the new Mrs. Green; lawyers pictured themselves pleading her cases in court; ladies floated in daydreams of new dresses they would wear when she invited them to tea; children held out their hands pretending to catch the coins she would sprinkle around the town.

Expectations rose with each letter Edward wrote home from England. Hetty's name was well known; that she was Mrs. Edward Green made her something of a folk hero even before she stepped onto the platform. But the whiff of riches and royalty that came from Edward hardly fit his plebeian wife. The starched and flounced crowd waiting to greet her gave an almost audible gasp when, disheveled and layered in dust, she emerged from the train. The residents may have dreamed of a princess swooping down on Bellows Falls, but what they saw was a stepdaughter covered in soot. Nothing disappointed the villagers as much as Hetty's arrival. Her appearance augured an uneasy relationship with the town.

As pleased as she may have been to return to New England, which she preferred over New York, Hetty's disenchantment was just as great. After the family deaths, the wills, the accusations of forgery, and the persistent sense that people hungered after her fortune, she had enjoyed her anonymity in England. After years of taking orders from Aunt Sylvia, she had finally experienced independence in London. She had run her household with a free hand and paid the bills with a purse full of Edward's money. Now they were to make their home with their two children under her mother-in-law's roof. Once again, as she had in New Bedford, Hetty would have to evade the public's envy, and once again she would have to bow to another woman's demands. Worse, Edward's purse had shrunk with his Wall Street losses. Hetty simmered with resentment, and her paranoia seemed to return.

Just as she had argued with her aunt over domestic expenses, now she quarreled with Edward's mother, and had little patience with Mary, the Irish maid. When, at their first meal in the house, Mary presented herself with her black hair curled and her uniform starched and ruffled, Hetty saw it as frivolous. The churchgoing Anna Green, who played the organ at Immanuel Episcopal, was too extravagant, she said. Hetty set her frugal mind to lowering the household costs and turned on Edward to lower his style of living. Hetty felt that the merchants sometimes raised their prices, the lawyers sometimes raised their rates, and the doctors sometimes increased their fees when they knew she was the customer. Wary of the men who ran the general store and certain they tried to overcharge the maid, she refused to let Mary go shopping in town and insisted instead on sending a friend or going herself.

Once more, as they had in New Bedford, ugly rumors mottled her path. It was true that Hetty skimped in her spending, but instead of calling her frugal, gossips clucked their tongues and called her mean. When her milliner made her first trip to New York, Hetty gave her the name of a restaurant in Washington Square that charged ten cents for a plate of soup "good and thick on the bottom" or the same low price for "well-cooked oatmeal with real milk." Instead of thanking her for the advice, the woman mocked her for being cheap. When her cleaning lady gave birth to a son, Hetty gave her a gold piece and told her to deposit it in the bank. Keep it there until he is twenty-one, she advised. Instead of understanding the lesson of compound interest, the woman scorned her for saving instead of spending.

Stories spread that, with six year-old Ned and three-year-old Sylvie by her side, she bought sacks of broken graham crackers from the grocer Patrick Keane, asked the butcher for free bones for the dog, and bargained over a peck of potatoes at the store on Westminster Street. But at least one clerk who waited on her in the general store swore that she never haggled. "Watch your pennies and the dollars will take care of themselves," she often told her children in thrifty New England style. S. J. Cray, who owned the fish and meat market, admitted she was a regular customer, but said she was no different from most. Years later, when Mr. Cray's son earned his way to millionaire status, the townsfolk smiled at his rumpled suits and hats and his reputation for being a tightwad; but they frowned when they mentioned Hetty.

Hetty prided herself on her bargaining skills. After a few jaunts in Edward's fringe-covered brougham, she prevailed on him to sell the fancy carriage and found a smaller cart for sale. Using the skills she had learned from her father, she discovered a man who had a grudge against its owner and convinced him to tell her every fault of the horse and rig. And then she approached the seller. "With the knowledge I gained I succeeded in depreciating the owner's opinion of his property," she explained, bringing his price down even lower than what she would have been willing to pay. She bought the old horse and worn-out wagon for less than half the $200 he initially asked.

Whether it was a horse and buggy or stocks and bonds, her canny habit of investigating every possible facet before she bought helped make her successful. "Before deciding on an investment, I seek out every kind of information about it," she said. But her methods enraged those who hoped she would spread her wealth with a blind and generous hand. Worse, she embarrassed her mother-in-law, who seethed as Hetty usurped her position in the house and undermined her standing in Bellows Falls. The millionaire daughter-in-law who was supposed to raise her status with her friends instead made her feel like a fool.

While Anna Green suffered Hetty with indignation, others enjoyed her as a friend. Solon Goodridge, who had introduced Hetty and Edward, lived in Brooklyn and summered in Bellows Falls; so, too, did his daughter Mary, who had married Herbert Bancroft just a month before the Greens were wed. Hetty was also close to Mr. and Mrs. James Williams, head of the Bellows Falls bank, and to Cynthia Nims, a longtime friend of Edward's.

Edward's niece Agnes Elmendorf, eldest of his sister's twelve children, had moved back from the Midwest, graduated from the local high school in 1874, and worked as a teacher in town. Eighteen-year-old Agnes, the only one of her siblings living in Bellows Falls, cared more about being close to her family than being close to their fortune. Hetty treated her kindly. But almost everyone else, she believed, was after her money; she was always grateful to those who were friendly to her just for herself. She shared stories with Agnes of life in London,

Paris, and New York, and invited the young woman to visit them at home.

After Edward's mother died in the summer of 1875, the Greens sat down to dinner one day at a dining room table set only with simple kitchenware instead of Anna's elaborate crystal, silver, and china. When Edward questioned his wife about his mother's belongings, she told him she had packed them up and put them away. The usually mild-tempered Edward took the goblet in his hand and threw it against the dining room wall. Then he stood up and left.

The next two months were tense as Edward's investments turned sour. The Bank of California had borrowed money from the London and San Francisco Bank and used it recklessly. In August, when the California bank declared itself in default and its president drowned himself in the ocean, its huge loans were revealed, and depositors made a run on the bank. The directors of the London and San Francisco were responsible for covering the losses, and Edward, still on the board, was caught short. As a wave of defaults struck the state, the value of his holdings declined, and his mining stocks, bought on margin, suddenly dropped. Edward looked to his wife for help, and although she rebuked him for his risky speculations, Hetty gave him a lifeline.

Salvation had its revenge. That winter, before they left for New York, Hetty asked Agnes Elmendorf for her help: she wanted to open the crates holding her mother-in-law's belongings. The young woman yearned for some of her grandmother's objects. But instead of offering them to Agnes and her family, Hetty announced she was putting everything up at auction. A shocked and saddened Agnes refused to assist her. But the gavel banged fast as the townsfolk bid at the sale.

In return for rescuing Edward, Hetty reckoned she was owed more than just the few dollars brought in at the auction: she was named an executor of his mother's estate. It was not the only time they made this kind of arrangement. "Hetty went in and saved him three or four times," said a stockbroker friend. "She would lecture him about the chances he was taking, but time after time the turn in the market confirmed his judgment. He disobeyed her once too often, though, and she got rid of him." But that would come later. For now they were still Mr. and Mrs. Edward Green, and despite the disagreements, their marriage remained intact.

Chapter 10

====

A Forceful Woman

Worried over Wall Street, the Greens left Bellows Falls to spend part of the winter of 1875 in New York, starting a pattern they repeated for years. Edward had business meetings with colleagues at his club; Hetty had business to take care of downtown. While Edward dined with his friends and chewed over ideas for investing, Hetty journeyed to Wall Street on the horse-drawn omnibus. On one occasion she trundled down with a satchel stuffed with $200,000 worth of bonds and handed them over to John Cisco. Her banker admonished her for carrying negotiable securities on public transportation. "It's dangerous," he told her. "You should have taken a carriage." Hetty shot him a look with her steely eyes and replied, "A carriage, indeed! Perhaps you can afford to ride in a carriage—I cannot."

All was not business for the Greens: New York offered a wonderland for adults and children alike. At the American Museum of Natural History, founded by Pierpont Morgan, Moses Grinnell, Theodore Roosevelt Sr., and others, wide-eyed youngsters could encounter specimens of twelve thousand birds, one thousand mammals, and three thousand reptiles and fish. In one room an Armenian camel proudly showed off his humps, a Nova Scotia moose glared from his girth, and a Rocky Mountain deer posed between them. Buffaloes, monkeys, and grizzly bears stood in another hall alongside rats, bats, and other rodents. A third room held a collection of shells, donated by Hetty's friend Catherine Lorillard Wolfe. The quiet Miss Wolfe gave millions of dollars to religious and educational institutions and to the arts: she supported the Episcopal Church in America; the Theological Seminary in Alexandria, Egypt; the Protestant Church in Paris; and the American School in Athens, Greece. She underwrote archaeological explorations in Babylonia, helped homeless children in Manhattan, gave land for a hospital in the Bronx, and bequeathed her paintings to the Metropolitan Museum of Art.

Outdoors in Central Park, Hetty and her family could join the crowd of New Yorkers walking for hours through the eight hundred acres of meadows, hills, and labyrinthine paths, or they could watch the parade of open equipages on the carriage road. On Saturday afternoons, men with pince-nez tapped their canes to their top hats to say hello, and women in capes and shawls nodded beneath their ribboned bonnets, taking their seats as the band began a concert on the mall. Children lined up for bumpy rides in goat carts, rode round and round on carousel horses, whooshed in the air on swings, or sailed on the lake in small boats. When winter came and snow covered the hills, they hauled their sleds to the top and, mufflers flying, swooped down the white slopes, piercing the cold air with screams of joy. But when young Ned, built like his father, big and tall, jumped onto his sled and banged his knee, his screams were cries of pain. His parents smoothed his tears and soothed his wound, but the damage was done.

When the weather turned warm, Edward shuttled back and forth on the train from Vermont to New York, while Hetty and the children relished the mountain air in Bellows Falls. Spring and summer, the boisterous Ned scrambled over the hills, raced in the fields, and played his favorite game of baseball. But a few years after the sledding accident, he fell from a tree and injured his knee again. This time his screams were worse.

Hetty quickly called for a doctor, but his house was miles away. Waiting for the man to arrive, she applied a warm bandage to the wound; proud of her nursing skills, she thought the poultice had helped. "I went outside and stood at the gate," she explained, fending off stories that she had been too cheap to call a physician. "When the doctor came, I waved him away and called to him that he wasn't needed. If he'd gotten out of his buggy, I'd have had to pay him even if he didn't do anything, you know." Hetty never paid for something she did not receive, though the question of whether she received it was often under debate. On the other hand, her friends said, she never forgot a kind service and always rewarded those to whom she felt attached. She gave local children nickels for their birthdays and piggy banks to store them in; she brought soup and medicine to neighbors who were sick and sent money to those who had shown her consideration or done her a favor.

Sadly, Ned's injury refused to heal, and the boy remained in pain. His parents tried every home remedy they knew, from Carter's pills to Squibb oil to hot sand. When all proved fruitless, they took him to different doctors, but he had dislocated his knee and every physician recommended the same course: amputation. Too many Civil War soldiers had suffered without anesthetic while their limbs were sawed; too many peg-legged sailors hobbled down New Bedford's streets; Hetty refused to allow her son Captain Ahab's fate.

When Hetty learned that Edward's friend Cynthia Nims was married to a farmer who grew tobacco, she was eager to pay them a call. She had heard that the dry leaves wound around the leg would loosen the ligaments. On a warm day, Edward hitched up the horses and drove the family out to the country.

As soon as Hetty Green arrived at the door, the Nimses' eight-year-old daughter, Mamie, riddled with curiosity, ran to the living room window and peeked out from behind the blinds to see the fabled woman. The girl watched as two children—the boy Ned, big and lame, and the girl Sylvie, wearing glasses and a sailor hat—played in the garden; Mrs. Green talked at the door, Mr. Green sat in the cart. A little later, he and her father spoke about Edward's adventures in the East. Shortly afterward, the Greens drove off, their wagon heaped with tobacco leaves, their hearts filled with hope.

But once more, the wished-for cure did not work, and once more, when Ned cried in pain, Hetty carried him in her arms or sat with him through the night. She and Edward took their son from one doctor to another, desperate to find someone who had a good solution. When her husband did not join them, she put on a costume of shabby clothes so she would not be charged extra for being rich, and went alone with Ned. Often the doctors felt sorry for her but sometimes she was found out. Wrapped in her cloak of poverty, she called on specialists in New

York and took the train to Baltimore to see Dr. McLean, a leading orthopedist. Her experience with William Gordon, her aunt's physician, may have soured her feelings toward doctors, but she was willing to go anywhere to save her son's leg, willing to try anything from medicines to mechanical devices in his shoe.

Always worried about Ned, his parents indulged him in whatever ways they could. In the winter of 1877, when Hetty decided to switch her Midwestern lawyers from her father's representatives to Edward's agents, the family traveled together to Chicago. Hetty held mortgages and real estate, including the entire town of Cicero, which eventually became the headquarters of the gangster Al Capone, and land downtown that would become the Loop. The Greens rode by private train across the flat Midwest and were met at the end by the fiery glow of steel mills and iron foundries, the pounding clank of new factories, and the bloody smell of the stockyards, all of which enriched the city.

The family checked into Matteson House, a leading hotel even before the Chicago fire, with gas lighting, steam heat, elevators, and French chefs serving guests three meals a day on the American Plan. Its newly redone elegance offered Hetty and Edward a reminder of the years they had stayed at the Langham in London. For Ned and Sylvie, the fancy hotel was a perfect place to play in the corridors or hide their unusual pet, a hen. Their understanding parents did not object. But the management felt otherwise. Tired of the eggs the hen laid under the bed, disgusted with the dirt it dropped on the carpets, they went to extreme measures. When the Greens came back to the room one day, they discovered the chicken was dead: someone had wrung its neck.

The following morning the family checked out. They left for St. Louis, the newspapers said, another terminus for the transcontinental rail, another town where Hetty owned land. On future trips to Chicago, the Greens stayed at Palmer House, owned by Hetty's friends, which was the city's finest hotel. One night, Ned and some friends engaged in a furious pillow fight; feathers flew and two sets of pillows were destroyed. When the chambermaid complained, Hetty gave her the money to buy new pillows and told her to send them to the boys. "As long as they're making noise in the room, I'm satisfied," she said. "If they had been still, I would have been suspicious."

The Greens' travels left little time for the children's proper schooling. Like bathers dipping their toes into the sea, they took tentative steps into public school classrooms in New York; other times they studied with private tutors. In Bellows Falls, the children enrolled in the school of the Immanuel Episcopal Church. Seated at one of the double desks in the boys' front room, Ned studied history and mathematics, while Sylvie sat in the back parlor with her best friend, Mamie Nims, and a handful of other girls, learning to do their needlework by stitching red thread onto muslin.

Ned loved playing baseball with his friends, but when his leg prevented him from running, his mother allowed him to stand in the outfield on the chance a stray ball might come his way. When other boys came to the house, he could throw a ball in the backyard, but he wasn't permitted to run. Whatever he did, from playing catch to organizing games around town, his mother kept a vigilant eye on him. "Be careful, Ned!" or "Don't throw the ball so hard to Ned," she would call out whenever he played with his friends. His parents gave him permission to drive his friends around in their old horse and cart, and once in a while, he was driven around by his sister in a toy wagon. Hetty and Edward gave Ned a larger allowance than most of the boys received, but Hetty's generosity had its limits. She dressed her children in hand-me-down clothes and was adamant that they watch their pennies. She was pleased when her son and his friends earned money by cleaning bottles for a local distillery; but when Ned lost his coins in a pile of leaves, she insisted he help her search through the heap to find them.

As surely as balls bounce up and down, Edward's finances sprang high and low. In 1879, when his stocks were moving in the right direction, he purchased Tucker House, the Greek Revival mansion that rose on a hill on Church Street. Once owned by his grandfather, the imposing yellow brick house, with its grand staircase and large central hall, stood like a dowager welcoming the Greens and their friends.

To the right, in the parlor, candles in the crystal chandelier lit up a portrait of Hetty done in her youth. Guests moving about the rooms could see paintings of Edward's forefathers by John Singleton Copley and Gilbert Stuart hanging over the mantels, and tapestries sewn by Aunt Sylvia hanging on the walls. Around the house mahogany tables and lowboys held silver candlesticks and signed silver pieces from Boston; fainting couches offered a respite for women whose corsets were pulled too tight; and in the dining room, Queen Anne chairs lined the table where family and friends took their places. Upstairs, a seven-foot bed accommodated the large frame of its owner, Edward Green.

The substantial house boasted a square widow's walk on the roof and a wide porch in the front, where the outgoing Ned and his shy sister Sylvie sat with his friends on rocking chairs, looking out on the canal and across to the steep face of Mount Kilburn in New Hampshire. In the garden the children grew fruits and vegetables and all around the property they let their pets—cats, dogs, birds, and other animals—run free. But there was no free run for the children: wherever they were, in Bellows Falls, Chicago, or New York, or traveling by railroad in between, Ned and Sylvie lived under the protective gaze of their forceful mother.

Chapter 11

Changing Times

"Our country's prosperity depends on its having an efficient and well-maintained rail system," said the investment genius Warren Buffett in 2010 when he invested $34 billion in the Burlington Northern Santa Fe Corporation. "They are the only mode of freight transportation that can handle growth." Over a century earlier, railroads changed the course of American life. They inspired innovation and energized the economy. They brought farm goods to urban markets, raw materials to factories, finished goods to towns. They ventured into far-flung corners of the country and made them accessible, created cities and linked them together, compressed the vast space between the oceans and laced the populace into a single nation. Then they synchronized the clocks from end to end.

As towns cropped up across the landscape, each decided on its own time. Aldermen in the East and sheriffs in the West—and the jewelers of any town—looked up to the sky, shielded their eyes with their hands, and gazed at the sun: when it appeared to be at its highest point, they declared the hour to be high noon and set their watches. Residents checked the hands on their church steeple or peered in the window of the jewelry store to find the correct time.

But even when towns were in touching distance, time was unreliable and varied from place to place. The situation created havoc for the railroads. With three hundred different time zones across the country, trains that met at various terminals could not coordinate their schedules, nor could they even keep to a schedule because it was so confusing.

Travelers in Pittsburgh would find six different clocks at the station. In Buffalo, New York, four clocks showed four different times. A man from Portland, Maine, who was catching a train might well ask an innocent question: "What time is it?" Checking his watch, he would see that it was 12:15. But looking up at the New York Central Railroad clock he would see that it was noon, while the Lake Shore and Michigan Railroad clock announced it was 11:25 and the Buffalo city clock stated it was 11:40.

Travelers from the East might have to reset their watches two hundred times before reaching California. Trains might wait at one stop for farmers to arrive with their freight and then, at the next, find farmers who had been waiting with freight for a long time. Cities a mile apart geographically could be several minutes apart chronometrically. Twelve o'clock in New York was four and a half minutes past twelve in Newark; five past the hour in Boston was seven past the hour in Lewiston, Maine. Confused passengers could not calculate what time they would arrive or what time they would depart.

The problem had become so horrific that doctors declared it was driving people crazy: they blamed the time confusion (as well as everything from dyspepsia to insomnia to tooth decay, and the stress from other modern technology, such as steam engines and telegraph wires) for a new illness called "neurasthenia." The American neurologist George Miller Beard declared it "the disease of the age." Though beneficial to some, "railway travel is injurious" to others, he said. "We are under constant strain," he went on, "to get somewhere or do something at some definite moment."

Yet the definite moment differed from place to place. The situation was so chaotic that the editor of a railroad guide appealed to a convention of railroad officials to standardize their clocks. After much argumentation, they agreed to four time zones across the country that would be based on Greenwich Mean Time.

At noon on November 18, 1883, at Union Station in Chicago, the assembled crowd watched and waited as the timekeeper stopped the clock. Hours seemed to go by until, exactly nine minutes and thirty-two seconds later, a telegraph signal from the U.S. Naval Observatory announced the new noon. Americans across the continent reset their pocket watches and reconfigured the hands on their tall case clocks. Although some fearful souls declared it would bring on the wrath of God, and some dissident cities refused to go along, the country now functioned on the same system. Workers at offices and factories toiled by the same clock, businessmen arranged their meetings with synchronized watches, and salesmen planned their travels around similar schedules. The new zones set a new pace for the country; the railroad revolution raced ahead and America sped ahead with it.

Hetty Green put her money in the race. The railroads' dynamic potential, their promised return on capital, their unregulated operation, and their untaxed profits provided infinite possibilities for financiers. Since the end of the Civil War, Hetty had been investing in, among others, the Reading, Rock Island, Connecticut River Valley, and Louisville and Nashville railroads. The latter, based in the Union state of Kentucky, owned routes that ran straight through the South: occasionally during the Civil War it transported the Confederate army and was paid in Confederate notes; most of the time, however, it carried men and matériel from the North and received payment in greenbacks. By the end of the war its southern competition had been destroyed, but the L&N not only survived, it emerged financially strong. The profitable line was in a unique position to extend its reach.

Hetty's investments were not always known: she purchased property under fictitious names, bought stocks under other identities, and was praised by shrewd observers for how closely she held her positions. By 1879 Edward Green owned thirty thousand shares—one-third of the stock—of the Louisville and Nashville Railroad: he was the company's single largest shareholder. It is not known whether he bought it with his own money or Hetty really owned the shares, or if she owned a large block of bonds. But with his huge chunk of stock, in December 1879 Edward was elected to the board of directors and appointed second vice president. But Edward was doing more than buying stock in the L&N; he was secretly sweeping up shares of the competition. With his clever maneuvering and his talent for raising money, he was put in charge of the New York office, the financial end of the railroad's operations.

The L&N expanded dramatically, laying new track and gobbling up smaller lines. In a series of secret moves, Edward and a group of major financiers, including John Jacob Astor, managed to gain control of track that gave the L&N a direct line from Chicago to Mobile, Montgomery, and New Orleans, and an unbroken line from Chicago to Pensacola Bay in the Florida Panhandle. They were paving the way, said the *New York Times,* for the railroad to become "the largest aggregate under one management in the world." At a time when no regulations existed, when oversight was unheard of, when the industry had the feel of the Wild West, this was "one of the most gigantic railroad operations of the age." The newspaper called it "a brilliant coup."

Within a short period, the Louisville and Nashville quadrupled its track to 3,500 miles extending from St. Louis, Missouri, to Savannah, Georgia, and from the freshwater lakes in the north to the Gulf of Mexico in the south, making it the only line to have an inlet to New Orleans. The lucrative monopoly was not only carrying profitable freight north to south, it was buying land, building towns, and developing coal and iron mines, making its operations more cost-effective and more self-sufficient. The routes were so extensive that the New York Central Railroad was eager to lease them. With the success of the line, Edward was elected president and given an annual salary of $5,000.

Edward's reign was short-lived. After a few months as president, he was demoted to vice president, and then, a few months later, with his financial ties still needed, he was asked to take on the chief post once again. By the end of 1881, however, the stock was down, he had mortgaged his house, and his official duties were over. Nonetheless, he remained an important member of the board of directors: "E. H. Green," said a historian of the railroad, was "an erratic financier whose influence upon the L&N extended far beyond his brief Presidency."

As an officer of the L&N, Edward was expected to make inspection tours of the roads, and Hetty and the children sometimes traveled with him. For Hetty, an investor who kept a careful eye on her assets, it was an opportune way to see the railroad in full operation from its roadbeds to its rolling stock. Standing on the open platform at the rear of the company's private car or sitting on the plush seats in its private, windowed lounge, she could look out, examine the track, and survey the bridges as the train rolled by. The trips also allowed her a chance to visit her properties in the Midwest, which increased with the expansion of the railroads from Chicago to St. Louis to Cincinnati.

Young Ned and Sylvie loved steaming around the country with their parents in the opulent train. In the dining room, they sat at tables set with starched white cloths, sparkling crystal, and gleaming silver, while crisply uniformed Negro waiters served them tasty food; at night, they slept curled up in the new Pullman beds carefully arranged by the Negro porters as the rhythmic roll of the train rocked them to sleep. They weren't the only ones who enjoyed the sumptuous private car: the sociable Edward often entertained other guests along the route.

Agnes Elmendorf and other members of his sister's family were invited to join them if their travel plans coincided, and friends of Edward's and Hetty's were sometimes asked to come along. As always, Edward made an amiable and charming host. In fact, he was sometimes too charming, especially with other women. Hetty had known of his reputation as a bachelor in the Philippines, but she thought he had finished his womanizing by the time he returned from the East. Along with his "loose habits" of drinking and playing cards, however, she discovered that not only was he very courteous to ladies when his wife was with him, he was touring with other women when she was not.

"I had heard stories about his life in Manila before I married him, about his sowing his wild oats out there, but those stories never bothered me. That was all before my time," she told a friend. "But when I was traveling with him, I noticed he was always exceedingly polite to women. After I got back to New York, rumors about his doings came to me. When I thought it over, I thought that he had been a little too polite." Deeply hurt by Edward's deception, Hetty hired a detective from Chicago to follow him around. "I got a report on him," she said. "It told me everything I needed to know."

Hetty needed time away from Edward. In the summer of 1882, and again the following year, while he scampered around the country or lodged near the Union Club in New York, Hetty took the children on a six-week trip to New Bedford. Stepping off the train and into a carriage in the town where she grew up, she ordered the driver to take them to Pleasant Street. It would cost her more money, the man protested, but she brushed him off and told him to do as she said. Riding along the familiar streets, she reminisced with Ned and Sylvie, point-ing out the different sites: "Here is the house where I was born." She motioned as they passed the big house on Seventh and Walnut streets. "And here is where your grandpa and I used to walk," she recalled.

Hetty told the driver to turn onto a narrow road leading to Round Hills. Halfway there, she ordered him to stop and led the children a few feet from the side of the road to a thicket of bushes. Beyond the trees were rocks leaning along the banks of a brook. "Here is where Mama—that's your grandma—used to take us picnicking when she felt well enough," Hetty said. It was one of the few times she men-tioned her mother; it was one of the few good memories she had of her. Hetty took off her shoes and stockings and told the children to do the same. The threesome dipped their feet into the sparkling water. A few minutes later they scrambled back into the cab.

She had inherited 140 acres and the house at Round Hills after Aunt Sylvia's death. This was the place she always enjoyed as a child, where she learned to drive a horse and cart at the age of six, where she learned to ride sidesaddle, where she ran free in the fields. Her daugh-ter Sylvie liked to ride too, but fourteen-year-old Ned was no longer able to ride or run; he and his sister enjoyed the salty air and the ocean breeze. Some of the time Hetty took him around to local doctors to see what they could do about his leg, but their response was always the same: they shook their heads and recommended amputation. Out at Round Hills, where Sylvie rode her horse, Ned sat on the big rocks, dangling his fishing rod in the waters of Buzzards Bay.

While Hetty was with her children, Edward still struggled with the L&N. Like so many other speculators, he and his friends at the Union Club had bought their shares on margin, and like so many other railroads, the Louisville and Nashville had overexpanded and built unprofitable lines. The company fell into debt, and the stock fell with it. In the autumn of 1883, Jay Gould tried to bring down the price of the stock even further, hoping to buy up shares, take control, and enhance his own Union Pacific and Missouri Pacific lines. Over the next twelve months Edward and the other members of the L&N's finance committee fought hard against Gould, trying to support the price of the stock, but the debt kept growing and the earnings continued to shrink.

Edward was a gambler at heart, and his adrenaline soared with every risky move he made. When Henry Watterson, editor of the *Louisville Courier-Journal,* came to see him in his office, he told Edward that he had bought some stocks. Edward asked him how he bought them. Watterson did not understand the question. "Do you buy long or short?" Edward asked. "You are talking Greek to me," said the editor. "Didn't you ever put up any money on margin?" "Never," Watterson said. "Bless me! You're a virgin," Edward exclaimed, adding that he wanted Watterson to look over a list of stocks and pick one. He wanted to try the editor's luck; whichever stock he chose Edward would buy for himself and Watterson. "All I make we'll divide, and all we lose I'll pay," he said. The editor told him that he could do even better; he was having lunch with Jay Gould and would ask him for a tip. Edward paused for a minute. "I don't want any tip—especially from that bunch. I want to try your virgin luck," he said. But his curiosity was piqued; he told the man to let him know that afternoon what Gould recommended.

At lunch, when Watterson asked Gould what stock he liked, the infamous operator leaned over and said, "Buy Texas Pacific." The editor relayed the message. Within two days, the stock dropped sixty points. Six months later, Edward sent Watterson a check for thousands of dollars, half the profit on his purchase.

When Watterson relayed the story to Gould two years later, the stock manipulator admitted that he thought someone else had bought the shares that day; he had pushed the price down to get even with the man. When Gould heard who the buyer was, he was taken aback. Edward Green was a popular fellow. "Dear, dear," he said. "Ned Green! Big Green. Well, well! You do surprise me. I would rather have done him a favor than an injury." He was pleased to learn that no harm was done and that, even though the stock had dropped, it had come back, and "after all, you and he came out ahead." Edward won the admiration of Watterson and was held in esteem by investors and scoundrels alike. But his wanton ways lost him the respect of his wife.

In May 1884, when Edward's colleague and friend C. C. Baldwin, the prominent head of the Louisville and Nashville, was accused of irregularities, the stock dropped fifteen points in a week. Baldwin later admitted to the board of directors that he had borrowed more against company stock than had been avowed; furthermore, he had falsified the company's statements, claiming far less debt than the real amount. In truth, the losses were $5 million, not the $2 million he reported. The directors were responsible for covering the difference. Many of Baldwin's friends, including Edward and other members of the Union Club, were caught in the mesh of Baldwin's lies: they had used the stock as collateral and were now forced to cover their margin accounts. "The Union Club is a funereal assemblage," said the *New York Times*. Edward was in mourning.

Inside the management of the L&N, the fighting continued between the Louisville office, which oversaw the railroad operations, and the New York office, which backed them. The financiers in the East, obliged to raise more money, issued more stock and bonds, but rumors flew that the railroad was verging on bankruptcy. The money men found it difficult to find buyers for the bonds. Weak business conditions in 1884 did not help. Factories were forced to cut their wages, coal miners declared a strike, and freight receipts were dropping. The price of L&N shares was in free fall.

As the value of Edward Green's shares declined, the Cisco bank demanded more money to cover his losses. Forced to provide more collateral on his margin accounts, Edward delivered more shares of the L&N and gave Cisco the deed on his house in Bellows Falls. But the shares kept heading downward and Edward was drowning in debt. Once again he called on Hetty to bail him out. In return she demanded the house. Edward may have been her husband, but business was business. In June 1884 the deed for Tucker House was turned over to her.

John A. Cisco, son of the founder, was not only Edward's banker; he was his partner as well. Along with Frederick Foote, the other member of the firm, they had purchased a large block of bonds of the Houston and Texas Central Railroad. When the California railroad magnate Collis Huntington and his cohorts stepped in to take over the Houston and Texas, dollar signs flashed in the eyes of the Cisco partners. They had watched the price of another railroad, the Central Pacific, escalate when Huntington made it part of a transcontinental line; now the Cisco team hoped he would do the same for the

Houston and Texas. Instead, to their dismay the ruthless Huntington announced the railroad's earnings were weaker than he had thought: he declared he was canceling the 7 percent dividend due shortly. The bonds plummeted and so did their wealth. Their Houston and Texas holdings, which had once been worth over $300,000 to the bank, were now worth almost half. At the same time, Louisville and Nashville shares continued to drop. The Cisco team wore glum faces as they toasted the new year of 1885.

Cisco's troubles were quickly known on Wall Street. News of its shaky condition raced across the wires as far away as Europe, where the bank had a number of clients. Cisco responded indignantly to the rumors, denying any problems and claiming its assets were strong, but depositors demanded their money. Hetty had half a million dollars on deposit, and $26 million in stocks, bonds, mortgages, deeds, and other goods stashed away in Cisco's vaults. When word about Cisco lit up the new switchboard in the rear of the Bellows Falls drugstore, Hetty sent a letter to the bank. She wasn't taking any chances. At her desk at Tucker House she dipped the nib of her pen in ink and wrote: "Please close my account and remove my funds of $550,000 on deposit as I wish to transfer them to the Chemical National Bank."

Cisco refused. Instead they informed her that her husband was more than $700,000 in debt and that the money he had borrowed had been backed by the collateral of his Louisville and National stock. Her money represented one-quarter of the bank's assets on deposit. Cisco begged her to keep her deposits with them, not only to offset the loan but to calm their creditors' fears. If depositors learned she was pulling her money out, they would panic. Hetty reminded them that she had always kept her money separate from her husband's. She threatened to sue. On January 15, 1885, Cisco announced it was closing its doors. Hetty packed her bags and took the train to New York.

"Mrs. E. H. Green is well-known, by reputation, at least, on Wall Street. She is believed to be the richest woman in America, a title earned by her own business sagacity, energy and watchfulness," wrote the *New York Times* two days later. "She has lived a frugal life, exercised extraordinary keenness in her investments, and by embracing every good opportunity that the stock market afforded her, she has more than quintupled her heritage."

The paper continued: "Old Wall Street operators give Mrs. Green credit for having as intimate a knowledge of railroad securities as any personality they know. . . . She is so largely invested in the Louisville and Nashville securities that it has been frequently said that she practically owns the road."

Bundled in a black cape and black gloves to fight the brutal wind and the cold, Hetty emerged from a black and tan cab and appeared at Cisco's doors. She stood at the iron gate in front of the private office and scanned the room. Her piercing blue eyes landed on Lewis May. "I've come to get what's mine," she announced to the assignee for the firm. A white collar peeked out from her black wool dress, her gray hair, twisted in a French knot, was covered with a black bonnet and veil, and her legs were covered in black cotton stockings, her feet in black sensible shoes. She demanded that he transfer her funds to the Chemical National Bank. May informed her that he could not transfer her money, as it was covering her husband's losses. Indeed, he said, he required more. Hetty walked out in a rage.

The following day she returned. Her voice as chilly as the January air, she reminded May that her husband had no legal right to use her money as collateral; the bank could not claim her funds. She demanded her deposits and called for the valuables in her vault. But May refused again. Hetty's temper rose, her nostrils flared as she replayed scenes from the past: she screamed, she cried, she stamped her feet, but May remained unruffled. Outside Cisco's offices, curious bystanders watched through the windows; newspapers reported the scene the following day; the *Chicago Tribune* called her "the Queen of the Street."

In the end, Hetty had no choice: she paid her husband's debt. The next day, with Edward on hand to assist her, she stuffed her $25 million worth of certificates into her satchels, lugged four boxes of heavy silver objects that had long been in the vault, and loaded it all into a yellow cab. The lone horse pulling the heavy cab lumbered along for a block and suddenly stopped: stuck in the mushy snow, the cab could not move. The driver hailed another hack, transferred part of the load, and the two cabs continued.

At the corner of Broadway and Chambers streets, Hetty descended from the cab and was met by George Gilbert Williams, president of the Chemical Bank. The picture of a Victorian gentleman with his starched round collar, full mustache, and beard, Williams greeted his new customer with all the courtesy and respect due a woman of her wealth. "I have observed that many a tattered garment hides a package of bonds and that gorgeous clothing does not always cover a millionaire," he told his colleagues.

But as warmly as Hetty felt welcomed, revenge ran like ice water through her veins. She would never forgive Edward Green for using her money without her permission; she would never absolve Lewis May for forcing her hand; she would never forget Collis Huntington for defaulting on the Houston and Texas bonds and forcing down the price of its shares. Her Quaker tradition may have frowned on lawsuits, but Hetty had already established a tradition of her own. Huntington would pay a price and May would face her in court. As for her husband, he was the one person she had counted on. He had stood by her at funerals, sworn for her in lawsuits, advised her in finance, and fathered her children. But in the end, he had crossed the line: she could live with his philandering, his drinking, his card playing, and his chancy speculations, but she could not tolerate something far worse: Edward had betrayed her. He had risked her money for his own return. He had squandered some of her wealth, and, in doing that, he had cost her some of her worth. Hetty bade him a fond farewell.

Chapter 12

Against the Trend

Hetty and Edward stayed married, but their life together was over. For much of the time that Hetty was living with the children at Tucker House in Bellows Falls, Edward was lodging near the Union Club in New York. Being part of the city's oldest club implied "social recognition" and "the highest respectability," one observer said: its membership was small, its waiting list long. Among its names were a slew of Astors and Aspinwalls; Biddles, Belmonts, Delanos, and Delafields; Gardiners, Griswolds, and Grinnells; Heckshers and Jeromes; Livingstons, Lorillards, Morrises, and Pells; Roosevelts and Schermerhorns; Stuyvesants and Townsends; Van Alens, Van Rensselaers, and Vanderbilts; Wilmerdings and Whitneys. No matter how rich an applicant was, his views, political and otherwise, had to concur with those of the other members. Upon occasion, even a Vanderbilt or a Morgan was refused.

Inside the splendid brownstone on Fifth Avenue and Twenty-first Street, the paneled walls held the secrets of powerful men seeking solace, safety, and conversation. A long-standing member, Edward had enjoyed many a leisurely hour and many a business meeting in the comfortable club, catching up with friends on the latest railroad news, real estate speculations, stocks and bonds and defalcations.

In the evening, "Big Green," as he was known, dressed in the requisite formal attire, and in the frescoed dining room fit for a prince he ate his lobster or saddle of lamb and washed it down with some good red wine. Then, lighted cigar in his mouth, brandy snifter at hand, he adjourned to the library to read, or the card room for cribbage, or the billiard room to smack a ball. Always ready to tell a good story or laugh at a good joke, he drew attention for his six-and-a-half-foot frame, won affection for his congeniality, earned admiration for his shrewdness and respect for his dignified ways.

Now after handing his coat to the servant guarding the cloak-room, he headed down the hall for the reading room; ensconced in a leather chair overlooking Fifth Avenue, he snapped open the *London Times* or *Le Monde* and scanned the news. Once in a while, gazing out the window, he saw his wife go by, dashed outside, and caught up with her over lunch. But most often he stayed indoors, his head down and his cigar dry.

While Edward secluded himself at his club, Hetty spent time with Annie Leary. A Catholic philanthropist whose generosity eventually brought her the title of Papal Countess, Annie was as close as a sister to Hetty and almost a mother to Sylvie and Ned. Devoted to Hetty's children, she persuaded her friend to give them a Catholic education. In September 1885, at the age of seventeen, Ned enrolled at St. John's College at Fordham. Although he won no honors and the school has no record of a degree, his classes in the "Belles Lettres" demanded attention: Latin and Greek, including the works of Horace, Homer, Cicero, Plato, and Sophocles; Comstock's elocution; modern history; geometry and chemistry. While Ned endured his studies, fifteen-year-old Sylvie's struggles at the Convent of the Sacred Heart recall those of Mark Twain's Ruth Bolton in *The Gilded Age,* who described her school as "a place to turn young people into dried fruit."

With her children at school, Hetty scurried off each morning, uncorseted and unknown, clad in a costume of black clothes. The woman who had been called Mrs. Edward Green was now Mrs. Hetty Green, one of the wage earners on her way to Wall Street. At the Chemical Bank on Broadway she strode past the iron bars separating the outside world from the inner workings of the bankers and headed toward the clerks. She scoffed at the offer of a private office and, instead, chose a seat at an empty desk or settled herself on the floor. With a mouthful of baked onions to ward off colds (as the Moldovan army still chews on today), she promptly went to work: she clipped her coupons for dividends, read her newspapers thoroughly, scoured trade papers, perused periodicals, checked pertinent journals, probed the men in the office, and conversed with male colleagues such as Russell Sage or Chauncey Depew, who came to call.

When she had read, quizzed, grilled, interrogated, and investigated enough, when she had studied the costs, analyzed the assets, and dug through the debts, when she had found the answers to suit her, when she knew the true worth of a company and understood its weaknesses, when she was satisfied that its basic values were sound and its assets strong, that the downside risk was low and the upside high, then she invested her money. Over the course of a few years, choosing among railroad stocks and bonds, real estate (both land and mortgages), mining companies, and government bonds, she bought and sold securities: more than $1 million of Reading Railroad bonds; thousands of shares of Louisville and Nashville stock; 6,400 shares of Georgia Central Railroad; $1.25 million in Houston and Texas first mortgage and regular bonds; 2,200 shares and bonds of the Ohio & Mississippi; shares of the St. Paul and Duluth; initial shares of Hathaway Mills; and at least $3 million worth of mortgages in downtown Chicago, all traded in her accounts.

Sometimes at noon she ate a bowl of oatmeal or stole a sandwich out of her pocket; sometimes, surprisingly, her husband joined her and they ventured out, still friends. Sometimes she went alone, not to Delmonico's or Sherry's, where ladies lunched at damask-covered tables, but to restaurants with bare tabletops where hardworking men scarfed down their midday meal. They not only offered an economical repast, they kept her in touch with the real world. She much preferred common people to the stuffy socialites of the upper class. What she preferred most was her work. She loved digging up the dirt on businesses and she loved the nitty-gritty of finance. "I have a head for numbers. They light up and tell me a story," said Muriel Siebert, a later female success on Wall Street. Hetty's numbers told a golden tale.

I know of no profession, art or trade that women are working on today as taxing for mental resources as being a leader of Society," said Alva Belmont at the time. Married first to the grandson of Cornelius

Vanderbilt and then to Oliver Perry Belmont, son of the Rothschilds' agent in New York, Alva led an exhausting life, an endless round of fittings and coiffures, lunches, teas, dinners, and social calls. Snubbed by the upper class, she worked hard to snub them back. Turned down for a box at the Academy of Music, she helped found the Metropolitan Opera Company; on opening night in October 1883, the scent of money was as strong as the strains from *Faust*. Rebuffed by Mrs. Astor, Alva commissioned Marble House, one of the most spectacular mansions in Newport, replete with Siena marble and a Titian-style ceiling, right next door to her. Excluded from the smart parties, she spent $3 million and transformed her New York château to host the most glittering fancy dress ball America had ever seen.

Mrs. Astor practically had to beg to be invited. Not that it would have mattered so much, she might have said, except for the fact that her daughter Carrie was of marriageable age. Heaven forbid, if she did not attend the ball of the decade. The party consumed the thoughts, the dreams, the conversations of the upper crust. For weeks before the event, guests obsessed over what costume to wear: men could not decide between Cardinal Richelieu and the Count of Monte Cristo; women anguished over whether to appear as Mary Stuart or Marie Antoinette. In the end, they ranged from kings and queens to monks and dairymaids, the hostess herself a glittering Venetian princess.

In truth, no one could outshine Caroline Astor. The pudgy girl who married William Backhouse Astor Jr. the year Hetty made her debut now ruled as the queen of New York society. Wearing a wig of black hair topped by a diamond tiara, dripping in ropes of diamonds, rubies, and pearls, swathed in a royal purple gown by Worth, she flew into a room like a shooting star, perched with aloofness on a ballroom divan, and reigned over the groveling rich.

In the drawing rooms and dining rooms of New York's aspiring aristocracy, social acolytes whispered her name in awe, sought her approval with trepidation. Some, like Collis Huntington, paid thousands of dollars to be in her company. Mentored by Ward McAllister, who organized the Patriarchs, for twenty years she decided New York's Four Hundred and deemed who was worthy of inclusion. But as magnificent as her houses were, as gorgeous as her dresses were, as dazzling as her jewels were, Mrs. Astor could not electrify her own husband. William stayed with her long enough to father five children and then escaped from her overwhelming ambitions, fleeing to Ferncliff, his mansion on the Hudson, or to the *Ambassadress*, his yacht.

If Mr. Astor did not appear at his wife's glittering balls, neither did many of his colleagues. While their wives and daughters, wearing Parisian gowns (and paying a 50 percent import tax for the privilege), descended from their brownstones and townhouses in the dark of night and, under the gaze of the gossip columnists, partied with idle males till 2 a.m., the men who made the money supped early and went to sleep. Jay Gould, James Lenox, and William Vanderbilt, recoiling at the word "cotillion," retreated to their private clubs. Henry James understood: "The highest luxury of all, the supremely expensive thing, is constituted privacy," he declared.

Hetty agreed with the men. She shunned the trivial entertainment, the exorbitantly expensive clothes, the aura of excess, and favored a simple life. Her Quaker God shone his smile on her fortune; she dared not risk his wrath on frivolity. She weighed her wealth and balanced the brilliant gold on one side with a leaden social life on the other.

But if her evenings were unexciting, her mind was certainly not dull. Henry Clews, the famed investment banker, wrote that Wall Street "is not the place for a lady to find either fortune or character." Women, he claimed, were "impulsive and impressionable, and not able to reason in the way that is indispensable to a successful speculator." With one exception, however: Hetty Green. "Her unaided sagacity has placed her among the most successful of our millionaire speculators. She is, however, made up of a powerful masculine brain in an otherwise female constitution. She is one among a million of her sex." In other words, suggested Clews, she thinks like a man.

Like many men, she had no interest in keeping house. Instead, Hetty boarded. She lived in houses with snug rooms, comfortable parlors, and home-cooked food, owned by women who could have been her. Like William Dean Howells's Mrs. Leighton, who faced the loss of her fortune, thousands of ladies in financial ruin opened their private homes and quietly offered rooms for respectable people. For gentlemen, single women and widows, newlyweds, and families not ready to live in one of the new apartment flats, the boardinghouse allowed them to reside with others of similar mind. Many doctors, lawyers, and wealthy businessmen took their warm breakfasts and hot suppers at their boardinghouse table, including Henry Hyde, founder of Equitable Life Assurance Society, the largest insurer in the world; James Alexander, president of the company; Frank Leslie, publisher of *Popular Monthly,* and his wife, Minnie Leslie, editor of the *Illustrated Ladies Gazette*; and Adolph Ochs, publisher of the *New York Times,* and his family.

While some fashionable places, furnished by people who had lived in wealth, welcomed their genteel guests, or "family," as they preferred to call them, with plush sofas and polished silver, others were upholstered in the tears and tatters of their impoverished owners; faded and threadbare, the quarters were small, the meals measly, and the food badly cooked, and the boarders were working class. These dingy places gave boardinghouses a bad name. Responding to a nasty piece in the *New York Times,* a young woman defended her residence: "That 'cheerless' boarding house is often a much happier home and the business girl more contented than very many of those who have decided to become 'queens of homes.' I don't object for one minute to any girl's choosing to be a 'queen' if she wishes to, but I do solemnly object to her saying that the boarding house girl misses all the fun of life and is cheerless and discontented." It was far less lonely, she wrote, to be in the company of others than to wait at home alone while one's "companion" was out at his private club. "There are some girls who prefer to be in boardinghouses and some who prefer to be queens," she said. "I prefer the calm comfort of the boardinghouse to the tie that binds uncomfortably."

Hetty had little desire to be a queen or to be tied down. Nor did she wish to concern herself with the daily problems of domesticity. But the press, deprived of a monarch and bewildered by her ways, made fun of her meager quarters and scorned her for her boardinghouse tastes. That other millionaires, like James Lenox or Edward Schermerhorn, hid in seclusion or lived amid clutter, did not matter. Reporters rarely mentioned them; Hetty, a woman, was fair game.

Ignoring her wish for privacy, often not even sure where she lived, they hunted down her address, hounded her doorway, and, whenever possible, revealed her residence. Disclosure drew hundreds of letters begging for money, or suggesting ransom, or threatening murder.

Suspicious to begin with, afraid to settle in, she constantly felt forced to flee. She was Ishmael; she was the Wandering Jew. She was used to shuttling between places; she moved like a nomad from boarding-houses to flats to hotels, from Brooklyn to the Bowery, Hempstead to Hoboken, changing her name, evading the press, the public, and also the tax man. Like thousands of New Yorkers then and now, she escaped state and city taxes by refusing to establish a residence. Where she lived mattered little to her. Days were a whirlwind of transactions; at night all she wanted was refuge. More important issues occupied her thoughts.

Railroads were constantly on her mind: they were costly, conspiratorial, competitive, cutthroat, and corrupt. Those who ran them were like thirsty men near a bar, elbowing their way to the front, imbibing all they could, gobbling up fare along the way. No better example existed than the Louisville and Nashville. As many of the smaller railroads were swallowed up in the early 1880s, the L&N consumed or controlled or leased, among others (and sometimes in secret): the Great Southern Railroad; the Mobile and Montgomery Railroad; the New Orleans and Mobile Railroad; the Nashville, Chattanooga, and St. Louis Railroad; the Western and Atlantic Railroad; and the Georgia Central Railroad. Through these transactions, the L&N gained a monopoly on the produce, the provisions, and the passengers traveling through South Carolina and Georgia and on to the West.

Railroad men like Colonel E. W. Cole, former president of the Nashville, Chattanooga, and St. Louis, could almost taste the profits. Organizing a group of friends, he put together the financing to form the East Tennessee Railroad, and took on the L&N. Despite strong opposition, he obtained a charter from the state of Georgia for the new line, and with millions of dollars and in minimum time, blasted through the mountains and laid tracks to the sea.

But expenses overwhelmed the income, and shortly afterward the East Tennessee found itself in receivership. That, however, spurred it to slash its fees, just to spite the L&N. The East Tennessee behaved like a monster toward the Louisville and Nashville and menaced the harmony that prevailed among the Southern roads, said the *New York Times*. "Freight rates have been frozzled out time and again." By September 1885 both lines were offering free delivery of cargo in Atlanta and both cut their passenger rates more than once. The rancor had reached the point of siege; even the L&N's allies were set to fight the East Tennessee. "It will be war to the knife and knife to the hilt," said the *Times*. "This is the way the rails are laid and the wires are working in the South."

The way that railroad stocks were trading seemed hardly better. In 1886 when word leaked that the Richmond Terminal Railroad wanted to expand its lines and consolidate its position in the South, its stock bounded out of control. When the opening bell rang at the Stock Exchange on the morning of November 20, no one could figure out how much the shares cost: a dozen different opening prices were quoted at the same time. The same brokers were selling the same stock at anywhere from 68 to 76. The hurly-burly was driving the investing public to distraction.

Hetty Green owned a considerable number of Georgia Central shares. When the Richmond Terminal Railroad made its move to take control, Hetty's stock was in demand. Two officers of the Richmond Terminal paid her a visit at the Chemical Bank, where her office was a few desks at the back of the room. She may have been one of the largest shareholders of the bank, but hers was a simple bureau. In the area where the cashiers, tellers, and clerks sat behind their gilded barriers, she sat in the open, in a corner, at her rolltop desk. Bonds, stocks, cash, letters, and notes were stuffed in the desk's side drawers, overflowed its pigeonholes, and sat chock-a-block in a black tin box on the top. Here, where light streamed in from a skylight in the roof, she dictated letters to her stenographer or clipped coupons from her bonds. On a typical day, Hetty, dressed in a black silk shirtwaist trimmed with rusty velvet and a black sateen skirt dotted in white, met with businessmen who called on her by the hour.

The two men from the Richmond Terminal made her an offer that seemed too good to refuse. She had bought the stock at $70; now it was selling at $100. The officers of the railroad offered to buy her 6,400 shares at $115, fifteen dollars over the market; to seal the deal they showed her a certified check. Hetty wrinkled her nose at the cash and declared she would be willing to sell, but only if they paid her more: she would accept the deal at $125 a share. They declined and left, but soon appeared again. This time they said that if she would agree to support their candidate for president of the railroad, they would sign a contract secured by collateral to buy her shares at $125. Oh no, she sniffed, dismissing their bid, she could not do that: their offer was not in cash. If they wanted her vote, they would have to pay her $130. Further negotiations led to triumph: in true Hetty style, she sold her stock for $127.50.

It was hard to know which Hetty enjoyed more: making money or outsmarting men. Around this time she achieved another coup. Once again, as the stock market retreated and the Louisville and Nashville headed downward, Hetty went against the trend. The bears were selling, and she was buying. One of the best-known bears was Addison Cammack, a former stockbroker who earned the nickname "Ursa Major" for his negative positions in the market. Cammack had heard that the Louisville and Nashville would report a loss and sold the stock short, that is, he borrowed shares he did not own, sold them at what he thought was the high, and then waited for the stock to fall so he could buy it at a lower price. Gleefully he watched the shares plummet. But Hetty was cornering the market, aggressively buying up stock; with fewer shares available, the market started to turn.

Cammack tried to buy shares to cover his short sale, but the more he tried to buy, the more the price went up. The words of the infamous Wall Street bear Daniel Drew hissed in his ear: "He who sells what isn't his'n, must buy it back or go to prison." Worried that the stock would go even higher and he would be squeezed even more, he approached Hetty: he wanted to buy forty thousand shares. She was willing to sell, she said, if he would pay her a difference of ten dollars per share. Cammack considered it a reasonable offer; he had expected her to demand a higher price. Surprised that she didn't ask for more of a profit, he gladly wrote her a check for $400,000. Cammack had treated her with respect and Hetty returned the favor. But those who acted condescendingly to her were treated with disdain.

Lewis May was one who had behaved badly. In January 1887, Hetty filed a lawsuit against May, the assignee for the Cisco bank. In the course of the suit, which lasted more than a year, Hetty often ignored her own attorney and interrogated May at the hearings. She charged him with taking illegal commissions and implied that he had committed fraud. When she had no success with May, she attacked

John A. Cisco, who had proved to be far more of a gambler than his cautious father.

The heat of New York City in July 1888 hardly compared with the sizzling atmosphere of the hearings. Wearing a black dress and a battered hat, Hetty faced the younger man: Did he know his father was writing to her? she demanded. Did he know his father had said that none of her money would be used in anything, and yet Mr. Green was using it all the time? Why did he send someone to follow her in Bellows Falls? she wanted to know. Her nostrils flaring, her eyes burning, she hurled out her suspicions: "Did you think I had a tendency to heart disease, and you would put me out of the way and get all the money?" she asked. "She went for him like a tigress and nothing could hold her back," one observer said.

Although she lost the case and was forced to pay all costs, Hetty took pleasure facing her enemies in court. When Cisco denied any knowledge of her claims, she defended herself: "I come of good old Quaker blood. All I care for is to do right. Then I am sure to go to heaven," she said. The judge's decision may have gone against her, but the court was her meetinghouse, and she had been heard by the High and Mighty.

A few weeks after she initiated the lawsuit, the Reading Railroad, which had suffered severe losses, announced a reorganization plan. Satisfied that the idea would succeed, Hetty agreed to support it. In February 1887 she marched into the offices of Brown Brothers and handed over a satchel filled with a million dollars' worth of stock certificates; in line with the plan, she would exchange her old shares for the new. Would there be any costs for the transfer? she asked. Yes, she was told, the transfer charges from New York to Philadelphia would be $100. "A hundred dollars!" she screeched. "Why, I can go to Philadelphia and return for four dollars." The bankers neither denied her claim nor offered to lower the cost. Dismayed, Hetty picked up her securities, stuffed them back in her bag, rushed to the Grand Central Station, and bought a ticket for the next train to Philadelphia.

When word of her dealings reached the Stock Exchange, the Wall Street men were taken aback. What surprised them was not that Hetty took the train to save the money; rather, it was that she had secretly acquired far more shares of Reading than anyone knew. She was a rare woman who could hold her tongue, they said, and they sheepishly had to admit she managed her business far better than most men.

Hetty accepted reorganization of the Reading Railroad, but she refused to go along with such a scheme for the Houston and Texas Central Railroad. When Collis Huntington, still in control, offered to exchange existing bonds of the defaulting railroad for new bonds yielding 2 percent less, some bondholders resigned themselves to the plan. But Huntington had hurt Hetty once in 1885 when he stopped paying dividends on the railroad's bonds, causing the price to plunge; two years later she would not let him get away with it again. With her large holding of first mortgage bonds, she could take control of the railroad if it went into total bankruptcy.

The "Queen of Wall Street," as Hetty was called by the *Times* and other papers, opposed the Central Railroad reorganization. When Huntington said that he did not care whether or not she went along and that he would proceed as planned, the paper scoffed at him. "Other big men have talked in just this way about Mrs. Green in times past, but somehow she usually contrives to come out ahead whenever the fighting notion strikes her." Indeed, after almost a year of hard negotiation, Huntington caved in to Hetty's demands and she agreed to the reorganization. But Huntington stuck like a thorn in her side. Several years later, she would outbid him to take control of part of the railroad.

Hetty's life extended well beyond her New York City office. Besides visits to Vermont and Massachusetts, in the summer of 1887 she and her son resided in Hempstead, New York, and later, in the autumn, the *Chicago Daily Tribune* reported that they were living in Chicago. She was working out of her agent's office on Dearborn Street and sometimes arrived as early as 7 a.m. to oversee her properties, such as the Howland block. Known as the Honore and erected after the Great Fire, the block was a massive stone building that housed the Real Estate Exchange. Hetty had loaned its well-known owner, H. H. Honore, $250,000 some years before, but when he became overextended and was unable to make his payments, she took the property back. A local broker told the *Tribune* he'd like to own it now and could sell it for three times the price.

Hetty also held a $250,000 mortgage on the Major Block, a large office building that housed the National Weather Service. Her properties included, along with an aggregate of mortgages worth around $3 million, the Gower Block, the Reed Block, and other block-long buildings downtown that became a significant part of the Loop. Whenever interest on a loan could not be met, Hetty claimed the property.

In early 1888, when the managers of her father's trust insisted on selling 650 acres in nearby Cicero, Hetty was furious. She believed the land was worth far more and saw no reason to sell it. She filed suit and the matter was brought to court. When the case was heard, Hetty sent Ned to represent her in Chicago. But Judge Collins, who was in charge of hearing the case, refused to stop the transaction, and the acreage was sold to the Grant Locomotive Works. Hetty vowed revenge.

Few knew exactly how much money Hetty really had or what exactly she invested in. "No broker or operator who is not very new at the business ever attempts to get the better of Mrs. Green," said one observer. "Her methods are so quiet and straightforward that she mystifies the very elect among railroad men." So secretive was she that for a while they did not even know where she lived. In January 1888 the *Brooklyn Eagle* discovered the peripatetic woman was residing in its own backyard, and had been living there for several months. Her companions were her daughter and her Newfoundland dog, which had recently produced a litter of pups. Her son Ned was still in Chicago, her husband still in New York; on Sundays, Edward visited his wife and daughter in Brooklyn.

Hetty's choice of Brooklyn was not as surprising as it sounded. The third-largest city in the nation, Brooklyn offered a gentle alternative to Manhattan's hullabaloo. It was "as quiet as New York is bewildering and noisy," wrote Fredrika Bremer years before. "On Broadway," she said, one finds "endless tumult and stir, crowds and bustle . . . and the most detestable fumes poison the air." New York, she wrote, is "the last place on earth I would live. But thank Heaven! I know Brooklyn!"

The Brooklyn Bridge, the longest bridge in the world, gave easy access to Manhattan. Completed in 1883, its span of steel cables suspended across the East River competed with the continuous ferries that rushed back and forth on the water. At a penny a ride, six hundred passengers crammed each steamer for the five-minute trip, and seventy-five thousand people commuted on the floating platforms every day. With its leafy streets and numerous churches, Brooklyn, independent until 1898, provided a civilized place for wage earners and Wall Street bankers alike; "a kind of sleeping place for New York," wrote Charles Dickens.

Although she lived in Brooklyn Heights, a neighborhood of elegant Gothic Revival houses with expansive views over the East River, Hetty was seeking neither sophistication nor luxury. "She has a modest room in a comfortable boarding house on Pierrepont Street, and lives in a quiet, unpretentious manner," said the *Brooklyn Eagle*. Indeed, few she passed going up and down the steep front steps of her brownstone or walked by on her way to Wall Street knew who she was. Not more than half a dozen people in the neighborhood, and "not one in a hundred who brush by her on the ferry" each day, recognized the famous lady, said the *Eagle*. "This shrewd operator" and "keen financier" is a "well preserved looking woman, with a rather pleasant face, and dresses very plainly," the paper reported. At fifty-four, on her morning walk along the cobblestone streets to the ferry, Hetty looked like an ordinary woman doing ordinary chores.

It came as a surprise to Alice Bonta, the owner of the boardinghouse, when a well-known millionaire came to call. Mary Garrett, whose friends included several Quaker women, was a shrewd businesswoman and heiress from Baltimore who had served as her father's assistant when he was head of the Baltimore and Ohio Railroad. She had inherited several million dollars from his estate, and, with the proviso that women be allowed to enroll as students, donated some of the money to help create the Johns Hopkins University School of Medicine. Together with the president of the university, Mary Garrett was on a national campaign to raise funds for the medical school. Now she was calling on Hetty Green in Brooklyn.

The following evening the two visitors hosted a dinner in Hetty's honor. To the surprise of the boardinghouse owner, Hetty emerged from her room dressed in an elegant evening gown and exquisite jewels. Her gift to the university may not have been made public, but when Mrs. Bonta realized that the hardworking lady living in her house was the rich and famous Hetty Green, she made her tenant's presence known to all.

Hetty and Sylvie spent three months in Hempstead in the summer of 1887; the following year they stayed at the Ocean Hotel in Far Rockaway. When Hetty returned to the city, she faced a long-dreaded situation. Limping across the busy thoroughfare of Ninth Avenue, Ned was struck by a fast-moving cart. Dragged to the ground and pinned down by the boy driver and his St. Bernard dog, Ned suffered further damage to his leg.

Soon after, at the Union Club, where he was celebrating the Fourth of July with his father, he hurried to the window to watch the festivities, twisted his leg, and fell down some stairs. The young man was carried to a room and confined to the club until Edward's doctor arrived. The distinguished physician Charles McBurney examined the leg and saw the onset of gangrene; he declared he had no choice but to amputate, ending all hopes for a recovery. The operation at Roosevelt Hospital severed Ned's leg above the knee. But it did not stop Ned from living a life as rich and full as those of his parents: he was as robust and outgoing as his father, as shrewd and astute as his mother, and most important, as self-reliant as they all wished him to be.

Ned's recuperation took place in Bellows Falls, where he and his father and sister spent several weeks that summer. Happy to be back in the bucolic countryside where she could roam freely and ride her horse, Sylvie invited some friends to the Towns Hotel for a party. Dressed in a gray crepe dress, she entertained some of the young people she had known at school and took a fancy to one of the males in her class. When a friend accused him of being facetious, Sylvie showed surprise. "Never with me," she replied, indicating that he fancied her too. But the romance never went far and Sylvie soon returned to her mother.

Hetty never stayed in one place very long. In October 1887 she was discovered by the *Chicago Herald*, which announced she had been in the city for several weeks, her son at her side. Countering reports that she was thin, angular, and poorly dressed, "she is a big, plump woman," the paper declared, "and her togs are first class." She declined to stay in hotels, and instead paid rent to reside with her business agent, who lived on the South Side. She left his house at dawn to ride the streetcar and arrived downtown early in the day. After spending time at her desk one morning, at nine o'clock she left to go down the street and encountered a broker, who assumed that, like the stream of workers filing into their offices, Hetty was on her way to work. Certain of a coup, he told her about a mortgage he could arrange. But Hetty harrumphed. "That was offered to me at seven o'clock this morning," she snapped, "and I refused it." With that she shrugged him off and marched away.

Hetty had brought Ned along to train him in real estate investing. The best way to understand what a mortgage was really worth, she believed, was through hands-on experience. She wanted him to know the cost of a building and what it involved, not just from a financial aspect, but in terms of materials and labor. She assigned him work on a warehouse she was building. "I bought a pair of overalls for him, gave him a brush and a keg of white lead, and hired a man to teach him to paint," she told a friend.

Unfortunately, it was at the time of the anarchists' riots in Chicago. When one of the laborers saw Ned, he accused him of taking the bread out of the workingman's mouth; what's more, he threatened to throw him into Lake Michigan. Hetty was protective of her son, but she also sympathized with the poor and understood their rage. "I reasoned with the man and showed him that Ned was not getting any money for his work; that the job had already been let out by contract, and that the painters would get all there was in it," she explained. As a result, she said, "he went away satisfied." And Ned, she said, "got along fine with the anarchists."

Years later, when the trolley workers went on strike in Brooklyn, Hetty took the side of the workers. "The poor have no chance in this country," she said. "No wonder Anarchists and Socialists are so numerous. The longer we live, the more discontented we all get, and no wonder, too. Some blame the rich, but all the rich are not to blame."

Hetty was determined to educate her children on the value of money. Her approach was similar to that of the modern billionaire Alice Walton, the third-wealthiest woman in the world. "One of the great responsibilities that I have is to manage my assets wisely, so that they create value," says the heiress to the Walmart fortune. "I know the price of lettuce. You need to understand price and value. You buy the best lettuce you can at the best price you can."

Intent on teaching her children to be clever investors, from time to time Hetty brought them to the Chemical Bank in New York or asked them to join her in meetings elsewhere. Sylvie trudged along, wearing a faded frock and a sad expression. Investing sparked no interest in the girl; if anything, it made her more eager to be with her school friends in Bellows Falls than with the moneymen on Wall Street. For Ned, however, the downtown adventures served as a fantasy peek into the world of finance: "I sometimes thought that it would be nice if mother made me president of the Chemical Bank of New York," he confessed. But he had only "a vague idea concerning the future." He dabbled on Broadway, investing in plays, and dabbled with showgirls, playing at night. Hetty took control of things: worried that her son would fall for a pretty young thing who would quickly consume his fortune, she extracted a promise from Ned that he would not marry for twenty years. What's more, she made him swear he would never speculate on Wall Street.

Even his father was more restrained with his money now. Operating on a far more moderate scale, Edward was seen two or three times a week in the canyons of Wall Street, often in the company of his wife. On one occasion he sat beside her at the back of the Chemical Bank while she clipped away at her coupons, cutting them off the bond certificates, dropping them into her satchel; she would redeem the pieces of paper for the interest due on the scheduled date. When she finished snipping the bonds, she counted the slips and found that one was missing. They searched the floor, the desks, the bag, until they discovered the coupon, stuck to the bottom of Edward's boot. With a cry of joy, Hetty grabbed the paper and put it in her satchel, but not before casting a look of mistrust at her husband. Assured that he was innocent, she locked her bag and trotted off, her money and man in tow.

Chapter 13

═══

The Education of Children

From the day their son was born, Hetty had a singular goal: to see Ned become the richest man in America. With railroads propelling the country, she wanted him at the forefront. But she knew he needed an education in how the railroads functioned before he could captain his future along the gilded track.

For years she had owned shares of the Connecticut River Railroad, and from the time Ned was a boy he had traveled the line linking Bellows Falls with New York. The time had come for him to see its operations from the inside. Limping along the tracks with his new cork leg, he toiled as a section hand and foreman on the Connecticut River Railroad, weeding and clearing the tracks, running a locomotive, eating lunch with the workingmen. A quick student, he learned the ways of the railroad and, after several months, gained an understanding of the process. From there he was sent to Cincinnati, where he worked as a superintendent and then as managing director of the Ohio and Mississippi Railroad. Now his mother felt he was ready to take on bigger tasks.

Over six feet tall with a hefty build, Ned Green was an extroverted twenty-two-year-old when Hetty sent him off to the Midwest in 1890. Handing him a satchel filled with valuable papers, she ordered him to deliver them to Frank Chandler, her agent, in Chicago. On the twenty-three-hour train ride out west, Ned fought hard to stay awake all night. He tucked the bag under the mattress in his Pullman berth and did not close his eyes, lest the satchel be lost or stolen.

From the window of his car the next morning, Ned could see the open prairie landscape morph into a maze of stockyards and railroad tracks, could watch the tall poles and telegraph wires give way to smokestacks and factories. When the train pulled into Union Station, the young man grabbed his bag and went directly to the agent's office. Along State Street, LaSalle, Madison, and Monroe, he saw tall structures rising on "streets long and flat and without end," as Rudyard Kipling described them at the time; "interminable vistas flanked with nine, ten, and fifteen storied houses, and crowded with men and women."

The Great Fire had destroyed acres of land and structures, and out of its ashes arose an array of new buildings designed by leading architects such as Charles McKim and Richard Morris Hunt, who re-created the classic Roman style, and Louis Sullivan, father of the skyscraper. New laws prohibited the use of wood, causing builders to put up huge stone or iron structures, mounds of masonry with plate-glass fronts and brass nameplates, which now stretched across entire blocks. Eager young women and impatient young men, fair-haired and wide-eyed, fresh off the farms of Iowa, Kansas, and Oklahoma, dashed from the speeding, clanging streetcars and darted along the sidewalks: off to work, rushing to make a life for themselves.

Weary from the sleepless journey, relieved to have made the trip unscathed, Ned reached the agent's office and handed over the package. He watched with pride as the man carefully unwrapped the precious parcel. To Ned's surprise, the agent let out a loud guffaw. "What do you mean, telling me you have bonds here?" he asked, showing Ned the stack. Hetty's valuable papers were nothing more than a pile of outdated insurance policies. "My mother always dearly loved a joke," Ned said later with a laugh, "but I'll say she had a very practical way of testing me out."

Teasing and practical jokes were a regular part of the Greens' family life. On one occasion when Ned went to visit Hetty and Sylvie, he arrived with an enormous box. His mother quickly admonished him for his habit of buying things in large quantities. "You don't need all those dress shirts," she scolded. Her son protested and proceeded to open the package: the carton was filled with her favorite doughnuts.

Although Hetty often lived at less than distinguished places, she instructed Ned to pay six dollars a day at the Auditorium Hotel. Designed by Louis Sullivan, it was attached to the new Auditorium Theatre, where Grand Opera was performed and the Republican Party had recently held its convention. But the fancy four-hundred-room hotel on Michigan Avenue was too much for Ned. After a short while, he moved to a hotel on Madison that cost half the price. Ned may have wanted to enjoy his money his own way, but as soon as his mother heard, she dashed off a quick reprimand: "I notice that you are not staying at the hotel I suggest," she wrote. "It's all right, but I have reduced your daily allowance to $3," she said, cutting his stipend in half. She warned him to watch his pennies. "You are not to have any more spending money than the amount decided on originally."

Her affable son adjusted quickly to life in Chicago. He dressed nattily and wore his fake leg as gamely as he sported his thin mustache and wire spectacles. He joined the Elks, attended the theater, wooed the actresses, and favored a red-haired girl named Mabel Harlow. He might have run into Sister Carrie at McVicker's Theatre, or dined with Charles Drouet at the glittering Rector's, or swilled drinks with their creator, Theodore Dreiser, at Fitzgerald and Moy's. Self-assured and confident, he chatted easily with actors, businessmen, politicians, and the press. When a reporter from the *Herald* interviewed him, he boasted about his plans to open a bank.

Relaxing in his office at the Owings Building, a neo-Gothic structure owned by Hetty, he repeated his plans to the *New York Times*: "Arrangements are practically completed for the new business," he said, noting it would be a mortgage bank loaning money on securities. "We will loan at a reasonable rate of interest and borrowers may take up their paper at any time. Ours will be a sort of private bank." Ned assured the writer that he and his mother would have a controlling interest. "We never invest in anything unless we have control of it," he said.

Some people viewed such banking operations as high finance, but the young man made short shrift of it: "This loaning business is nothing more nor less than a pawnbroker's shop on a large scale, except that the borrowers have to hock a good piece of real estate instead of a watch. Some men get mad when you call them pawnbrokers," he said, "but loaning money as I do is nothing more nor less." Ned also spoke of buying a major newspaper, but despite his big talk, neither the newspaper nor the bank came to fruition. As much as Ned boasted, his mother kept her lips sealed tight. Her remarks were never heard. Ned noted that she was usually nice to him in public, but in private she "gave me hell."

Hetty knew it was a propitious time to be in Chicago. Not only was the city "the capital of the railroads," as one French writer observed, it was the bustling center of the West. Innovative and industrial, Chicago introduced steel-framed skyscrapers to the world, established major department stores like Marshall Field's and Sears Roebuck, and boasted manufacturers like Armour and Company meatpackers, McCormick Reapers, and Pullman Palace sleeping cars. It had twenty-five grain elevators that could hold 25 million bushels of corn. It had Lincoln Park with acres of green and a sand beach lapping Lake Michigan, a lake as large as an ocean. It had grand hotels like the Tremont and the palatial Palmer House, with its barber shop, billiards room, bowling alley, telegraph office, and its own ticker tape. It had banks with weekly clearings of millions of dollars, and the Board of Trade, where men bought and sold commodities—hogs and cattle, wheat and corn—as if they were penny candy. In this dynamic atmosphere, Ned announced he would run his mother's operations and make Chicago his home. He was right that the city would flourish, but wrong that it would be his home.

Hetty sent Ned to Chicago to sniff out new opportunities and to oversee her mortgages. She charged her son with collecting the payments due, and before he left, she proffered some advice. She counseled him to memorize the amount of principal and interest owed on each mortgage. Whatever someone owed, she warned, don't take a penny less. And not a penny more. It would only mess up his books. When her son wanted to entertain his associates, his mother cautioned: "After your business is over you may take him to dinner and the theater, or allow him to take you, but wait until the transaction has been closed and the money paid."

His other responsibility was buying and selling new properties and mortgages. Hetty held him accountable for his every decision but offered her own recommendations before making a deal: "If anyone is fool enough to offer you the full amount, take it. If you are offered less, tell the man you will give him the answer in the morning." She believed in giving things a second look. "Think the matter over carefully in the evening. If you decide that it will be to our advantage to accept the offer, say so the next day." Then she repeated one of her favorite maxims: "In business generally, don't close a bargain until you have reflected on it overnight."

Not only did Ned purchase mortgages for his mother, he also bought them for his father. E. H. Green became the owner of at least one Chicago mortgage, a $12,000 loan on the First Baptist Church at Thirtieth Street and Indiana Avenue. Whether Hetty had given Ned permission is unknown, but she had a soft spot for Edward, and his name cropped up every so often.

As much as Ned savored his independence, his mother often surprised him and arrived at his side. Hetty commuted between New York and Chicago as though they were two stops on a suburban train. No other woman traveled as much as she did, it was said. Wearing costumes like the brown dress and black cloak trimmed in cheap plush that the *Tribune* dismissed as clothes "a society lady's maid would not covet," she appeared in Chicago courts for her lawsuits, attended meetings in her agent's office, and scouted locations for investment.

In December 1890, when the builder of the town of Colehour defaulted on his payments and the whole property was to be sold under court order, Hetty and Ned were quick to visit the site. Before daybreak on the morning of the sale, they caught the train for South Chicago and rode out to the suburban town. They inspected the property carefully, walking around the homes of the clerks and mechanics who lived in the town, until they had seen it all. The sale was to take place at 10 a.m. and they had to make a decision.

Before the bidding began, they contacted the banks, arranged for some ready funds, and quickly informed the sellers they had the money. Later that day they met with their lawyer: Hetty plopped down a newspaper bundle on his desk; buried inside was $100,000, enough to finance a mortgage on the entire town. Critics claimed she had snaffled the land. But it was more the action of a shrewd businesswoman. Indeed, a similar event took place in 2006 when it was rumored that the Lord & Taylor chain would be put up for sale by Federated Department Stores. One man acted aggressively: "Before Federated even asked for bids, Mr. Baker kicked the tires and lined up financing, letting him close the deal before other parties had completed their bids," said the *New York Times*. Hetty assured the press there was no evil in her maneuver. Indeed, she said with a twinkle in her eye, it was more than a tactic for making money: it was an act of humanity. She had saved the town, she told reporters, and saved the four hundred families who lived there.

When others were failing, Hetty often stepped in and saved them by buying their mortgages. The secret, of course, was available cash. She loved a bargain, and having money on hand to pick up distressed assets gave her a distinct advantage in the marketplace. Then, when the banks allowed foreclosure on her mortgages, Hetty assumed the property.

Such was the case when she was sued for a mortgage she had purchased years before. In 1873, Hetty had loaned $150,000 for a mortgage, and after three years of nonpayment the bank foreclosed; she bought the property at a bargain price. By 1890 its value had grown to $1 million and the original owners challenged her in court. A federal judge in Chicago dismissed the lawsuit and the property remained in her hands.

More than a century later the *New York Times* reported, "Loans on Distressed Properties Become a Burden and an Opportunity." The 2009 story referred to the Drake Hotel in Manhattan, owned by real estate magnate Harry Macklowe, who had suffered from the severe credit crunch and defaulted on his loans. As the paper pointed out, however, the hotel itself was not for sale; what was available was a $200 million mortgage. "If Macklowe defaults on that mortgage, the owner of the mortgage will be in the best position to take ownership of the property," said the *Times*.

Numerous defaults took place in 1890. In August that year, the U.S. Congress passed the Sherman Silver Act, ordering the Treasury to make monthly purchases of four and a half million ounces of silver produced in the West and turn it into coins. But foreign governments did not view silver as equal to gold and two months later the country suffered the consequences.

Baring Brothers, the most important financial institution in London after the Bank of England, had lost millions of dollars on South American adventures. The usually conservative bank had put aside its cautious approach and taken high risks in Argentina and Uruguay. When the investments collapsed, Baring's holdings plummeted.

The bank paid the price, and Americans paid too. No longer able to use its foreign investments as collateral, Baring Brothers, a major investor in U.S. railroads, was forced to sell its shares in American stocks. In return, it demanded its money back in gold, draining some of the gold supply. Even worse, rumors spread that Baring Brothers had failed. On Wall Street, men's teeth chattered and their knuckles turned white as they contemplated the meaning of such a cataclysmic event.

The stock market dropped, and real estate prices fell with it. Hetty and other shrewd financiers found bargains galore. In Chicago, Hetty bought up mortgages. In New York, J. P. Morgan and Andrew Carnegie bought Madison Square Garden for only $400,000. Fortunately, Baring Brothers was rescued, and after a year the American markets seemed more secure. New Yorkers built bigger, more splendid mansions all along Fifth Avenue and rode in their horse-drawn carriages uptown. At Fifty-seventh Street and Seventh Avenue, Andrew Carnegie built his new Music Hall for $1.25 million. Over the course of a week in May 1891, thousands of people packed the auditorium: Walter Damrosch led the orchestra in a Beethoven overture; the Oratorio Society's voices rang out; and Tchaikovsky conducted his *Festival Coronation March*.

Culture flourished and commerce boomed in Chicago too: the city was the focal point of the railroads, "the Rome of the Great West," as the writer Charles Dudley Warner called it. Chicago was "the place where most of the great lines meet," where agriculture was shipped, where cattle were congregated, where raw materials merged, and where the rolling stock was produced to transport it all. Chicago's industries were thriving, its population increasing to over a million people, its business surpassing a billion dollars a year.

Against strenuous competition from St. Louis, Washington, and New York, Chicago had won the right to hold the Columbian Exposition: the World's Fair, a celebration of the four-hundredth anniversary of Christopher Columbus's discovery of the New World. To do so, it promised to raise $10 million through stocks and bonds. Opening in 1893, the World's Fair, laid out by Frederick Law Olmsted, creator of Central Park, included two hundred buildings in the beaux arts style; it hosted forty-three countries and in less than a year attracted twenty-six million people, almost half the nation's population.

The fair made an impact on every aspect of American life, from agriculture and advertising to transportation and technology, from manufacturing and marketing to classrooms and culture. Families saw the brilliance of electricity that would transform their homes and workplaces, children heard the pledge of allegiance they would soon recite in schools, and everyone sent postcards home to their friends. They chewed on Juicy Fruit gum, slurped the new Cream of Wheat, munched on hamburgers, shrieked on the Ferris wheel, and heard the oompah-pah of John Philip Sousa's marching songs. Antonín Dvořák and Scott Joplin, who composed music as varied as the *New World Symphony* and ragtime, and writers such as Henry Adams and L. Frank Baum, who wrote books as different as *The Education of Henry Adams* and *The Wonderful Wizard of Oz*, were all inspired by the exposition.

The fair brought to life de Tocqueville's earlier writings on America's "exceptional" and "eminently democratic" system—the egalitarian, individualistic, and free spirit that made it unique. American exceptionalism, a term recently revived, recalls the country's remarkable character, its atmosphere bursting with artistic, creative, industrial, and technological brilliance. The country in general, and Chicago in particular, was rich with opportunities and Hetty scooped them up like pennies raining down from heaven. "My mother was business, business, business," said Ned.

I hate business," Hetty told a reporter. "I just attend to it for my children's sake. I would a great deal rather be a society woman." As much time and effort as Hetty spent doing well in the business world,

Hetty Howland Robinson. The striking twenty-six-year-old, on her way to a dinner party at the home of former President McKinley, was known to be a good dancer and a witty conversationalist. *(Courtesy of the New Bedford Whaling Museum)*

Edward Mott Robinson, Hetty's father. A shrewd man who loved making money more than anything else, he berated his wife and thwarted his daughter.

(Right) Abby Slocum Howland Robinson, Hetty's mother. Dominated by her husband and depressed over not bearing him a son, she spent many years bedridden and under a doctor's care.

(Left) Sylvia Ann Howland, Hetty's aunt. Sickly from birth, she clashed constantly with Hetty's father and was frustrated in her attempts to turn Hetty into a proper lady.

Delmonico's. The smart restaurant where champagne flowed, elegant parties were held, and the upper crust showed themselves off. *(© Bettmann/Corbis)*

The Astor residence. The home of Caroline Schermerhorn Astor at Thirty-fourth Street and Fifth Avenue set the standard for the Gilded Age and was where Mrs. Astor determined who was to be part of her famous Four Hundred.

Edward Henry Green, Hetty's husband. A generous man who feasted on life, he did himself in by assuming too much risk and did his marriage in by using his wife's funds.

Annie Leary, a Catholic philanthropist. Hetty's best friend, who guided her debutante daughter, Sylvia Green, through society.

Madison Square Park cab stand. The center of fashionable New York, where ladies shopped and the smart set rode in hansom cabs.

The Breakers. The Vanderbilt home in Newport was the scene of fabulous parties. Based on a sixteenth-century Italian palazzo, it was built to rival Mrs. Astor's residence. *(Collection of the New-York Historical Society)*

The Elms. Inspired by a French château, it was another of the Newport palaces where American entrepreneurs and their wives could pretend to be European nobility.

Hetty and her dog. Fond of children and dogs, she fed her pets steak and said she liked them because they didn't care how rich she was.

Hetty and her daughter. Taken at the time of her wedding, Sylvia Green was thirty-eight when she married Matthew Astor Wilks, a kindly clubman and member of the prominent Astor family.

(© Bettmann/Corbis)

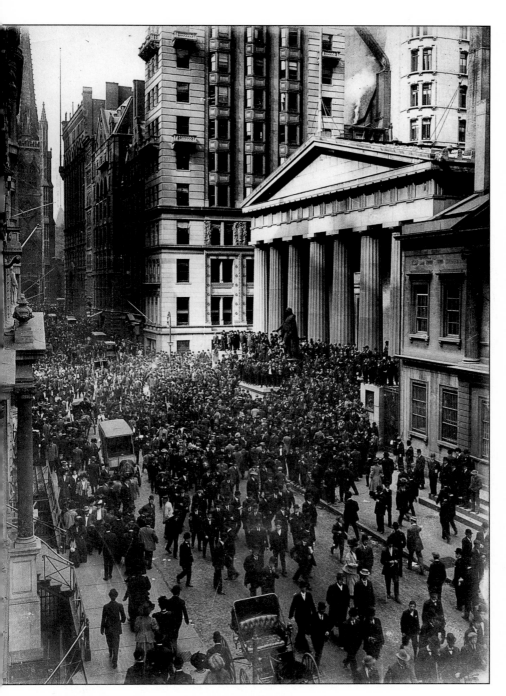

Panic of 1907 in front of the Sub-Treasury. Wild speculation and heavy borrowing led to a steep rise in interest rates and a collapse of banks and businesses.

The 1907 run on the Lincoln Trust Co. When the bubble burst, people rushed to withdraw their money, but the banks ran out of funds and shut their doors.

Ned and Mabel. Hetty had called her "Miss Harlot," and Ned Green waited until his mother died before marrying his longtime love Mabel Harlow.

her friend Annie Leary spent doing good in the social world. Annie was the Jekyll to Hetty's Hyde. A philanthropist and fun-loving woman who crammed her days with lunches, teas, and charitable events and filled her evenings with dinner parties, dances, concerts, and balls, she raised money for the poor, aided Italian immigrants in Greenwich Village, created schools, commissioned public art works, and generously supported the Catholic Church.

As much attention as Hetty gave to her son Ned, Annie gave to Hetty's daughter Sylvie. Like Henry James's character in *Washington Square,* the widowed Dr. Sloper, who disdained his daughter, Hetty might have said, "Try to make a clever woman of her. I should like her to be a clever woman." And like Sloper's sister, Aunt Lavinia, Annie tried. At her home at 90 Fifth Avenue, just a few blocks north of Washington Square, the lighthearted spinster took Sylvie under her wing. Determined that she be given a proper introduction to society, Annie acted as Sylvie's chaperone. She supervised the selection of her wardrobe and oversaw the numerous fittings of tailored luncheon suits, floating tea dresses, beaded evening gowns, ball gowns, plumed hats, wraps, gloves, and ostrich feather fans required of any debutante, even the thickset, six-foot Sylvie.

Although Hetty may have frowned at the thought of her daughter swathed in expensive taffetas and tulles, she understood the social rituals. "As for society," she said, "I believe in it. When a young woman, I went out a great deal myself." She clarified her words: "I don't think society means what some rich people would have us believe. I should get very tired of living in one of the great houses in New York, going out all night and sleeping all day. They don't have any real pleasure. It's intercourse with people that I like."

But while Hetty was a clever conversationalist when she chose to be, her daughter was too self-conscious to speak up. Although many considered her intelligent, her sad countenance and dour disposition made some regard her as Dr. Sloper viewed his own offspring: "My daughter is a wealthy woman with a large fortune," he said. "She is about as intelligent as a bundle of shawls."

Witty or not, Sylvie took part in Annie Leary's more sociable world. Miss Leary was described in *Town and Country* magazine as "an ideal hostess [who] takes the greatest interest in the lighter side of life." Her Thursday at-homes featured musical performances; her dinner parties were decorated by Hodgson and catered by Pinard; her after-dinner guests were entertained by Lander's Orchestra. What's more, the sewing circle she started, which ran year after year from Lent to Easter, was noted in the papers and copied by other prominent ladies. Once a fortnight, the group of debutantes—dance class students of Mrs. Stebbins's, who trained their bodies "to express a beautiful soul," or of Mrs. Shrady's, who taught them the more traditional waltz—gathered in Miss Leary's drawing room. In between gossip and giggles they stitched simple clothes to donate to hospitals, homes, and prisons.

In the redbrick house she shared with her bachelor brother Arthur, an accomplished athlete, fine dancer, and successful businessman, Annie introduced the twenty-year-old Sylvie to the Learys' friends, their daughters, and their unmarried sons. It may not have been a trumpeted coming out, but dressed in a debutante's virginal gown, Sylvie stepped timidly into a round of social events at which she was constantly on display, expected to flaunt her charms and attract her future husband.

The Patriarchs' Ball she attended in January 1892 dazzled the guests and the press. Held at Delmonico's at the height of the Gilded Age, as Mark Twain dubbed the era, it occurred at the start of the year, when Ward McAllister announced his famous list of Four Hundred. The most exclusive register of New York society was "not unlike Dante's description of Paradise," said Mrs. Winthrop Astor Chanler, one of its members.

Along with James Roosevelt, Withington Whitehouse, Matthew Astor Wilks, and an assemblage of Astors, Geolets, Peabodys, and Pells, the fashionable Mr. Arthur Leary, an original member of the Patriarchs, together with Miss Leary and Miss Green, arrived to find Delmonico's awash in pink. Garlands of pink roses filled the ballrooms and festooned the chandeliers; the tables were bursting with bouquets of roses and orchids. Pink flowers and lush plants bloomed everywhere, and rare ferns and palm fronds quivered in the nooks.

Almost all the 150 invited guests attended a Metropolitan Opera performance and then swooped in at 11:30 p.m., danced for an hour, and sat down to a dinner of roast duck and English wines. Later, not one but two orchestras, the Hungarian band in the red ballroom and Lander's in the white and gold room, provided music for the many couples who performed the cotillion. At 3:30 a.m. the strains of "Goodnight Ladies" wafted through the air. Sylvie, ungainly in her delicate dress, uncomfortable in her dancing shoes, joined the rest of the guests as they put on their wraps and faded away. She had endured her first Patriarchs' Ball. Like Edith Jones (the future Edith Wharton) a few years later, she had suffered through "the long cold agony of shyness"; she had survived, but she did not succumb to the Patriarchs again.

Still, there were the requisite dinners, for which an invitation, said Ward McAllister, "is a social obligation. If you die before the dinner takes place, your executor must attend." And there were special occasions, such as the evening hosted by Mme. de Barrios, widow of the Guatemalan president, who transformed her drawing room into a theater and provided her guests, including Arthur and Annie Leary, Mrs. Green and Miss Green, with an operatic performance of *Faust*. When the Italian orchestra commenced to play and the red velvet curtain rose, the audience gushed at the cottage, the gate, and the gardens created on the miniature stage. Later, at supper provided by Sherry's, they had a chance to chat with the hostess, bedecked in opals and diamonds, and appraise her new fiancé, Señor de Roda. But a few months later, when word leaked that Sylvie Green had a suitor, Hetty found little to celebrate.

Annie Leary had invited the diffident Sylvie to spend the month of August in Newport. The ocean resort, reached by train and then by connecting boat, was the favorite watering hole of the upper crust. Residents and visitors alike rushed from one activity to another and changed their clothes as frequently as butterflies flutter their wings. With Annie as her guide, the lumbering Sylvie might take a leisurely breakfast in flowered cottons, change into her riding habit for a morning ride, and then don her bathing clothes for the ladies' swimming hour on Bailey's Beach. There were informal lunches in pretty frocks with friends; social calls to make and quick stops to drop off cards at the homes of yesterday's hostesses; naps; and then afternoon tennis in petticoats, long skirts, and parasols, or viewing the polo matches in nipped jackets, crisp shirts, and long skirts.

At home again they changed for a carriage drive, part of the daily procession along the ocean avenues, then into loose-fitting tea gowns for friends at five, and then a rest before arraying themselves in evening attire. Their corsets pulled tight, their sleeves puffed, their gowns smoothed over their hips, they slipped on their satin shoes, grabbed their lacy fans, drew in their breath, and proclaimed themselves ready to face the festivities: dinner at friends', followed by dancing and midnight supper at the casino. One day required as many as seven different outfits and each one cost at least several hundred dollars.

For Astors, Belmonts, and Vanderbilts, Newport provided a broad stage on which to parade their riches. Miles of imported marble wrapped the facades, lapped the floors, and coated the walls of the Newport "cottages"; vast lawns greener than money led to the sea. In regal homes with names like "Beaulieu," "Marble House," and "Chateau-Sur-Mer," crystal stalactites dripped from the chandeliers; broad staircases swirled to the upstairs chambers; satins draped the windows; and silks covered the plump sofas and thronelike chairs.

In these seaside palaces, the wives of America's leading entrepreneurs lived like English aristocrats with their liveried servants and lavish balls. In the competitive urge to outdo one another, hostesses invited guests to sumptuous dinners where course after course was served on gold plates, and footmen stood behind the chairs, ready to fetch the salt. At one party, tropical fish swam in a pond down the center of the table; at another, guests were given tiny silver shovels and pails with which to dig for jewels in the sandbox that stretched from end to end. Even the guest of honor became a foil; the race was finally over when Mrs. Stuyvesant Fish announced the titled guest of honor, brought in a monkey in white tie and tails, and seated him at the table.

The purpose of all this spectacle was to enhance the social status of the hostess and increase her daughter's chances of marrying well. At her own dinner parties on fashionable Bellevue Avenue, Annie Leary was known to tie red ribbons on everything from the chandeliers to the clocks to her white dress and red wig. As surrogate mother, she wished for Sylvie Green to meet the most eligible young men. At her Thursday afternoons, at lunches, and at teas she made certain that her charge was introduced to Newport's best.

The last week of August, she invited friends to the largest fete she had ever held and decorated her house to celebrate the event: she covered her walls with red silk, swagged lace curtains over fake windows, trailed artificial ivy over the roof, and hung a gold revolving electric fan from the ceiling to cool her guests. She lined her dinner table, which ran the length of several rooms, with as many friends and bachelors as she could, and then opened her house to one hundred guests for an after-dinner dance, hoping that Sylvie would find a suitable mate. To Annie's relief, one young man made himself available and courted Miss Green. As soon as Hetty heard about it, she checked him out; a disappointed Sylvie was soon headed back to New York.

"I found that your young man is very nice and proper," Hetty told her daughter in words later made public, "but if it wasn't for his father, the world wouldn't know a thing about him. He has never earned a dollar and doesn't have the value of money."

Hetty had only disdain for self-indulgent socialites and said to Sylvie: "I want to say right here and now that you should never marry a society man with my consent. I want to see you happily married and in a home of your own, but I want you to marry a poor young man of good principles who is making an honest hard fight for success. I don't care whether he's got $100 or not, provided he is made of the right stuff. You will have more money than you'll ever need and it isn't necessary to look for a young man with money. Now you know my wish and I hope I won't hear anything more about your young man in Newport who knows just about enough to part his hair in the middle and spend his father's money."

With that, Hetty went back to business. Others might fritter away their time and money on the conspicuous consumption of the Gilded Age, but she had scores to settle, buildings to buy, and railroads to run.

Chapter 14

Texas

A man could travel the state of Texas for hours and count no more human beings than fingers on his hand. As sparse with people as it was thick with cattle, it was as cold and dry as a desert in some parts; in others, as hot and damp as a swamp. Texas stretched 773 miles from east to west and 800 miles from north to south; at its farthest points, from Beaumont, on the border of Louisiana, to El Paso, on the border of New Mexico, the distance was greater than that from Chicago to New York.

Mexican cowboys, whose roots went back to Spain, rustled the longhorn cattle and drove them north toward the stockyards. Germans and Czechs settled the hill country, where the soil was rich, and farmed the earth. Southerners brought their slaves with them to the Confederate state, planted their favorite crops, and watched them flourish. Cotton sprouted like daisies in the rich soil. Cattle fed happily on the green grass. Coal mined underground fueled the trains bringing the cotton to market and the cattle to slaughter.

Six thousand miles of railroads crisscrossed the state. Some belonged to major lines, others to small independents that charged high fees to link the larger ones. Some ran at a profit; others went bust. Hetty Green spent four years negotiating to buy a bankrupt branch of the Texas Central Railway. Her insolvent part came with fifty-four miles of track and almost half a million acres of land. Now she wanted Ned to take charge of the line.

In addition, she was eager to own a branch of the Waco and North-western Texas Railroad, a defunct piece that was of particular interest to Collis Huntington, her old enemy, who owned major amounts of track around the state. It would enable him to link his lines across Texas, connect them with grain states like Kansas and mining states like Colorado, and garner the lucrative fees for freight. Huntington was keen to own the branch. And so was Hetty. She wanted the fees, wanted badly to outwit Huntington, and ordered her son to buy the bankrupt line.

Shortly before the opening of the World's Fair, Hetty dispatched Ned to the Lone Star State. The young man carried out his mother's orders with the ease of an experienced entrepreneur. Looking older than his age and more dignified than his boldness might suggest, he appeared in the railroad town of Waco a few days before the sale. Streetcars, some pulled by mules, others fueled by electric power, rumbled through the town; cotton farmers drove their wagons to the depot to ship their crops; settlers stopped to buy goods on their way out west; and everyone gathered at the Old Corner Drugstore, where the pharmacist Charles Alderton, born in Brooklyn, created his drink Dr Pepper. Ned took a hotel room and scouted around. In his amiable way, he chatted with the locals and sought out the railroad buffs.

On the morning of the auction, he lumbered up the steps of the brick courthouse where the sale was being held. His competitors were three other men, but it soon became clear that his chief rival was Julius Kruttschnitt, Collis Huntington's representative. As soon as the bidding started, the auction took off at a fevered pitch. Kruttschnitt made the $800,000 opening bid and Ned immediately upped the offer. Kruttschnitt raised his hand at $1,250,000, certain he had won, but Ned increased his bid to $1,375,000. Only then did the auction screech to a halt: Huntington's man lacked the authority to go higher. With the bang of the hammer, twenty-four-year-old Ned Green won the railroad. His success meant more than just the track and the quarter million acres around it: the win was a triumph for his mother over her nemesis. But the victory was short-lived.

Collis Huntington had as much antipathy toward Hetty as she had toward him. He quickly announced that the Greens could not own the line until they paid almost $100,000 in liens against the property that he claimed were due him. Just as quickly, the state announced that the liens belonged to Texas. Ned responded that as far as he knew, there were no liens, but if they did exist, he had no interest in owning the railroad. Huntington tried to force the sale on Hetty and Ned with or without the liens.

The case continued for three years and made news around the country. In California, where the crafty Huntington had made his fortune at the expense of many farmers, the feelings against him were so strong that a group wrote to Hetty: if she came to California, they said, they would welcome her as a hero. In the meantime, to reward her for her victory they sent her a gift: a forty-four-caliber revolver, a holster, and plenty of cartridges. They hoped she would use it on Huntington. She almost did.

In the course of the dispute over the liens, Ned refused to make payments on the property. Angry and eager to prosecute, Huntington, who had built a mansion on Fifth Avenue, made his way down to Wall Street to visit Hetty. As the bushy-bearded man reached her desk, she offered him a hard-backed seat and some friendly conversation. But when he made threats against Ned, Hetty flashed her steely eyes and said: "Up to now, Huntington, you have dealt with Hetty Green, the business woman. Now you are fighting Hetty Green, the mother. Harm one hair of Ned's hair and I'll put a bullet through your heart." With that, she reached for the gun she kept on her desk. The bald-headed Huntington ran out the door, leaving his top hat behind him.

Not much later, Ned returned the deeds. Huntington bought the branch, paying more than the original price. But by then Ned was busy with the other Texas railroad Hetty had recently purchased.

One month after the auction, Ned traveled north from Waco on a hundred-mile trip past endless fields of white fluff. At Terrell, a transit point for local cotton, cattle, and timber, the broad streets were filled with carts carrying bales of cotton, waiting for the buyers who made the town rich. With three thousand people, two banks, three weekly newspapers, nine churches, and three cotton gins, Terrell would become the headquarters for the northeast portion of the Houston and Texas Central Railway.

Ned arrived at the start of 1893, carrying a check from his mother for a half million dollars. He deposited the funds like a New Year's gift to the bank. Despite its grand name, the American National Bank had few assets. Stunned by the size of the check, and aware that their deposits had just tripled, its officers quickly made the young man a vice president.

The money was to be used to improve Hetty's insolvent portion of the Houston and Texas Central. The new board of directors, which included her husband, Edward H. Green, and the Chemical Bank president, George G. Williams, renamed the line the Texas Midland Railroad and appointed Ned as president. Although older men joked that the road was little more than a pile of iron, the youngest railroad president in the country boldly announced he would turn it into "one of the best railroads in the Southwest."

The Texas Midland consisted of fifty-two miles of north–south track running east of Dallas between the tiny communities of Roberts and Garrett. But Ned had bigger plans in mind. Years of his mother's training had taught him to study every aspect of the subject, from the condition of the roadbeds to the state of the rolling stock to the rates to charge for freight. But he was sometimes too nervous to make a decision and telegraphed Hetty for advice. "You are on the ground," she answered. "Mind your own business."

Once when he was visiting his mother, she told him about the New Bedford whaling captain whose two sons served as officers on his ship. They carried the titles and wore the uniforms but stood aside while their father did the work. When their father died, the two young men tried to steer the ship, but, without experience, they lost control; the boat ran aground and all was destroyed. The story may have been apocryphal but the message was clear: Ned had to learn how to take command. "I sent you to Texas to learn the railway business," Hetty said. "I can't teach you by telegraph from New York."

She wanted him to learn from his own mistakes and urged him to use the railroad money as he wished. When he returned to Texas, she treated him like an experienced sailor, allowing him to find his strength, giving him slack to make his own way. But Hetty also knew how a young sailor could go astray; when conditions seemed questionable, she tightened her control. In a note to his mother in August 1893 Ned made a poignant plea for her to loosen her grip:

Dear Mama:

I am 25 years old today. I think you might send me money so I could go to the fair at Chicago in about two weeks, before the Fall rush comes. It would only cost about $200. I can get passes to Chicago and return. Let me know as soon as you can, so I can get ready. I want to see the fair so bad. Please let me go.

Your affect. son,
Ned.

The highlight of Ned's trip to the fair was his visit to the United States government pavilion; he was mesmerized by the exhibit of valuable postage stamps, some worth as much as $1,000 each. Excited by the display, he purchased a full set of Columbus commemorative issues, the start of a stamp and coin collection that in his lifetime became one of the most rare and treasured in the world.

Within a year of Ned's arrival in Terrell, he bought the old Opera House, turned it into offices, and created a handsomely furnished apartment. He lined the walls with books, hung a portrait of the actress Lillian Russell over his bed, and for his kitchen, furbished with everything up-to-date, he hired the best chef in the state to prepare his meals. But his special residence was his private train car, the "Lone Star": "a palace on wheels," said the *Dallas Morning News*.

To expand the railroad, he purchased additional track to the north and south, connecting the small Midland road with major lines that ran perpendicular to it, east to west across the state. Before he built the rail from Garrett to Waco, he rode the eighty miles on horseback to assess the valuable land along the right-of-way. Hiring experts, listening to the needs of his clients, he heavied up the run-down rails and replaced the worn-out ties, strengthened the sagging wooden bridges with steel, introduced electric headlights, improved the passenger cars, added café lounges and observation cars, built new stations, and provided customers with scheduled, on-time service.

Besieged by people wanting free passage on the railways, Ned turned again to his mother for help. She spoke to Chauncey Depew, head of the New York Central Railroad, who offered some biblical wisdom. Hetty suggested Ned hand out cards with these phrases:

Monday—"Thou shalt not pass." Numbers, xx, 18
Tuesday—"Suffer not a mass to pass." Judges, iii, 28
Wednesday—"The wicked shall no more pass." Nahum 1, 15
Thursday—"This generation shall not pass." Mark, xiii, 30
Friday—"By a perpetual decree it can not pass." Jeremiah, v, 22
Saturday—"None shall pass." Isaiah, xxxiv, 10
Sunday—"So he paid the fare thereof and went." Jonah 1, 3

In the months and years that followed, Ned became a popular figure around town. A generous host, he entertained on an elaborate scale and spent money lavishly to make friends with the local people; he bought uniforms for baseball teams in towns along the railroad line, supported theatrical groups, and started a brass band. "Eddie," as he was known all over Texas, "is a capital fellow—hail-fellow-well-met with everyone," said the *Dallas Morning News* a few years later. "He is generous, though level-headed, very charitable, especially thoughtful of his men in times of trouble, and a father to the orphans of his men who are killed on duty." The paper added, "Eddie Green is his mother's boy. She has the utmost confidence and pride in him."

Despite his showmanship and boisterous living, he had his mother's ability to focus on his work. "He has the reputation of being one of the shrewdest railroad managers in the country, and his business keenness is phenomenal," reported the *New York Times*. The Texas Midland, serving as the connecting line between the St. Louis–San Francisco and the Southern Pacific Railroads, carried more cotton per mile than any other railway in the country. Passengers could board one of its dark green Pullmans furnished in green, gold, and buff, ride for five hundred miles, from Terrell to St. Louis, and never change cars. "The lighting in the cars is so good," said the *Dallas Morning News,* that "passengers may read as comfortably as at home and the conductor has no need to carry a lantern to read the tickets." By 1895 the once-insolvent line was earning $28,000 a year from passenger traffic and $165,000 from freight. Over the course of several years Ned turned the Texas Midland into the most efficient railroad in the state.

Efficiency was a rare commodity among the railroads. The bankruptcies of the two Texas roads that Hetty bought presaged the failure of many others. Excessive building of track, unwarranted buying of lines and equipment, and overextension of credit in the 1880s led the way to ruin. No longer able to fuel their expenses, in the 1890s they ran out of steam.

Chapter 15

The Glitter of Gold

A generation of Americans owed its way of life and its liveli-
hood to the railroads, said Henry Adams. Furnace workers and financiers, shopkeepers and technicians, miners and
manufacturers were all "mortgaged to the railways." And the
railways were mortgaged to the world. But after the Baring
Brothers disaster in 1890, the withdrawal of European funds
dried up an oasis of available money. In addition, although the
railroads had enjoyed good profits transporting American crops
across the country and overseas, by 1893 the crops were failing and freight traffic dropped. The Pennsylvania and Reading,
unable to pay the $125 million debt on its loans, declared itself insol-
vent; the announcement tossed the stock market into turmoil. Three
other major lines, the Northern Pacific, the Union Pacific, and the
Atchison, Topeka and Santa Fe, all declared they were broke when
their loans were called by the banks.

Bankers were nervous, with good reason. They had risked huge
sums loaning money to railroads and other enterprises with weak
financial underpinnings. Adding to their concerns, American exports
were down while imports were up markedly. As Thorstein Veblen
pointed out a few years later, the rich needed to spend more money
in order to improve their social position; the newer their money, the
more they spent. They were spreading their dollars abroad, buying
more clothes, more jewels, more furnishings, more food, and more

wines from Europe, creating a demand for more payments in gold from American banks.

Ships were sailing into the East River filled with fancy goods and leaving the New York harbor laden with gold. But because of the Sherman Silver Act, the ship of state at the Treasury was flooded with silver. Dollars may have been redeemable in both, but with much of the world on the gold standard, financiers everywhere requested their funds in bullion. They worried that American paper money was sinking in value.

With not enough gold in reserve to fill the demand, many financial institutions were forced to close their doors. The bankruptcies ruined railroads, injured investors, stranded farmers without enough funds to sustain themselves until harvest, and left small businesses without money to purchase goods or meet their payrolls. The rich still imported expensive clothes, dined on Lobster Newberg at Delmonico's, and drank to their health and wealth at the new Waldorf Hotel, but the rest of the country bit their nails and spat out fear. "Everyone is in a blue fit of terror," said Henry Adams, "and each individual thinks himself more ruined than his neighbor."

Companies whose stocks had skyrocketed, whose dividends defied gravity, collapsed when their lack of capital was revealed. Money became so tight that short-term interest rates soared as high as 75 percent. The National Cordage Company, one of the most heavily traded stocks on the exchange, could not get credit and declared insolvency. The market plunged. Investors panicked. The Gilded Age, like other eras of avarice, opulence, and easy credit, burst from gluttony.

The New York Clearing House, a group of bankers led by George Williams of the Chemical Bank, put together an emergency fund to ease the flow of money. When Williams asked Hetty Green to help, she agreed. She would lend money to the fund, she said with an innocent air, if they would sell her Chicago railroad notes that were payable on demand. Williams consented, and Hetty provided millions of dollars to the fund. But as soon as she received the notes, she called them in for payment. When the railroad men complained they did not have the money to pay her back, she made them a counteroffer they couldn't refuse.

For many years, the Chicago men had supported Judge Collins in his campaigns for the Illinois Supreme Court. But he was the judge who had let her down on the sale of her land in Cicero: now she could settle the score. She would forgive their payments, she told the railroad executives, if they would assist her with Collins. "You put him on the bench," she declared, and now, she told them, "you can take him off." "Or," she said with a shrug of indifference, "you can pay your loans to me." The men had little choice. They flattered Collins, suggested he was worthy of a higher position, and proposed that he run as Republican candidate for governor. Collins agreed and resigned from the judgeship. But the railroad men never gave him the financial support they promised and backed his opponent instead. Collins withdrew; Hetty won. "There's been dirty work at the crossroads," said his advisers.

The influx of funds from the Clearing House brought interest rates down, but financial institutions had risked their funds and caused "a loss of confidence in the solvency of the banks," wrote the former Treasury comptroller Thomas Kane. Investors remained agnostic. Their doubts were "inspired by a general knowledge of the unsound conditions in private and public life and the speculative and venturesome character of the investments and loans." As a result, fortunes were lost, thousands of depositors left destitute. But in their perpetual greed for profits, bankers would repeat those risks again and again. The Great Recession of 2008, brought about by hazardous speculation and high-risk loans, and followed by years of high unemployment, harkened back to those times. Referring to 2008, the financial writer Andrew Ross Sorkin said, "The single most important factor was too much leverage." Too much money borrowed, too much money loaned, and not enough assets behind it.

The crisis of 1893 forced the closure of companies around the country. Manufacturers and merchants slowly turned the key in their door for the last time as fifteen thousand businesses went under. Bankers slammed their heavy vaults shut; more than five hundred banks were in ruins. Firms of every kind suffered, even A. T. Stewart's department store. The marble retail palace that opened on Chambers Street a few years before Hetty Robinson arrived in New York in 1854 had followed the fashionable uptown. For more than a quarter of a century, the store served as a mecca for upper-class women who used it as much as a social club as a place to shop.

When A. T. Stewart died in 1876, the business, with buildings and factories around the world, was sold to a former adviser, Henry Hilton, who gave the firm to his two sons. But the Hiltons lacked Stewart's marketing skills, and the business slid from $60 million to $8 million in annual sales. By the time of the financial crisis in 1893, the company had more than $1 million in accounts receivable that it could not collect.

The senior Hilton did everything he could to rescue his sons: hat in hand, he appealed to banks, insurance companies, and individual investors, but every man he went to turned him down. Only Hetty Green was willing to help. A shrewd bargainer, she sat across the table and demanded the original Stewart building as security. Offering him more than he wanted—$1,800,000 for five years—she insisted on discounting the loan and took 6 percent interest in advance, leaving Hilton with the amount he had asked for. They shook hands on the largest mortgage ever given on a single piece of property in New York. In the end, said the *Times*, both sides did well: "Ex Judge Hilton saved his sons' firm and Mrs. Green had the best mortgage in New York."

Hetty prospered, but the country endured the most serious depression it had ever experienced: unemployment rose to 18 percent in 1894, went down slightly to 14 percent in 1896, and stayed at over 10 percent for two more years. In New York, seventy-five thousand people lost their jobs and twenty thousand were living in the streets. In Chicago, the Pullman Palace Car Company, which manufactured sleeping cars for the railroads, cut its wages, and three thousand union members went on strike. As anger spread, more workers joined and violence erupted; eventually 125,000 people around the country protested in sympathy. Railroad traffic in the Midwest came to a standstill, threatening the mails and menacing the economy. From Ohio, an army of five hundred unemployed men, led by Jacob Coxey, marched all the way to Washington, demanding that the government provide jobs through public works.

Monetary issues divided the country. In the West, where mining spurred the economy, Democrats and Populists pushed for support of silver. In the East, where exports played a major role, Republican businessmen feared that a bimetallic system, one that was based on both silver and gold, would make small change of the dollar.

The Wonderful Wizard of Oz, by L. Frank Baum, told the tale of the times. Both a children's fable and, many critics believe, an adult allegory, it portrayed the political machinations, the social inequities, and the economic distress of the period. The author grew up in a wealthy family in the East but worked in the late 1880s as the editor of a newspaper in South Dakota. Living in Aberdeen with his wife and children, he wrote about the farmers and their families. Moving to Chicago in 1891, he saw the financial crisis of 1893 and the depression that followed devastate millions of people. He empathized with the Populist Party that arose and supported William Jennings Bryan, who campaigned against McKinley and spoke "against the encroachments of aggregated wealth." In his Cross of Gold speech, the senator from Nebraska drew the nation's attention to "the brave pioneer," "the attorney in a country town," "the merchant at the crossroads store," "the farmer who goes forth in the morning and toils all day," "the miners who go 1,000 feet into the earth"—the little man who struggled against the force of big businessmen and financiers.

Frank Baum set his story on the impoverished Kansas prairie, where an almost biblical series of plagues tested the people and challenged their survival: across the Midwest, farmers suffered as freight fees rose and agricultural prices fell while grasshoppers devoured the crops, blizzards withered new plantings, and drought desiccated much of what was left. Despite the sense of despair drawn in the lined faces of the citizens and across the somber landscape, the book's heroine, the orphaned girl Dorothy, sparkles—a spirited symbol of the country itself.

As the book begins, we are introduced to Dorothy's family: her grim Uncle Henry, stern and solemn in his long beard and rough boots, and her Aunt Em, thin and gaunt and never smiling, living in a one-room house furnished with only a rusty-looking stove, a cupboard, a table and chairs, and beds. Looking out from the doorway, Dorothy "could see nothing but the great gray prairie on every side. Not a tree nor a house broke the broad sweep of flat country." The sun had baked the ground and burned the grass and blistered the paint on the house. Everything, including the people, was dull and gray.

When a cyclone hits the farm, Dorothy is swept up in a swirl of conflicting interests, dropped into a world of naïveté; she has arrived in the Land of Oz. The girl is bewildered: the fertile landscape, filled with "stately trees bearing rich and luscious fruits," beautiful flowers, and colorfully feathered birds, she learns, is bewitched by the evil forces of East and West. The little girl yearns to go back to Kansas. No matter how enchanting other places may be, she says in all-American earnestness, "There is no place like home."

With no road map to follow, she is told she will learn the way back from the Wizard of Oz. Adorned with silver slippers, alighting on a path of gold, she is at once, unknowingly, treading on the currency conflict as she sets off to the Emerald City. There, she hopes, she will find the answers to her problems from the all-knowing Wizard. Along the way she encounters personalities who embody the characteristics of the Midwest: the unemployed worker, turned by industrialists from human to automaton and personified in the Tin Man, is eager to be a human being back on the job; the undervalued, simple-minded farmer, symbolized by the Scarecrow, isn't even aware that he has a wellspring of good common sense; the fearful citizen, come to life in the Cowardly Lion, discovers he has the courage to lead. This ragtag band became Dorothy's own Coxey's Army marching to Washington for help.

In the Emerald City, the money-obsessed capital where greenbacks are printed and government officials paid off, all who enter wear green-colored glasses and all that they see, from the people's faces to the food they eat, is tainted by money and tinted green. At the Emerald Palace, the Wizard of Oz reveals himself as little more than a circus trickster who came into power carried aloft in a hot-air balloon. He is the true politician promising all things to all people.

A country-fair promoter, the Wizard sits in his office, avoiding the public, hidden behind a paper screen. Like Mark Hanna, the rich political operative from Ohio who orchestrated McKinley's campaign, he is the puppeteer pulling the strings, presenting a different image to each person he meets: a man with an enormous head to Dorothy; a lovely lady to the Scarecrow; a monstrous beast to the Tin Man; a ball of fire to the Cowardly Lion. But once the curtain is pulled back, the real president is revealed: a decent man who doles out good advice, telling the Scarecrow that "experience is the only thing that brings knowledge"; counseling the Cowardly Lion that "true courage is facing danger"; warning the Tin Man that having a heart can be painful.

Scary adventures and strange escapades ensue, but with the help of a golden cap, each character in the book finds his or her rightful place. The wise Scarecrow takes charge of Washington; the brave Lion becomes king of the beasts; the hardworking Tin Man rules the West. And Dorothy, minus her silver slippers, finds her way back to Kansas. On the farm, content to be with her family, she turns to her aunt. "Oh, Aunt Em!" she exclaims, "I'm so glad to be at home again!"

It took years until the real financial crisis was over, the gold standard set, and the country on solid ground. Not until 1900, when *The Wizard of Oz* was published, could America say it was at home again.

=====

Chapter 16

Crazy as a Fox

Hetty Green never seemed at home anywhere: not in New York, or Chicago, or New Bedford, where she still retained her Howland properties. Despite the hundreds of acres and numerous buildings she owned in Massachusetts, the town had embittered her memories. She visited every few years and never stayed longer than several days.

Peripatetic, she constantly scuttled from east to west inspecting her assets. In 1894 she crisscrossed the country by train from Boston to Dallas to St. Louis to San Francisco, with constant stops in between. "I traveled for two years and stayed at forty hotels," she said. Her holdings included thousands of acres of valuable land, mortgages on factories, ranches, churches, and "blocks of businesses, houses, theatres, livery stables, hotels, restaurants, farms, and nearly everything you could mention—all good mortgages," she vowed.

With her properties spread far and wide, her headquarters, she declared, were in Vermont. In the summer of 1895 she was in Bellows Falls. Coming in from her garden, wearing a tidy dress, couching a basket of tomatoes in her arms, she encountered a reporter, who asked why she was there. "I'm here because folks can't find me out without coming a long way," she replied. "I'm here for my husband's rheumatism, and I'm here because my daughter isn't strong." But "more than all," she added, "I'm here for the reason that I'm a born farmer and I love to work the ground and raise crops." Indeed, she said, with a wry air, everything her family had eaten for the past month had been raised on their farm: "We live on chickens, and ducks, and turkeys, and eggs."

Like her daughter, she claimed she much preferred the slow pace of the countryside to the frantic rush of New York. For all the hostility she felt from some of the local people, she did appreciate the small town and the friends she had there. But the burden of wealth prevented her from remaining in Vermont. "I've other interests, but some day I'm going to live here," she said. "If I hadn't had a fortune in real estate in town left to me, you may be sure I'd never been driven from Eden to the noisy city—either for comfort or to make money."

"Time is money," Hetty told another reporter, "and I never leave my business for long." Most of the time, her business was at the Chemical Bank on lower Broadway. Wearing a neat black dress and small black hat, gold brooch, small diamond earrings, and a diamond and emerald ring, she was spied by a writer as she was speaking to a clerk. Her "tall and stately" figure, delicate features, and refined bearing impressed the viewer. Nothing about her, he said with surprise, matched the stories of the terrible Hetty Green.

Although she regularly spent her days downtown, her nights were unpredictable, scattered around Brooklyn, New York, and New Jersey. Lodging at a daily rate at boardinghouses or hotels, leaving behind none of her belongings, she worried about the tax man, fretted over letters begging her for money, and feared being physically attacked. She tried to remain anonymous and listed herself under assorted names: Mrs. Norton, Mrs. Hickey, Mrs. Nash, Mrs. Warrington, Mrs. Dewey. As soon as her identity was revealed she hurried away.

Or so it was thought. In December 1895 she was discovered at the St. George in Brooklyn. The posh new apartment hotel on Pineapple Street boasted the largest dining room in the country and its own electric plant. She and her daughter had registered as Mrs. and Miss Gray, the head clerk said; for several weeks they occupied one of the most expensive suites.

The day the newspaper published the story, Mr. Nible went on, Hetty became an object of curiosity in the hotel. Recognized by other guests and the staff, she was followed by inquisitive eyes in the foyer and bombarded with stares in the dining room. The next morning, under the watchful gaze of breakfasters, she finished her coffee and rolls, paid her bill, and bustled off. She and Sylvie would eat their Christmas dinner with Edward Green, who was staying at the Union Club, the clerk revealed. They may have all dined in New York. But more than once the clerk was covering up her whereabouts; although he confided she had left, she was still residing at the hotel.

Many believed Hetty refused to establish a permanent residence in New York to avoid paying personal property taxes to the city. Despite her protests, New York was where she made most of her money. Yet for years she scurried from place to place, evading the tax man like the mouse eluding the cat. And like modern New Yorkers who claim residence in other states, she was hardly alone in her efforts to escape the payments.

Even prominent people like Theodore Roosevelt avoided payment by taking an oath and "swearing off" their personal property. In 1895 New York's acting tax collector announced that Jay Gould had declared his home to be in New Jersey; William Vanderbilt's payment had not been seen; and two thousand people in Brooklyn were delinquent. Assessed by New York for $1.5 million, Hetty appealed to the city mayor to have the tax commissioners indicted. She swore she was not a resident of New York and showed that she paid her taxes in Vermont. With records to prove her innocence, she won her case.

As frequent a litigant as she was an investor, lawsuits were her yellow brick road to justice. Although they were often costly, she pursued them with religious zeal. She studied every detail with her attorneys and sought advice from her friends, among them George Williams of the Chemical Bank, Clarence Kelsey of the Title Guarantee and Trust Company, Chauncey Depew of the New York Central and Harlem Railroad, Russell Sage of Wall Street fame, and her husband, Edward Green. She claimed she never took on a lawsuit if she did not think she could win. "If my friends and lawyers tell me there is no chance for me," she said, "I would rather compromise than take the chance of succeeding by fighting."

Some legal cases were settled quickly; others stretched out for years. Just before the start of 1895 she handed the New York Superior

Court a complaint that the *Times* called "one of the most remarkable papers ever filed in court." It covered ten thousand typewritten pages and was estimated to contain three million words. The suit, which had started earlier in Illinois, against the executors of her father's estate, charged the men with reckless expenditures and bad investments. She demanded an accounting. The case dragged on for years.

The trustee Henry Barling accused of her being crazy. "She certainly talked rationally enough," countered a reporter covering the case, "convincingly and without the slightest show of vindictiveness. She did a great deal of business yesterday, and was as keen and shrewd in making her business as ever she was in her life." Added her lawyer, William Slayton: "Mr. Barling is welcome to the opinion that Mrs. Green is crazy. She is the brightest woman financier in this country today."

Perceptions of Hetty were as varied as those of the Wizard of Oz. Readers of the *Brooklyn Eagle* chuckled over the paper's view: Mrs. G: "I've been reading of that Hetty Green. I think she must be crazy." Mr. G: "Why, she's worth 40 millions." Mrs. G: "Then she can't be crazy. She's only eccentric." Said Hetty, "Probably I am a bit eccentric, but everybody has some peculiarity."

Opinions of her appearance were poles apart. In early January 1895 she was portrayed in the *Boston Evening Transcript*: "The Richest Woman in America, Mrs. Hetty Green, went to a public office in New York the other day on business, but she was dressed in such shabby clothes that a policeman was about to direct her to the charity bureau." "This eccentric woman," the paper said, "certainly proves that the possession of money and its use for personal adornment are not inseparable in the makeup of womankind."

Another day, walking briskly to her lawyer's office during the lawsuit, she wore a dark green dress, a velvet-trimmed cloth cape, and a violet-speckled hat. Two reporters who saw her offered their views: "Stories about her cheapness of clothing are true," wrote one. "As she walked down Cedar Street she looked for all the world like some old servant going to market, prepared to carry home coffee, sugar and soap in her arms." The other observed: "She was not fashionably dressed, as things go nowadays, but she was certainly comfortably and appropriately clad." Both agreed on one thing: she stood straight, her step was as sprightly as that of a forty-year-old, and she looked more than a decade younger than her sixty years.

The case against the trustees of Edward Robinson's estate was first brought about by the sale of property in Cicero, near Chicago, in 1888. The executors had insisted on selling the vacant land for $650,000 although they had been offered $800,000 for the same acreage. The sale roused Hetty's suspicions: she accused the men of investing her father's money with their own interests in mind. Fees they charged for managing the trust seemed excessive and included payments to their own relatives. Money they paid to public officials "for improving the morals of the city" went toward procuring improvements on the trustees' property. Improvements they made had no effect on her land but clearly enhanced their own. Claims were made for repairs but no vouchers were produced. And no accounting of the trust had been made in more than a decade. When Hetty asked to see the papers, they balked at bringing them forth.

It was true that while the land around it had been improved, hers had remained untouched. Like John Jacob Astor almost a century earlier, her strategy on land was to let the weeds grow while others planted flowers; when the flowers bloomed and the surrounding property increased in market price, the value of her land went up too. And, most important to Hetty, as unimproved property, it stayed untaxed.

The next lawsuit, which began in 1891, was countered by the defendant, and reached a crucial point at the end of 1894, when Hetty filed her papers with the Superior Court of New York. She had long been apprehensive about the three original executors of her father's estate: Thomas Mandell and Abner Davis, both deceased, and the one still surviving, Henry Barling. The only other current trustee was her husband, Edward Green. Hetty brought no personal charges against Edward; indeed, she even paid his law fees, and had moved into his bachelor building for ten days while she nursed him through an attack of gout. But she was deeply suspicious of Barling.

She always believed her father and aunt had been murdered and worried that the executors were determined to do her harm as well. She stated in an affidavit that Edward Mott Robinson told her on his deathbed that he had been poisoned; he warned her to be careful and take precautions to protect herself. In the affidavit she included testimony from an elderly woman who had cared for her father. The former servant claimed that just before Edward Robinson took ill, some of his food had been fed to a dog: soon after, the animal died in agony. Hetty was wary of what she ate.

She was certain her aunt's death, two weeks after her father's, had also been planned. "I do believe that they were put out of the way by people who wanted to take control of the property and cheat me out of it," she said. Her suspicions were not without support. Her lawyer, William Slayton, told the *New York Tribune* in 1895: "It is common talk to this day among the older citizens of New Bedford that her will was juggled with. It was just as much a surprise to New Bedford people when they heard that Miss Howland had left half of her estate to an unknown doctor and lawyer," he said, "as it would have been for New York City people to find after Hetty Green's death that she had bequeathed half her estate to Tammany Hall."

The court assigned a referee, Henry Anderson, to oversee the examination of the accounts. Asked if she would attend the hearings, many of which took place in 1895, Hetty replied that she "never missed a session." Nor did she miss a chance to make a comment. She arrived one morning at the Mills Building, a huge structure across from the Stock Exchange, where Collis Huntington and other railroad moguls retained their offices, and entered the book-lined rooms of the referee. In her dark dress and dainty bonnet, she walked over to Henry Barling, the trustee. As reporters watched, she slapped him on the back, extended a friendly hand, and said, "How d'you do, Mr. Barling?" But a few minutes later, she changed her tone.

Questions arose about the late executor Abner Davis, who had been declared incompetent while serving as a trustee. Hetty once told him of her concerns about a conspiracy. "If you are not careful," he snapped, "you will be taken out of the house, feet foremost, just as your father was." Shortly afterward, Davis's doctors ordered him to a sanitarium, though he remained a paid trustee. As they sat in the referee's offices, his colleague Barling was asked to describe it: "An institution for repose—repose of mind and body," he said. Hetty drew a different picture: "An insane asylum for gibbering idiots, you mean."

When Barling said he had been there, Hetty broke out in a loud laugh. The referee begged her to be quiet. It wasn't the first time he made such a request.

Later, in the hall, with her daughter Sylvie by her side as usual, Hetty told the waiting reporters her opinion of the referee. "He didn't do much sleeping today," she jibed, promising to keep things lively with her new lawyer. Before she hired this forceful advocate, she noted, the hearing was so calm the referee could hardly stay awake. She spoke in the rough style she had picked up as a girl on the docks: "On one day he slept nineteen times, snored fourteen, and struck his nose on the desk three times. He wants me to stop talking, and I want him to stop snoring. He makes his noise with his nose, and I make mine with my mouth. It's nearly the same, ain't it?"

At a session when her lawyer was questioning Barling's counselor, Hetty interrupted. "No use lying," she snapped at the distinguished Joseph Choate.

The referee admonished her. "Now, Mrs. Green, I do not like to speak to a lady of your age in this way," he said.

"Oh," she answered, "you needn't mind me. I know I am in my second childhood, but you can't muzzle—"

"Mrs. Green!" the referee cried out in disgust. "You must not talk. I will keep order, and you have lawyers to talk for you."

But Hetty was right; she couldn't be muzzled. When Barling's attorney stated he "always tried to be accommodating," she called out again: "Oh, no one thinks so, but you."

On another occasion when her new lawyer, Charles Ogden, who had represented her against Collis Huntington, arrived from Texas, he began his presentation by saying, "This is not a small estate." Hetty quickly jumped in. "But it is getting smaller," she quipped, winking at the reporters.

Henry Barling's reluctance to cooperate tested the patience of Hetty's attorneys. When Ogden questioned him about the past, he repeated over and over again that he could not remember. Finally Ogden gave up: "I very much regret that I cannot remain with you in the case to its conclusion," he wrote to Hetty, "both because our relations have been so exceedingly pleasant, and because the facts already disclose a most shameful state of affairs in the administration of the estate, facts which, if made known to any honest jury, will invoke the most severe condemnation of every one connected with the administration of the estate or in any manner responsible for it."

Ogden was one of several counsels so frustrated they resigned from the case. But Hetty never quit. In the summer of 1895, in the office of the referee, a three-month adjournment was called. Hetty walked over to the window, and to the amusement of her daughter and the astonishment of the reporters, she fell to her knees, folded her hands, raised her eyes to heaven, and moved her lips in silent prayer. Minutes later, she stood up, brushed off her dress, took Sylvie's arm, and marched out.

A few days afterward, a reporter asked her what she was going to do for the summer. "I am going to get together all the religious persons I can," she said in a solemn voice, "and go to some quiet place, where we can all pray that my litigations with Mr. Barling may be ended within the next twenty years." In fact, she spent the summer in Bellows Falls, where she was interviewed in her garden, and Barling died one year later. Hetty took some credit for the event. "I'm a Quaker," she noted afterward. "In just a year after my prayers, that executor was found stone dead in his bed."

If lawsuits were her road to justice, lawyers were bumps along the way. Hetty saw them as obstructions that took up too much time and cost too much. More than once she found herself up against them in court, where they sued her for refusing to pay their fees. She often repeated one of her favorite riddles: "Why is a lawyer like a man who is restless in bed? Because both lie first on one side and then on the other."

Hetty expressed her venom to a reporter from the *Brooklyn Eagle* who visited her in a suite at the St. George Hotel. She greeted him in a dress of black brocaded silk with puffed black velvet sleeves, a plain wedding band on her left hand. Although she was often described as "a dowdy old creature," the writer declared she was "comfortably stout," with gray hair "stylishly curled." She looked like "a woman of quiet and refined tastes," he said.

During the interview Hetty proved "a voluble, intelligent, agreeable conversationalist." Other reporters agreed. On a visit to Fall River, Massachusetts, when she was featured in a story in the local paper, she sent the writer a thank-you. Years later, working for a major paper in New York, the same reporter met her at the Chemical Bank. He had come on assignment to interview someone else, but when he saw Hetty he turned his attention to her. He may have lost the scheduled interview, he said, but he was glad for the "extremely delightful chat I had with that brilliant and kind hearted woman."

Those who spent time with her admired her intelligence and industry. Yet stories persisted that she was miserable and malevolent, heartless and cruel. Instead of giving away her money lavishly like Annie Leary, she handed it out meagerly, providing jobs, not welfare, avoiding the publicity that led to more requests. "I believe in discreet charity," she said. "I wish I could show you the begging letters I receive." James Gerard, one of her lawyers, later explained: "Because she devoted her surplus income, and it was large, to the development of the country rather than to frivolous expenditures, [she] attracted the constant attention of the Press." C. W. de Lyon Nichols, an Episcopal chaplain who knew her, said, "Hetty Green has in secret done a vast deal more of philanthropy than the public can give her credit for."

Not so different from the modern Warren Buffett, who resides in a simple stucco house, eats his lunch in a local diner, and takes his pleasure in making money, she shunned the spendthrift ways of the rich. Like Buffett, she reveled in watching her money grow. "For him, it is a vocation," said the New York Review of Books. "He is called to it. If it's for anything, it is for getting more of. The man's a collector. He just happens to collect dollars. Getting money interests Buffett more than having money or spending money. It's an intellectual and moral pursuit." And so it was for Hetty. But as much as the press smiles at Buffett's habits, they smirked at Hetty's behavior.

What she wore, where she lived, how she did or did not spend her money were all fuel for the anti-Hetty fire. "I have been maligned, abused, and laughed at in the papers until nothing can injure me now," she said. Her reported habits of stuffing her clothes with newspapers to ward off the cold, of chewing onions and spewing bad breath, of cooking her pot of oatmeal on the office heater, of hiding in dingy rooms consumed the press, whether the reports were valid or not. Her penny-pinching ways left those who hoped to bask in the warmth of her wealth shivering in the chill of her thrift. If such a well-heeled woman did not live lavishly, why was she rich? Instead of providing the public with glamorous dreams, she offered them shadowy nightmares.

"Sensationalist newspapers made her notorious as a cranky, miserly old woman who hoarded her millions," wrote the *Eagle*. Disreputable publishers made her angry, but nothing goaded her more than lawyers. "Just because I dress plainly and do not spend a fortune on my gowns, they say I am cranky or insane," she complained. Her face hardened, her lips pursed at the thought. "All this is the fault of these lawyers," she groused. For thirty years, she said, she had been trying to get the lawyers to give her justice, "and I am as far off now as ever. I have gone over the books myself and I am pretty fair at accounts. I could make nothing of them." She added a note about the trustee's well-known attorney: "If I could save Choate's soul, I would earn my crown."

While Hetty was trying to save the soul of Joseph Choate, he was trying to save the marriage of Alva Vanderbilt. Although he advised Alva against her proceedings, after twenty years of marital misery, in March 1895 she officially ended her alliance with William K. Vanderbilt. "Divorces are a bad thing," declared Hetty Green.

As difficult as her own marriage may have been, she never discussed divorce. Indeed, as she and Edward grew older, they spent more of their time together. During the winters they sometimes lived in her quarters, and in summers they stayed with their daughter in Bellows Falls. Whether they dwelled high on the hill overlooking the mills and the river in their own Tucker House or took rooms in a local hotel, the Greens were a familiar sight: Sylvie out on the tree-lined streets of the town; Edward drinking and smoking with pals on the porch; Hetty striding the few blocks to town to purchase a sack of flour.

She was known by all for her frugal habits, her earthy tongue, and her impatience with snobs. When an English visitor crossed her farmland and was chased by a cow, he knocked at the door to protest. Hetty made no response. "Madam, do you know who I am?" he demanded. "I'm the Honorable Vivian Westleigh, of London." Hetty looked at him with her piercing eyes and replied, "Go tell that to the cow."

But as little time as she had for the snooty, she had plenty of patience with family and friends. When Edward suffered inflammation in his joints, Hetty took on the role of nurse, rubbing his sore spots with a mix of raw eggs and shells, vinegar, and alcohol, a remedy that sometimes seemed to work. But as hard as she may have massaged, as much care as she may have given, she could not rub away reality: their days together were coming to an end.

Chapter 17

A New Hetty

omething remarkable happened to Hetty Green. She became
more sociable, her wardrobe became more stylish, and her
words became more subdued. In February 1896 she appeared
in court wearing a new silk dress, a fur-trimmed wrap, and a
jaunty bonnet. "She looked many years younger for her finery
and did not interrupt the proceedings once," reported the *New
York Sun*. "She was as sedate as possible."

Perhaps it was the influence of her son. A larger-than-life
figure in Texas, Ned thought and acted on a grand scale. Taking the advice of his mother, he soon became involved in local
politics and won favors and influence for the Texas Midland Railroad.
When he announced to Bill McDonald, an influential black man in
the Republican Party, that he wanted to be a delegate to the convention, his friend advised him it would "take 75" to pay off the man he
replaced. Ned handed him a check for $7,500. "I only need $75," said
the startled McDonald.

An opportunity arose in 1896 to become state chairman of the
Republican Party, and Ned leaped at the chance. But he needed his
mother's help to gain the party leaders' support. With McKinley in the
White House and Mark Hanna pulling the strings, the newly revamped
Hetty traveled to Washington to lobby for her son. The richest woman
in the country worked to win them over. Her words and money had
an effect. Ned led the Texans at the Republican convention and told
reporters his party would throw their electoral votes to the president.

In Washington an astonished hotel owner exclaimed at how much Hetty had changed. "Her whole nature has been revolutionized," he said. "I never knew anybody to loosen up as Mrs. Green has of late." Eight months earlier she had been in the city on her own for a lawsuit. "When she came here, she haggled with me over the price of one of the cheapest rooms in the house," he recalled. This time, "she had on the finest sort of a dress, such a one as nobody had ever seen her wear, and this time my house was not good enough for her."

Instead, she went with Ned to the Shoreham, the most expensive hotel in town, and never asked the rate. Nonetheless, she could never resist a negotiation. When Ned's pet canary escaped from the room, she offered a five-dollar reward for its return. To her delight, a news-boy brought back the bird in a wooden cage. Hetty offered the freckle-faced boy one dollar for his efforts; reminding her of her pledge, he shook his head and refused. After futile attempts at bargaining, Hetty bestowed the five dollars and the boy handed over the bird.

Hetty returned to Brooklyn, took a sun-filled, five-room suite at the St. George Hotel, rented a separate suite for Sylvie, and, at her daughter's urging, invited Edward to move in upstairs. After years of shuttling between them, Sylvie was pushing Hetty to reconcile with her husband. Hetty agreed to have Edward nearby, but she still maintained her independence.

While she went off to work, Edward, often confined to his chambers with gout, spent much of his time reading his books and smoking cigars. And although he took his meals upstairs, Hetty preferred the dining room, which was adorned with her favorite pineapple plants. Despite her previous cries for privacy, after dinner she held court, amusing the ladies in the lobby. Dressed in plain black while the others wore pale, frilly frocks, she looked, said the writer Beatrice Fairfax, who was staying at the hotel, "like a very dark chocolate drop in a box of pastel-tinted candy."

When she wasn't gossiping about society, which she loved to do, she griped about the lawyer Joseph Choate. The year before, she claimed, one of Choate's assistants had thrown Sylvie against the door of a safe and left her an invalid. It may have been more a case of shattered nerves, but Hetty often presented her daughter as weak and frail, an unacknowledged reminder of her own mother and aunt. As a result of the lawyer's aggression, Hetty said, she was nursing her daughter as well as her husband, who suffered from a number of ailments. She admitted she enjoyed the role and noted that she helped other guests as well. Wherever she stayed, children with colds, neighbors with fevers, and the infirm elderly testified to her skills. "I never had a greater pleasure than seeing them get well under my care," she declared.

Her calm demeanor came in handy when a train she was on derailed. The surgeons who came for the wounded needed help and she was quick to volunteer. She borrowed the gloves of an engineer and held a passenger's leg while the doctors performed an amputation. Afterward the physicians praised her coolness. "The secret of good nursing is common sense," she said, "just as common sense is the secret of making money. Common sense I believe is the most valuable possession any one can have."

Ensconced in a chair in the hotel foyer, her Scotch terrier nestled in her arms, she was asked by Beatrice Fairfax why she loved the dog so much. She narrowed her eyes and replied: "He doesn't know how rich I am." Her money served as a constant source of conversation, as popular a subject at farmhouse tables as it was in formal boardrooms. Estimates were made that she had increased her wealth to somewhere between $40 million and $50 million. But her riches came at a price: the energy she spent on her work left little time for amusements. "I'm too busy to go to theaters or mingle in society. When I get home I am too tired as a rule to do anything but rest," she told a friend. "We are all slaves," observed Jay Gould, "and the man who has one million dollars is the greatest slave of all, except it be he who has two million."

Hetty may have been a slave to money, but she was determined to master her daughter's fate. The time had come, she said, for Sylvie to "come in closer contact with New York society." Even Hetty socialized more. She traveled to Newport as a guest of Annie Leary, and one evening accepted an invitation to a musical performance. Women in white décolleté dresses chatted in groups around the flower-filled room while Hetty stayed in the rear. She admired the bouquets of tuberoses on the tables and the banks of flowers along the far walls.

She enjoyed the music, took pleasure in the atmosphere, and wished that Sylvie were there.

In New York, she dined with friends and discussed her philosophy with George A. Plimpton, a well-regarded member of New York society. She quoted her favorite poem, "My Symphony," by William Henry Channing: "To live content with small means; To seek elegance rather than luxury, And refinement rather than fashion; To be worthy, not respectable, and wealthy, not rich." Plimpton, treasurer of the board of Columbia University, urged her to use her wealth to support a new college for women. Hetty responded with a challenge.

On letterhead from the Chemical National Bank, under the name "Wm. J. Quinlan jr. Cashier," dated July 1, 1896, Plimpton wrote: "I will give Barnard College twenty thousand dollars on condition that the treasurer Geo. A. Plimpton raises twenty thousand dollars additional by August 1st 1896." Under the note was written, "To be signed by Hetty Green." On August 1, the college received a gift of $20,000 from a donor in North East Harbor, Maine. Hetty's match is not recorded. A few years later Plimpton wrote her another note. *"I am coming down to ask you for a lot of money for Barnard College. I hope you and Miss Green are well this summer, a pleasant visit from your boy. Sincerely Yours."* Once again, her gift is unrecorded.

Hetty criticized her friend Annie Leary for her charitable ways: "She gives so much away needlessly and uselessly too, I tell her." Annie provided two suits of wool underwear to every man released from the Tombs city jail. "And she pays four dollars a suit!" Hetty exclaimed. "They only pawn the suits as soon as they get them. And goodness knows what they do with the money they get."

Her son was one of the few people who could convince his mother to give money away, either to him personally or for public purposes. He asked for her support for a group of physicians in New York, and Hetty not only loaned them funds, she helped find patients for their pediatric practice. It was reported that she donated $100,000 worth of lakeshore land in Chicago on which to build a home for aging and infirm actresses, an institution whose mission accorded with Ned's interests. And with the 1896 presidential campaign under way, Hetty contributed $100,000 to the Fusion Party in Texas.

Under Ned's direction as state chairman, the party, which combined Republicans, Populists, and National Democrats, worked to defeat William Jennings Bryan. The Democratic candidate supported the silver movement and favored a federal income tax. Bryan made Hetty Green a target: "She owns property estimated at $60 million and enjoys an income scarcely less than three million dollars," he railed in a speech. "This woman, under your indirect system of taxation, does not pay as much toward the support of the federal government as a laboring man whose income of $500 is spent upon his family." Hetty would pay anything to defeat him.

As eager as she was for McKinley to win, her support came at a price: she wanted something for Ned in return. "Green is said to be reasonably sure that he will be made a foreign Minister of some sort, or get something that will do to hand down to future generations of the Green family," said the *New York Times*. He may not have been made a foreign minister, but Ned had the privilege of riding a white horse at McKinley's inauguration. Soon after, Hetty took the train again to Washington to request the president's help. Ned was given full control of federal patronage in Texas.

Toward the end of March, Hetty traveled to Chicago with her bachelor son. In the Great Northern Hotel the skylighted lobby buzzed with financial talk, but some of the chatter spilled over to an ongoing trial. The city's headlines screeched about the actions of Adolph Luetgert: the butcher had poisoned his wife, ground up her body, and turned her into sausage. Meeting at the hotel with her real estate agent, Frank Chandler, Hetty ruminated on marriage: "I believe when persons get married it's for life," she said. "There wouldn't be any wives made into sausage if people were a little careful about whom they married."

She had great concern about the marriage of her children, keeping Ned to his pledge not to marry for twenty years, and wishing, at the same time, that Sylvie would find the right spouse. Young people needed a place to meet their future mates, she said to Chandler. "That's where society comes in. Lots of folderol and foolishness, but it's a pretty good thing. Not for me, understand. Too many people depending on me."

"But it's nice," she acknowledged, "especially at Newport. All flowers and music and a lot of nice girls like Sylvie and young men like

Ned. That's what it's for, you know. . . . How are they going to know what kind of life partner they are getting if they don't go out to these things and look each other over? If people were better acquainted with each other before they married, there wouldn't be so many divorces." Her daughter, she said, went to lots of parties and dinners in New-port. "I think she ought to," Hetty noted. "All young people ought to. That's where they find out who they ought to marry." A few days later, she returned to Brooklyn hoping to help her daughter find a mate.

She held Thanksgiving dinner in her apartment at the St. George Hotel with a reception afterward for friends: Annie Leary, her sister, and her niece Anna; Ruth Lawrence and her niece Ruth; and Miss Justine Cutting, whose father, Bayard Cutting, was a major investor in railroads and real estate. At other times Hetty arranged dinner par-ties or card games and invited Sylvie's friends, like Philip and Juliet Livingston, and eligible bachelors like James Gerard. Hetty may have been pursuing Gerard for Sylvie, but the lawyer, who came from a prominent family, had no interest in pursuing her daughter. Nonethe-less, at the end of an evening of cards, Hetty presented him with a gift. When he reminded her he had not won, she dismissed his protests. "Never mind, I bought it for you," she said, and handed him a silver calendar. With that, he recalled, she brought out supper, "with all the delicacies of the season and a bottle of vintage champagne."

Once again under Annie Leary's patronage, Sylvie was launched. She was seen with the social set at the horse shows at Madison Square Garden, at the opera, at private dinners, and chaperoned by a rela-tive, Mrs. Howland Pell, at the Knickerbocker Bowling Club, where, it was noted, Sylvie scored well. Her confidence increased, her ward-robe refreshed, hosted by Annie Leary or Amy Pell, she summered in Newport, coming into contact once again with New York's leading bachelors. Her mother approved.

To establish herself on her own, Sylvie moved away from Hetty to the Park Avenue Hotel in Manhattan. While she enjoyed her distance from Brooklyn, the third-largest city in the United States was mourn-ing its loss of independence. The merger of Brooklyn with New York, the Bronx, Staten Island, and Queens in 1898 made Greater New York, with a combined population of 3.5 million residents, the largest city in America, second only to London in the world. Many Brooklynites saw it as their darkest hour, but most New Yorkers marked it as the start of a brilliant era. "The sun will rise this morning on the greatest experiment in municipal government that the world has ever known," declared the *Tribune* on January 1, 1898.

The amalgamation had special significance for Hetty. It meant that residents of all the boroughs would be subject to New York personal property tax. Hetty made a dash across the Hudson River to Hoboken and never looked back. But business was business. In June of that year, when New York needed funds, she loaned the city $1 million at 2 percent interest on a four-month bond. "Two percent is considered a low rate," said the *Times*. "Three and a half percent are usually obtained by the city's bondholders." She kept the city tax men off her back, and the city benefited from her favorable rates.

Fine accommodations, friendly people, and an easy ferry ride to Wall Street made Hoboken a pleasant place for her to live. She chatted with neighbors and looked after them when they were ill, helped out local businessmen and sometimes loaned them money, made friends with children, and gave them piggy banks on their birthdays. Wherever she was, children held the highest place in her heart. She was seen one summer day in Bellows Falls on her way to buy her daily provisions: walking snappily down the street, she stopped to kiss a baby, gave advice to a mother about her sick child, and chatted with a group of curious youngsters who formed a circle around her.

Aside from her travels, her routine was as regular as the opening and closing of the Stock Exchange. The sky still dark, she awoke in her Hoboken flat, scarfed down her breakfast, and scurried to the boat slip two blocks away. Joining the throng of workers on the ferry, she debarked at Fourteenth Street and clambered aboard the crowded streetcar clanging its way downtown. At City Hall, hordes of men—merchants in derbies, clerks in caps, financiers in top hats—crammed the cavernous, narrow streets. Hetty brushed past the men, stepping away from the horse dung, steering clear of the carriages, her hem sweeping up the dust on the sidewalk as she strode the few blocks to the Chemical Bank on Broadway.

With a nod to the gentlemen tellers in their three-piece vested suits, she moved past the brass rails, slipped into the small office she used for storage, changed from her faded dress into another one she

sometimes used at work, and walked out into the long, narrow count-
ing room. Beyond the rows of starched collared clerks, near the window at the rear, she smoothed her long skirts, sat down at her rolltop
desk, and began her business.

Four times a day the letter carrier brought stacks of mail to the
bank. Hetty slid her knife across the envelopes, read the letters,
scanned the tabloids and broadsheets, sifted through piles of papers,
checked the mounds of coupons to clip, tracked her lawsuits, decided
which railroads, real estate, and bonds to buy or sell, and oversaw the
scores of payments on loans and mortgages to collect. As much as
she relished all that, she reveled in conversations with the officers of
the bank and the frock-coated men who came to call. Some days she
bundled herself up, took her bunch of keys, and went off to check on
her properties or visit investor friends like Russell Sage or Chauncey
Depew or Clarence Kelsey. Her eyes bright, her cheeks rosy, she bent
her square head toward them, asked their opinions, and learned the
news of the street. It was an opportunity she recognized as rare.

"A woman hasn't as many chances for making money as men
have," she told the *Woman's Home Companion*. "She isn't around or
among men, as a rule, and she doesn't hear of the opportunities for
investment which are talked of day by day, in Wall Street and other
financial centers." Her years with her father had given her the confidence to confront this world. "Most women are afraid to venture into
the regions where man reigns supreme," she said, calling it "foolish
timidity." If a woman conducted herself properly, and looked out for
herself, she believed, she could get along well. "I am able to manage
my affairs better than any man could manage them, and what man has
done, women do. It is the duty of every woman, I believe, to learn to
take care of her own business affairs."

Her single-minded resolve helped her make her fortune. But it also
made her a target of the press. "She has reduced money-making to a
fine art and let avarice replace some of women's highest attributes,"
said one paper. "This seems severe language in speaking of a woman,
but Mrs. Green has usurped the place of men and does not seek the
privileges of her sex."

True, she did not speak coyly, or flutter a fan flirtatiously, or pretend to be innocent to win help. Instead, she used her intelligence to

increase her wealth, her independence to live as she wished, and her strength to battle anyone who stood in her way. From her personal friends to the French lace maker to her father's lawyers, anyone who knew her knew how intense she was and how hard she worked. As for her appearance, the clothes she owned were of good quality, but, she explained, "If a thoroughbred were harnessed to an omnibus for forty years, it would begin to look like an ordinary hack. Taking care of a fortune," she said with a smile, was "something like omnibus work."

For as many years as she toiled at making money, she brought to it the passion of a woman for her lover. And at the end of another long day, she parted from the bank leaving behind the feel of crisp new bills, the sound of bonds being clipped, and her concerns over finance. "Business never disturbs me after business hours," she said. "I never worry about things. I do the best I can every day as I go along."

She strode to City Hall, climbed onto the streetcar that took her to the dock slip, and boarded the boat back to Hoboken. She loved the fresh air and the sail, and sometimes she even ferried on Sundays to attend the Quaker service on Fifteenth Street. Sitting silently on a bench in the spare meetinghouse of the Friends, she could contemplate the fate of her enemies and consider the future of her daughter and son.

Chapter 18

Family Matters

As much as Hetty was mocked, her son was admired. "Texans say there is no more popular man in the Lone Star State than Edward H. R. Green, son of Mrs. Hetty Green," wrote the *New York Times*. In August 1899, he joined Republicans from around the country convening in New York. Reporters waited near his suite at the Waldorf-Astoria, eager to catch a word. He was said to be spending money liberally in hopes of winning the governor's chair; from there he would try for a turn at the U.S. Senate. His popularity and his wealth afforded him a good chance to fulfill his political aspirations. "He is said to have $1,000 a month from his mother for pocket money and he spends it," said the *Dallas Morning Times*. But his mother soon put an end to his dream. He couldn't run for politics and run a railroad, she said.

His mother restrained him from marriage too, but she could not prevent him from pursuing romance. Soon after he moved to Texas, his former girlfriend Mabel Harlow, deemed a chorus girl by some, a call girl by others, arrived from Chicago. Ned made arrangements for her to live in an apartment in Terrell, but, at his neighbors' urging, he soon moved her to Dallas. The booming town, with electric streetcars, a six-story skyscraper, and a population of thirty thousand, was the largest city in the state and big enough for Mabel. At the Grand Windsor Hotel, a favorite of railroad men, his red-haired flame kept the rooms clean and her man happy. To Hetty's disdain, she was the love of Ned's life. Children adored her; Hetty called her "Miss Harlot."

With his usual aura of showmanship, Ned caused a sensation, driving the first horseless carriage in Texas from Terrell, where he still maintained his headquarters, to Dallas, where he established his home. At the sight of the automobile, the *Dallas Morning News* reported, cotton pickers abandoned their sacks and flew to the fences, pigs raced the machine, and horses reared on their hind legs. Ned sped along at the fast clip of fifteen miles an hour, his straw hat tilted back, his mustache bristling in the breeze; but a sudden jolt from a farm wagon pushed the car off the road and threw it into a gulley: the two-hour trip took five hours. By the time he arrived in Dallas, dusty but triumphant, the word was out: "Nothing that has passed along the streets of Dallas since the parade of the Kaliphs has attracted greater attention," said the *Morning News*. When a friend told Hetty he heard she had let her son buy a car, she replied, "Yes, it's cheaper than a wife."

While Ned dallied with Mabel, Sylvie still longed for a man. Despite her mother's prayers, no one seemed to spark her interest. Or vice versa. Until she met the Duc de la Torre. Tall, dark, and distinguished looking, the son of a revolutionary general who overthrew the queen of Spain, he arrived in New York at the start of 1900. Francisco Serrano y Domínguez spoke little English and claimed little money, but he had the dash of a Spanish nobleman and a swooning effect on the ladies.

Set to make his mark in the military and assume a role in society, he befriended Howland Pell, a captain in the National Guard. Pell's father was Hetty's cousin, a penurious man who seated his guests on rickety chairs and served them expensive wine poured into broken mugs. His son, well mannered, with an interest in warfare and weapons, was among the friends who introduced Hetty's daughter to the Duc de la Torre. The aristocrat's interest in the affluent Sylvie, said the *Evening World*, "was keen from the start."

Assiduous in his attentions, he organized numerous dinners in her honor, hosted her at theater parties, joined her at the Knickerbocker Bowling Club, and soon had his name linked with hers in the social news. Within two months of their meeting, rumors of their engagement ruffled New York.

The pairing of a European title and American wealth waltzed through the dreams of ambitious mothers and eager daughters. Role models already existed, the precedent set when Leonard Jerome paid Lord Randolph Churchill 50,000 pounds to wed his daughter Jennie. Jay Gould's daughter Anna married the French count Boni de Castellane, who spent her money at the rate of a million dollars a year. And only recently Consuelo Vanderbilt, daughter of Alva, had married the Duke of Marlborough after her father agreed to pay him $2.5 million in railroad stock with a guaranteed yield of 4 percent. The Duc de la Torre had an income of $4,000 a year; Sylvie Green was heiress to one of the world's largest fortunes.

The wedding of Sylvie and the duke, it was said, would take place in June in Newport or Bar Harbor. Before that, he was on his way to Mexico and would stop in Texas to meet her brother. But as quickly as the wick was sparked, the flame went out. Asked about her daughter's romance, Hetty replied curtly that she had never met the man. It was just another lie about her and her children. Indeed, she sniffed, "Dukes may be all right, but for my part, I'd rather my daughter would marry a good wide awake newspaper reporter than any duke in the world."

Soon after, Hetty was on the ferry to Hoboken when she was approached by a reporter for the *Ladies' Home Journal*. "Excuse me, are you Hetty Green?" he asked. She glared at him with the piercing look that turned full-grown men into short-pantsed boys. He apologized and moved away. For a fortnight he followed her to Hoboken, but like a cat being chased by a dog, she disappeared through an alley and scooted up the back stairs to the third floor of her yellow brick apartment house. A kind word and a dollar to the janitor revealed that the brass plate on her buzzer said "C. Dewey." After several evenings of knocks on her door, Hetty decided to answer. Dewey, her dog, barked, the reporter bent down, petted the animal, and pleaded with her not to scold it. She scowled at the familiar face: "Who are you, and what do you want?" she grumped and let him in.

Her tone belied the soft spot she had for the press. "Newspapers help the light in," she told one writer. "The press in law matters is to my mind like sunlight among spiders." She was glad to have reporters in the courtroom and answered their questions freely, but rarely did she give them interviews at home. Too many newsmen ran in packs, repeated rumors, scorned her as a miser, sneered at her quarters, or scoffed at her clothes. Still, she enjoyed speaking to those who paid her respect; she liked seeing her name in the papers and, for all her protests, she enjoyed the press; in later years, she hired an assistant to cut out her clippings.

Leigh Mitchell Hodges seemed to have a doggedness not so different from her own. She led him into her sparsely furnished parlor, nodded toward the vase of flowers on the mantel, and flashed her steel-gray eyes. "You think they're real, don't you?" she challenged. "Well, they're only dyed chicken feathers," she said, adding that they cost no more than fresh roses and outlived the real ones by years.

Directing her guest to the well-worn sofa, she sat down beside him on the haircloth seat and made room for Dewey, the Skye terrier, who jumped in between. His namesake was her husband's hero: the Vermont-born Commodore who defeated the Spanish and occupied the Philippines was rescuing the place where Edward Green had made his fortune. The dog was Hetty's playmate, an unconditional friend who lapped up rice pudding and rare steak and romped with her in the park.

After surveying the photographs in the room, of her son and herself in younger days, Hetty relaxed. With a childlike love of repetition, she eagerly told the stories she had told so many times before: her harsh childhood; her gay society years; her troubled marriage; her haranguing lawsuits; and her money—the sixty million she said she was now worth. "Words seem to come to her as easily as dollars," Hodges wrote.

What advice did she have for a young girl? he asked. "A girl should be brought up as to be able to make her own living, whether or not she's going to inherit a fortune," Hetty replied in a low, feminine voice. "But a woman's place is in the home, though some young women do better in business than men." Perhaps with the Duc de la Torre in mind, she continued: "A girl ought to be careful about the man she marries too, especially if she has money. She oughtn't to marry until she's old enough to know what she's doing anyway." Sylvie was nearing thirty and living in New York: her romance with the duke had come to an end. Despite another season with Annie Leary in Newport, there were no other prospects in sight.

Hetty dismissed the reporter and, eyes twinkling, bade him good night. As she spoke, her husband scuffed about in the flat above. She would take her dinner alone, as always, in her small dining room and then join him upstairs. Sometimes she bought him books from Isaac Mendoza's shop downtown and read to him, reminiscent of the times when she read the news to her father.

Edward Mott Robinson had trained her in business and given her good skills, but he had also imposed a responsibility she did not want for Sylvie. "My daughter hasn't been reared to be a business woman," she had told the reporter. "She knows a good deal about business and she'll be able to take care of what she may have, but I wouldn't want her to follow in my footsteps." With that she gave a hint about another life she might have preferred: a domestic world of husband, hearth, and home. And yet, business pulled her in like a magnet. And business, she claimed, helped her appreciate life.

"I have heard it stated that for a woman to get a business training is to crush all the poetry out of her life," she said. "This is sheer nonsense. A woman with a knowledge of business appreciates music, painting and other finer things of life just as much as the woman who is ignorant of all business matters. She has the advantage to secure more opportunities of seeing and appreciating these things. She can get more tickets to concerts and art galleries and will have more money to possess beautiful things. I have been a business woman for fifty years and I am just as fond of pictures and music as anyone my age." Two years earlier she had attended an auction at the Fifth Avenue Art Gallery. When a copy of a portrait of James Madison by Gilbert Stuart appeared, she raised her hand. "Seven fifty," she called out. "Twenty-five," someone else cried, and Hetty was out of the bidding.

Her interest in art hardly matched that of her rival Collis Huntington, who left his collection of paintings to the Metropolitan Museum of Art. But Hetty was not envious of his art; it was his business tactics that ate at her like termites gnawing at wood. In the summer of 1900, while she was in Vermont with Edward, news arrived of her nemesis. Hetty marched into the room where her husband sat with a friend. "The old devil Huntington is dead," she announced. The railroad mogul, seventy-nine, had died at his summer lodge in upstate New York. Edward listened and puffed on his cigar; the loss of a good businessman, he said. Hetty proclaimed it Satan's defeat. "Serves him right," she declared.

The following year Frank Norris gave a searing account of the railroad promoter's ruthless acts against the farmers of California. His book, *The Octopus,* was a vindication for Hetty. But no victory flags waved from the windows of the dark green train that brought Edward Green back to Bellows Falls that next autumn. He had been in poor health for years, and now, weak from heart and kidney ailments, he journeyed with his daughter in Ned's private railroad car, joined soon by his son, his wife, her private secretary, and a cluster of clerks.

Business never stopped for Hetty. She had just received $1.5 million at 5½ percent interest on a loan she made to New York a few months before. She lent the funds during summers when the financial markets were quiet and the city needed money, and she received a good return in the fall when she was paid back. "Hetty Green is smart," said an official in the Department of Finance.

The city comptroller, Bird S. Coler, later remarked: "Hetty Green had the best banking brain of anyone I ever knew. She carried all her knowledge in her head and never depended upon memoranda. She watched the money currents so closely that when I went to ask her for a loan she often knew how much I was going to require before I opened my mouth." Not only was she receiving interest, she was constantly investing her capital. In November, she joined the Vanderbilts and Goulds and pledged $4 million for a new iron- and steelworks in California.

For several months Hetty hovered over Edward, waking continually during the night to check on him; a serious inflammation of the kidneys seemed to foreshadow his end. The whole family stayed close to his side and then, under the care of a private nurse, he regained his strength. Convinced he was on his way to recovery, Ned returned to Texas, never to see his father again. Hetty resumed her old routine, commuting from Bellows Falls to New York, traveling in good weather and through the worst of storms.

In early March she stopped in Boston at the Parker House and met with lawyers representing her in a legal suit. Less than two weeks later, on March 19, 1902, while she was on the train on her way back from New York to Vermont, eighty-two-year-old Edward took a turn for the worse. Hetty arrived at the Bellows Falls station that evening, walked across the bridge and up the steep streets to Tucker House, but by the time she reached the house, Edward was dead.

The funeral in the cemetery of the Immanuel Episcopal Church marked the end of a disappointing life. A bold adventurer in his youth, a well-dressed clubman in his middle years, he had been shot down by the random swerves of the market and the straight arrows of his wife. She had had no patience with his womanizing, or his profligate use of her wealth. In the days when women were known by their husbands' names, she had long since given up calling herself "Mrs. Edward Green." Indeed, for years he had been known as "the husband of Hetty Green." And yet, they kept their marriage together.

Wearing a fine black dress and heavy widow's veil, Hetty graced him with a broken circle of laurel leaves and Easter lilies and said farewell to the father of her children, her financial adviser, her friend, and the guardian of her life. One month after Edward died, she visited the Leonard Street station and asked the police for a license to carry a gun. New York Pistol Permit #13854 was a rare certificate granted a woman for her own protection. In July she was in Far Rockaway with her daughter, and then in August, joined by Ned, she holidayed with Annie Leary in Newport. But in September Hetty sailed alone to London to settle up Edward's accounts. And perhaps in a final act of farewell, in December 1902 she sold twenty thousand shares of Louisville and Nashville Railroad stock to the Wall Street gambler John Gates. She doubled her money on the railroad that brought down her man; it was a fitting end to their life together.

Chapter 19

A Cool Head

The atmosphere that greeted America at the start of the twentieth century seemed as solid as the gold standard it now banked on and as bright as the electricity it now burned. New inventions, new technology, and new forms of transportation transformed the country and the customs of its people. While Hetty kept her Bellows Falls lanterns filled with kerosene, Americans lighted their homes with electric bulbs, listened to music on talking machines, rang each other on telephones, and lurched along in automobiles—all a dramatic change from the decade before.

After the panic of 1893 the country's economy had remained less than robust. For several years American companies had struggled to keep their profits up and their prices down: in the methods still practiced today, they fired workers, slashed paychecks, and cut costs on raw materials and overhead. With jobs scarce and wages low, customers counted out their pennies and snapped their purses shut. Mountains of merchandise rose on shelves; orders for new goods sputtered to a halt; factories were lifeless.

The economy stayed moribund until European industry came back to life. By 1897 business was flourishing in France and England; as their factories flooded with orders they could not fill, they turned to the United States for help. Slowly, American steel and iron mills were roused from their sleep, cotton mills hummed, railroads picked up steam transporting freight from coast to coast, and ships packed with cargo sailed to Europe. U.S. exports crawled out of a deficit of nearly

$20 million at the start of the crisis in 1893 and climbed to a surplus of almost $300 million over imports.

The Spanish-American War did little to derail the boom. From the congressional declaration of war in April 1898 to Commodore Dewey's swift destruction of the Spanish fleet in Manila Bay toward the end of May that year, the United States established itself as a world power. With its victory over Spain, America gained possession of the Philippines, Guam, and Puerto Rico; it guaranteed the sovereignty of Cuba and ensured the safety of American citizens residing and conducting business on the island ninety miles off the coast of Florida. That same year Congress passed legislation allowing the annexation of Hawaii, an important military base for actions in the Pacific. And by the end of 1898 American exports exceeded imports by $615 million. America had confirmed its superiority in both conflict and commerce.

The end of the war reignited commercial engines and invigorated entrepreneurs, who found new methods for making money. Where once they sought to finance rising industries like railroads and mining, now they saw the chance to consolidate existing firms. When promoters approached the banks for loans, the financial institutions scrambled to help. They saw new prospects for themselves: "Wall Street has furnished the money that has set the wheels of industry in motion over the vast continent," said the financier Henry Clews.

John Gates, a smooth-talking barbed-wire salesman turned daring entrepreneur, led the merger mania. In 1898, he combined seven factories in Illinois into the Consolidated Steel and Wire Company. Two months later, he sold that business to another new firm, the American Steel and Wire Company, which then bought an additional seven mills. But Gates was not satisfied to gain a hold on the wire business: he wanted to cash in on his assets by selling the stock to the public. With his salesman's showmanship and the help of banks that underwrote the issue, the new company offered shares at a market price of $24 million. Wall Street gobbled it up like cotton candy.

The following year Gates organized another business, American Steel and Wire of New Jersey, which bought the earlier American Steel and Wire Company for $33 million and then added another eleven wire plants to its name. Again with the help of bankers, Gates issued $90 million in new shares: eager buyers pushed up the common stock and doubled its price in two months. One of the most triumphant men of his time on Wall Street, Gates topped it all off with the sale of American Steel and Wire to United States Steel.

The success of Gates's consolidations inspired other entrepreneurs to follow his path. J. P. Morgan conducted a huge coup when he convinced Andrew Carnegie to sell him Carnegie Steelworks and then persuaded Wall Street to underwrite the purchase. As soon as the stocks and bonds were issued, the public grabbed its share: if it was good enough for Carnegie, it was good enough for the man on the street. In similar ways, John D. Rockefeller snapped up smaller companies to create Standard Oil, James Duke chewed up his rivals and spat out American Tobacco, Armour and Swift formed monopolies in meatpacking; others controlled sugar refining, utilities, and paper.

By 1901 hundreds of small businesses were folded into huge conglomerates. The number of companies within those fields shrunk from 1,800 to fewer than 200. As a result, America rose to become the world's largest supplier of copper, cotton, corn, coal, steel, iron, and oil; but its position came at a high cost to the country. Prices were fixed and politicians paid off: Chauncey Depew, elected to the Senate in 1899, later admitted under oath that the Equitable Insurance Company had paid him "a substantial annual retainer" while he was a legislator. To Hetty's fury, the small businessmen who made up much of the American economy could not compete and were sidelined; one or two men controlled entire industries. "They are ruining the chances of the people," Hetty said.

With money readily available, investors and manipulators borrowed from the banks to buy stocks. The rash of buying sent prices zooming: men whispered hot tips in one another's ears; rumors roiled of companies going sour; stories spread of huge amounts of money being made overnight. Hetty watched from the sidelines as America swirled in another carnival of speculation; rich and poor rushed to the carousel and reached for the brass ring. Corporate leaders and clerks bought and sold on margin; many bought shares being offered to bankroll the purchases of worthless firms. The irresponsible borrowing echoed the past: "I wasn't worth a cent two years ago, and now I owe two million dollars," mocked Mark Twain in *The Gilded Age*.

The reckless use of margin and the razzle-dazzle of new industrial stocks also predicted the future, foreshadowing the dot-com bubble and the frenzy for initial public offerings at the turn of the twenty-first century.

Everyone but Hetty seemed to be buying. She did not buy industrials, she said, and never bought with borrowed money. Once in a while she cornered a stock like Reading Railroad, but that was the exception, not the norm. "I don't believe in speculating as a rule, and I don't speculate as much as people think." Her approach was far more cautious: "When good things are so low that no one wants them, I buy them and lay them away in the safe; when owing to some new development, they go up and my shares are so needed that men will pay well for them, I am ready to sell."

She watched for bargains but never bought to be in style. In January 1903 when a prominent art collection was put up at auction, Hetty attended the sale. For two evenings in a row, the formally attired crowd, polished and powdered, arrived at Mendelsohn Hall, eager for the art that would enhance their status. As, one after another, paintings by Gainsborough, Delacroix, Corot, and Breughel came on the block, some of the richest men and women in New York, along with agents of some of the most important museums in the country, raised their hands in a frenzy. Hetty refrained from bidding.

In the frantic heat of the market Hetty kept a cool head. She attributed her success chiefly to her basic rule: "always buying when everyone wants to sell, and selling when everyone wants to buy." As easy as her motto appeared, it took restraint to keep from buying while others swooped up stocks in the euphoria of a boom; it took courage to remain calm while the crowd dumped their shares overboard in a wave of panic. She had stayed the course in the past; she would continue it into the future.

Along with her unruffled outlook and good judgment, her fierce focus, endless reading, and intensive research all helped her penetrate the complexities of the market. Determining when stocks were cheap demanded a thorough knowledge of "their history, their dividend-paying possibilities, and what they have sold for in the past," she said. "If one can buy a good thing at a lower cost than it has ever sold for before, he may be fairly sure of getting it cheap." She treated her holdings as if they were jewels: "I keep them just as I keep a considerable number of diamonds on hand until they go up and people are anxious to buy." Indeed, as one acquaintance attested, her vault in Bellows Falls held a glittering pile of diamonds, emeralds, rubies, and other stones, some inherited, some acquired in business deals. But the deals being done by many entrepreneurs were more dissolute than dazzling.

"The captains of industry who have driven the roadway systems across the continent, who have built up our commerce, who have developed our manufactures, have on the whole done great good to our people," said Theodore Roosevelt when he inherited the presidency after McKinley's assassination in 1901.

But corruption had corroded the country. He followed his praise by firing a warning shot: "Great corporations exist only because they are created and safeguarded by our institutions, and it is therefore our right and our duty to see that they work in harmony with those institutions." Roosevelt's trust busting had begun. It started with the support of men who knew how rotten the system was: Thomas Lawson had worked for thirty-four years as a banker, a broker, and a corporate man; he hoped, he said, that Roosevelt would "shake the largest trusts and corporations until their teeth chattered and their backbones rattled."

Almost immediately the Justice Department filed suit against Northern Securities, the railroad holding company that controlled three of the largest rails in the country: the Northern Pacific, Union Pacific, and Burlington railways. Formed by J. P. Morgan, E. H. Harriman, and James Hill, Northern Securities set the fees and left little room for smaller rails to transport freight or passengers. Within months of the case and for several years after, the government pursued monoliths like Standard Oil, American Tobacco, and more than forty other monopolies. Still, the president tried to find a balance between the need to stamp out fraud and the need to stimulate American enterprise. His aim was not to destroy business but to rein in the trusts. Hetty shook her head, calling Roosevelt "a trust buster who didn't bust trusts."

Hetty had no fear of standing up to large corporations or other institutions. Over the course of several years she had acquired mortgages on twenty-eight churches in Chicago; after the church of a wealthy congregation went into default, she announced she would foreclose. The church's pastor told her she would not be welcomed in heaven if she did. Hetty promptly wrote back, asking his help to get there: "as long as you are in a threatening mood, you'd better climb up on your cornerstone and pray for my soul, because I am going to foreclose." And she proceeded.

The story made news across the country. When the reverend criticized her on the pulpit for taking over the property of "a poor little church," a fellow Chicago pastor took umbrage at the charge. "To expect the holder of a church mortgage to cancel it upon the grounds of Christianity after the money has been borrowed in good faith is nothing less than a hold-up. Churches should expect to pay their debts," he was quoted in the *St. Louis Republic*. A New York editorial concurred: "If churches are to borrow money from people who make a business of lending it, there is no imaginable reason why they should not pay their debts." In March 1903, Hetty took over the property and sold it for the amount of its debts to another congregation.

Three months later the indomitable woman was portrayed in the *Chicago Daily Tribune*:

> Hetty Green has an automobile. It is a bright red, twenty horse-power one, and cost $12,800. Mrs. Green may be seen any afternoon riding up and down the Jersey turnpikes either side of Morristown. Her companion on these trips is either her son, Edward H. R. Green, president of the Texas Midland railroad, or her chauffeur. Thus far she has not been arrested for scorching [speeding]. The automobiling costume worn by Mrs. Green is a modest gown of dark material and a black poke bonnet. Here is her opinion of the sport:
>
> "Some people who do not know me or my fondness for progressive as well as practical things may be surprised at my advocating what some still choose to call a fad. But since my son purchased a motor—they say it is correct to call them motors—I have discovered the practical as well as the pleasant side of automobiling. Are they dangerous? No more so

than horses and carriages. More people are injured every day
by runaways than in a week or month by automobiles."

A lively Hetty Green turned seventy years old in 1904. As with
many events in her life, the press reported it wrong and pronounced
her a septuagenarian the following year. "Seventy years rest lightly
on Hetty Green," declared the *New York Times* in 1905. When a clerk
at the Chemical Bank tried to congratulate her, she told him, "If I
am seventy years old today, this must be my seventy-first birthday."
Whatever her age, she was spry, spirited, and assertive. In more than
one interview, she reflected on women and business:

"Every girl should be taught the ordinary lines of business investment," she said. Whether rich or poor, a young woman should know
how a bank account works, understand the composition of mortgages
and bonds, and know the value of interest and how it accumulates. For
the moment, at least, she suggested that men should be the ones to do
the teaching. "I think fathers should always talk such things over with
their daughters as well as with their sons. If they did so, girls would
learn to think along business lines, and not be at the mercy of business
sharps who prey upon the weaker sex." As for choosing investments,
"Railroads and real estate are the things I like," she said. "Government bonds are good," she acknowledged, then added, after a pause,
"though they do not pay very high interest. Still, for a woman safe and
low is better than risky and high."

She saw a rapidly changing role for women, who were replacing
men as stenographers and typists in banks and as cashiers in stores.
With a nod to herself and a hint of the future, she said, "There is no
reason why the married woman should not also be a business woman."
As important as business was, however, she agreed with the prevailing
attitude: "the chief sphere of woman is [the] home; her most important
duties are that of wife and mother." She added, with some exaggera-
tion: "I took care of my husband and his stomach and he lived to be
eighty-three years old."

She believed a knowledge of business would make a woman a better wife. In the past, said Hetty, at the end of the day the only thing
a woman could do to relieve her husband's strain was "to make her-

self as pretty as a wax doll. But there is no reason why that primitive idea . . . should continue to exist in the sense it once did." A woman who understood the pressures on her husband would be a far more sympathetic spouse.

In spite of her strong words, she had little support for women's suffrage and no desire to see a woman president. "I should hope not," she said, piercing the interviewer with her steely eyes. "I don't believe much in so-called women's rights. I am willing to leave politics to the men." Indeed, she had never taken office on any corporate board, nor had she been the public face of any company she controlled; she left it to her husband and son to hold those positions. Nonetheless, she wished women had more rights in the world of commerce. "I could have succeeded much easier had I been a man. I find men will take advantages of women in business that they would not attempt with men."

Still, she prized the life she led. "I enjoy being in the thick of things. I like to have a part in the great movements of the world and especially of this country. I like to deal with big things and with big men." Unlike society matrons, she said, "I would rather do [this] than play bridge or whist. Indeed, my work is my amusement, and I believe it is also my duty." Imagine, she said, if someone gave her money to invest and she stuck it in the bank or frittered it away. "What would you think of me?" she asked. "I feel that I am doing my duty in taking care of and increasing the trust left me by my family, and the Lord is blessing me in it."

John D. Rockefeller thought the Lord had done even more: "God gave me my money," he said. "I believe it is my duty to make money and still more money and to use the money I make for the good of my fellow man according to the dictates of my conscience."

Said Hetty: "One way is to give money and to make a big show. That is not my way of doing. I am of the Quaker belief and although the Quakers are about all dead, I still follow their example. An ordinary gift to be bragged about is not a gift in the eyes of the Lord." Despite her denials, it was reported that she had given half a million dollars to the Nurses Home in New York and $50,000 to their settlement house. And more often than not, her gifts were loans to public institutions and jobs for individuals.

Nevertheless, Hetty was happy to receive a gift from her friend Edwin Hatch. She had met the head of Lord & Taylor when she moved from her flat in Hoboken to Annie Leary's new house on Fifth Avenue at Eighty-fourth Street. Hatch, who lived next door and summered in Vermont, sometimes saw her at Annie's soirees and often joined her in an early-morning constitutional. If Hatch did not appear on time, Hetty would rap at his door and tell his butler to rouse him. Together the dapper merchant and the dowdy matron paced around the Central Park reservoir or down the street's smooth pavement. As they walked along one day, she turned to Hatch and asked, "Is it true that I look ragged and terrible as the newspapers say?" Hatch pondered the question for half a block. "Mrs. Green," he finally replied, "just consider that veil through which you are looking at me. It is torn. It is faded. It looks like hell. You come down to the store some morning and I'll give you one of the best veils we have in stock."

Hetty wasted no time. The next morning, making her way down Fifth Avenue to Nineteenth Street, she arrived at Lord & Taylor and told the liveried floor boy she wanted to see the head of the store. At Hatch's direction, the young woman behind the counter showed her the very best veils. When Hetty found the one she liked, Hatch told the clerk, "Charge it to me." Delighted by the gift, Hetty asked to see some skirts—"at reduced rates," she added. Upstairs, amid the ruffled shirtwaists and long skirts laid out on tables, the salesclerk found an item that had been returned. The ticket was marked eight dollars, but Hatch told Hetty it was fifty cents. She was more than pleased as she left the store, new clothes in hand, and worked her way down to Wall Street.

Chapter 20

Panic Again

In September 1905, Hetty arrived in Boston embroiled in lawsuits against her father's estate. During her stay at the Parker House, she agreed to attend a lecture with a friend at a Protestant church. "I was bred a Quaker, but I go to every kind of church," she confided to a reporter sitting nearby. What counted was not the denomination but that the followers kept the commandments. "I believe in simplicity. It's that, you know, that makes me what folks call 'mean.' The fact is, I prefer not to be extravagant." Extravagance was hardly an issue. Unlike the rest of the women in the pews that night in the early autumn frost, she wore no gloves on her hands and no furs over the shoulders of her plain dress.

She attended the daily courtroom proceedings and confessed on the way back from the church to her hotel that "all this litigation makes me very tired." She sighed and spoke in a plaintive voice: "I am all fagged out tonight. Yet I must be in court by ten o'clock tomorrow morning." After spending five years on the case she won a payment of $75,000 with a promise from her to drop all proceedings in court. "I usually get the better of all people who oppose me in lawsuits," she said.

Back in New York, in November 1905 she marked her birthday with another loan to City Hall. Once again, New York needed money, and it turned to the most dependable banker it had. Over the course of two weeks, Hetty loaned the city $2.5 million at 5 percent interest. "She is now," declared the *Los Angeles Herald,* "the largest money lender in New York."

From her perch at the rear of the Chemical Bank, Hetty carried out her moneymaking obligations. With the economy flourishing around the globe, from Europe to Asia to South America, demand was rising and prices escalating. U.S. railroads expanded their plans, increasing their need for new funds. Merchants and manufacturers widened the scope of their dreams, asking the banks for more money to build their businesses. As the boom continued, more and more Americans were eager to take part, borrowing money from the banks to buy stocks at prices that soared like out-of-control hot-air balloons.

At the same time, the cost of land skyrocketed around the country, as people raced to buy up real estate in cities, towns, and rural communities. Inevitably, the cost of borrowing the money to buy the land rose precipitously. While others bought, Hetty sold. "I saw the handwriting on the wall," she said later. "Every real estate deal which I could possibly close up was converted into cash."

In 1905 the call for money surpassed anything that had come before. The heavy requests pushed interest rates up, causing many people to owe the banks far more than they had. At the start of 1906, the financier Jacob Schiff was so outraged over the currency situation that he told the Chamber of Commerce: "If this condition of affairs is not changed, and changed soon, we will get a panic in this country compared with which the three which have preceded it would only be child's play." But businessmen and bankers continued to play.

Black clouds hung over the debtors; many had little choice but to divest their holdings. Hetty watched as rich men arrived at the Chemical; doffing their top hats, drawing out their expensive engraved cards, and handing them to the clerk at the door, they sought her out to sell off their possessions. As rates rose, more and more of "the solidest men in Wall Street," she said, from "financiers to legitimate businessmen," came to call, begging to unload everything from palatial mansions to automobiles.

"They came to me in droves," she recalled. "Some of them I lent money to, and some of them I didn't. That was my privilege." Stories spread that she was lending money at usurious rates. "Those to whom I loaned my money got it at six percent. I might just as easily have secured forty percent. But never in my life, no matter what has been said against me, have I practiced usury, and no one knows it bet-

ter than the wealthy men who have had business dealings with me."
Ironically, the woman who rarely shopped was besieged by retailers.
"Nearly all the big department stores came to me and I loaned them
money," she said. She knew "a panic was inevitable."

Opportunities emerged wherever she looked. Of all she was
offered, she felt most comfortable with real estate and mortgages. "I
would advise any young woman with $500 at her command to invest
in real estate," she said. "She should buy at auction on occasion when
circumstances have forced the sale. If she will look out for such opportunities, they will surely come, and she will find that she can buy a
parcel of land at one third its appraised value." She followed her own
advice and purchased land in upstate New York for $400,000, one-
third the normal price. She donated the land to build a school for boys;
Hetty was proud that the project gave work to many men at a time
when jobs were scarce.

She owned real estate and mortgages all around New York: hotels,
office buildings, brownstones, and townhouses such as 838 Fifth Avenue, 8 East Sixty-ninth Street, and 110 West Fifty-seventh Street; like
most big real estate investors in the city, then and now, she bought
them under various names to limit her liability. It was rumored that
she was the real purchaser of Annie Leary's new house; more likely,
she held the mortgage.

Whether she owned it or not, Hetty spent much of her time in the
lavish, five-story townhouse, where her daughter also lived. There, in
the marble house with its sixty-eight gilt-framed mirrors, the philan-
thropically minded Annie Leary, newly appointed a papal countess by
the Church, entertained Catholic leaders. And there she hosted New
York socialites and European aristocrats, praying that one of them
would marry the tall and stocky Sylvie Green. A brief glimmer of
hope arrived with the Prince del Drago, an Italian aristocrat working
on Wall Street, who devoted time to the heiress. But the romance soon
dried up. Three years later the twenty-seven-year-old prince married
a wealthy widow nearly twice his age.

The news of the San Francisco earthquake on April 8, 1906,
stunned the country and rocked its financial institutions. Within one

minute, the ground heaved and pressed, heaved and pressed, and with each groan, wooden structures disintegrated and tons of stone crashed from the steel frames of buildings. In that early-morning nightmare, families rushed from their beds to the streets: mothers clutched their babes; fathers stood agape watching their homes collapse. The rumbles brought the city to ruins.

The worst quake in the country's history destroyed two-thirds of San Francisco—everything from factories to office buildings to private houses to City Hall. A mass of rubble covered the streets; the water mains broke and cut off the water supply; fires broke out and for three days smoke belched from burning buildings; 2,500 people were killed; 250,000 people were displaced and destitute. As a result of the catastrophe, factories and businesses were forced to shut, and railroads suffered losses of hundreds of thousands of dollars. The calamity, which cost insurance companies $100 million, in due course drained hundreds of millions more from the banks. It took an immediate toll on Wall Street as fearful investors sold off stocks in its wake.

The increasing need for funds came at a high cost to municipalities and individuals. Banks raised their rates, forcing borrowers to pay more and more for their loans. Once again New York City came to Hetty; once again she loaned the money at favorable rates. "She is a grand little woman," said the deputy chamberlain. "We can always rely on her." Added one newspaper editorial: "With the aid of Mrs. Hetty Green, the richest woman in America, Controller Metz has been enabled to beat the financiers of Wall Street and save the city thousands upon thousands of dollars."

Months before, Hetty had loaned the city $4.5 million at a rate well below those established in Wall Street; "she would have been ready to lend more if the city needed it," noted the *New York World*. Indeed, with the death of Russell Sage, the city's leading lender, in July 1906, it was confirmed: Hetty Green was number one. For all his reputation as a shrewd financier of ready wealth, a cool, immovable calculator, a person who could deal with heartless corporations in a corresponding manner, Hetty was his equal, said the paper. "The King is Dead; Long Live the Queen," cried a Wall Street operator.

The balloon began to sink in the spring of 1907. A stock market crash in Egypt, which led to a run on the banks, was followed by bank failures in Japan, Germany, and Chile. Throughout the world, a hoarding panic seized the markets. But the phenomenal increase in America's economic strength, along with the establishment of the gold standard for its currency and the great resources of its banks, reassured everyone that the United States was safe from a similar fate.

With few regulations to restrain them, U.S. banks continued to loan more and more, lowering their reserves, at greater and greater risk of not having ready money if customers wished to redeem their deposits. But the bankers weren't worried. "It had been a cardinal doctrine, in American banking circles, that a panic like those of 1893 and 1873 would never again be witnessed in this country," wrote Alexander Noyes, the financial editor of the *New York Times*.

But in June an iron manufacturer in New York went bankrupt, and shortly afterward a deficit in the city budget, combined with a lack of confidence in the local government, caused the failure of two municipal bond offerings. At the boardinghouse on Madison Avenue where Hetty was staying, a neighbor asked her advice. The young woman had money in the Knickerbocker Trust. What did Mrs. Green think about that? she asked. Hetty looked at her sharply: "If you have any money in that place, get it out the first thing tomorrow," she said. "Why?" the young woman wanted to know. "The men in that bank are too good looking," Hetty said in a serious tone. "You mark my words." With that she marched off, a chunk of valuable papers, withdrawn from a shaky bank downtown, hidden in her bosom.

In the fall, the Metropolitan Street Railway, which ran the city's streetcars, went under; other companies followed. For four months more, short-term interest rates soared upward from 25 percent to 125 percent as the stock market spiraled downward. In early October, Annie Leary honored Hetty at a lavish dinner for twenty-six guests at her home in Newport, but back in New York, everyone chewed over events: J. P. Morgan took a sandwich and a glass of water at his desk; Hetty took comfort in a cup of custard and a glass of milk at a dairy restaurant on Broadway. Uptown, housewives shared their woes over chocolate sundaes at the new Schrafft's on Herald Square, and socialites sobbed into their champagne at the new Plaza Hotel. All had a bad taste in their mouths.

Men's brows darkened as the market declined. Not only were their shares in peril, a large number of banks had loaned money to speculators and taken stocks as collateral. Worse were the trust companies, institutions that invested money for the beneficiaries of estates and wills. They had also accepted demand deposits; with little regulation, and even less in cash reserves, they had traded in stocks, speculated in real estate, and loaned money for risky mortgages.

As Hetty predicted, the Knickerbocker Trust, one of the largest trust companies in New York, was in trouble. Rumors spread. Panic struck. The sidewalks of Wall Street overflowed as fearful depositors rushed to the banks to collect their funds. On the morning of Tuesday, October 22, 1907, dozens lined up on Broadway at the doors of the Knickerbocker's downtown branch. Well-dressed women on the verge of tears, nervous priests, their faces as white as their collars, and a mass of clerks and messengers carrying empty satchels stood waiting. Over the next few hours the line grew, snaking around to form an S in front of the bank. Slowly, people were ushered in to claim their money, but by that afternoon, when $8 million had been handed over, the bank called a halt to the distributions; no more money was given out.

Depositors at all the Knickerbocker's branches were left in despair. At the stately branch on Fifth Avenue at Thirty-fourth Street, where Roman columns and bronze doors ordinarily hailed its rich depositors, an anxious crowd clamored inside, their automobiles and carriages waiting for them on the street; at the Harlem branch, women wept and workingmen fought back their tears as they turned and walked back home. The Knickerbocker had shut its doors.

When a group of bankers, headed by J. P. Morgan, met to consider bailing out Knickerbocker with money from the U.S. Treasury, they studied the firm's books and announced it was too far in debt to save. Within two weeks, six New York banks and two more trusts were forced to close. When both the Trust Company of America and the Lincoln Trust declared themselves in trouble, Morgan took the lead and called for emergency meetings.

Throughout the day of November 5, 1907, somber-looking men scurried around the city conferring over the crisis. Bankers, business executives, and government officials huddled over what to do.

The most important meetings took place on Thirty-sixth Street at the baronial library of J. P. Morgan. Starting at 11 a.m., a string of automobiles and carriages lined up along the block from Madison Avenue to Park Avenue as their owners emerged and approached the classical white marble building. A few had been there before but most had never been past the bronze Italian doors. The magnificent structure, a masterpiece of Charles McKim, was the "most jealously guarded treasure-house in the world," wrote the *London Times*.

Clusters of four or five men, including the heads of banks such as Chase and First National, private bankers like August Belmont and Levi Morton, directors of trusts, and business leaders such as Henry Clay Frick of U.S. Steel passed through the gates into the high-ceilinged marble hall. From there they entered a lofty apartment, adorned with a carved wood fireplace, a splendid portrait of a Florentine girl, green tapestries, rich crimson furnishings, and two walls lined from floor to ceiling with the rarest volumes of fine books and manuscripts. From this space glowing with ancient leather bindings, the men strolled into a smaller but even more exquisite room, its Renaissance painted ceiling said to be brought from the Aldobrandini Palace; its fireplace carved in marble; its walls covered with crimson tapestries; its low bookcases filled with ancient relics and medieval treasures of marble, bronze, terra-cotta, faience, and enamel. In these hushed and sacred chambers, their voices murmured money.

Later, other groups came, and at 6 p.m. a mysterious woman veiled in black entered the building. Names were mentioned, gossip spread; later Morgan insisted it was the widow of Russell Sage, but rumors persisted it was Hetty Green. New groups arrived, each more important than the last; meetings continued into the night. When the clock struck twelve, a wagon appeared: six waiters from the Waldorf rolled in trays of edibles and urns of coffee. Finally, at 3 a.m., as the weary financiers emerged from behind the bronze doors, an announcement was made: they would give money to the two big institutions. The failing trusts would be saved.

The crisis was far from over. Around the country, banks with deposits in New York demanded their funds. Word of the New York closures caused a run on regional banks. Merchants in the Midwest wanted their money deposited in St. Louis; brewers in the West and tobacco growers in the South demanded certified checks to pay their taxes. Farmers in Oklahoma, miners in California, and mill workers in Massachusetts withdrew their funds from local banks. Hiding their money under their mattresses, they hoarded nearly $300 million.

In Terrell, Texas, a long line formed in front of the bank that held the funds of the Texas Midland Railroad. Ned Green walked in and plunked a cardboard box on the counter. "This is the safest bank in the country," he declared as he handed the clerk $30,000. The grim faces of the depositors melted into smiles as they realized their bank was safe. In New York, Morgan's committee used government funds to support the banks with $25 million in loans.

The clamor for money caused a selling epidemic on the floor of the Stock Exchange. Shareholders who had borrowed money by using stocks as collateral saw their security washed away; forced to put up more collateral, they could not cover their loans. Orders to sell piled up on brokers' desks, but few came forward to buy the shares. Stock prices plummeted to 50 percent less than their high the year before. The Exchange was on the verge of shutting its doors when the J. P. Morgan group stepped in again with $27 million to buy up shares and temporarily offset the losses. The *New York World* credited Hetty with providing some of that money.

The panic affected New York City. With expenses up and revenue down, worried financiers urged the mayor to lower the city's costs. "The budget must be reduced to the bone," Mayor McClellan announced: there would be no new policemen hired; no new city buildings constructed; no raises for the men who cleaned the streets. Jobs were cut, contracts were pushed aside, and contractors left unpaid. Once again, only when Morgan and a group of bankers agreed to buy $30 million of the city's bonds was New York saved. Hetty helped out with over a million dollars in loans to New York.

The turmoil continued into the first few months of 1908. A major corporation, the Westinghouse Electric Company, went into receivership. And when the Oriental Bank in New York announced it would have to close its doors, Hetty ordered the Chemical Bank to advance it money; she promised to stand behind the loan. Later her son revealed that in addition to all the loans she made to banks and businessmen in New York, she lent $6 million in Texas.

But she accused President Theodore Roosevelt of worsening the problems: "Mr. Roosevelt has not made good. What would you think if I were to declare every day for years that I was going to kill a musk-rat—and then never did it?" she asked. "What has he accomplished aside from helping to create the financial situation? Has he punished those dreadful corporations, has he cured the evils of high finance, as he said he would? What has he actually done except wield the big stick?"

Despite her doubts, confidence-building measures brought the money markets back into shape. At the urging of Morgan and his small circle of colleagues, the U.S. Treasury secretary, George Cortelyou, supplied money for the financiers to use in several ways: as loan certificates to banks, easing the way for them to settle their balances while keeping their cash reserves; to secure loans overseas; and to support stocks in solid corporations.

The crisis was over, but it offered valuable lessons for the future: exaggerated expectations, wild speculation, and high leverage would lead to disaster. The United States could continue to prosper, said the financial writer Noyes, if Americans kept a calm outlook on the use of the country's resources and restrained themselves from venturous experiments with capital. With that in mind, he wrote: "In the future, as in the past, the trend of the country's financial history will be fixed by the interplay of its natural resources, its capacity for production, [and] the industry, inventiveness and versatility of its people."

Hetty believed the problems could be traced to another source: "There's one reason why we have hard times: money easy coming and easy going! American children are not taught how to save money but how to spend it. Everything they want—give it to them so long as you know the price of the credit. That's the policy of the modern mother and she is raising a nation of spendthrifts whose one thought is to get what they want when they want it."

A few years later *Harper's Magazine* noted that the trouble was not unique to the nation or the times. "'Easy come easy go' is the maxim of all get-rich-quick civilizations," the editors wrote. More than a century later, the notion still applies. Referring to the stock market crash in 2008, Paul Volcker, the former chairman of the Federal Reserve, noted, "We had a big financial crisis. We'd overspent. We'd overborrowed. We'd overleveraged. It's tough to have a recovery."

As often happens, the 1907 financial crisis provided a catharsis: it cleansed the system of weaker banks; weeded out the speculators; strengthened sturdier institutions; and reenergized the markets. Once again, the country was on the go.

Chapter 21

Remarkable Changes

A nything, everything is possible," announced Thomas Alva Edison in 1908. Newspapers reported talk of war in Europe, Germany's increasing strength, a bomb in India, a coup in Persia, problems in Afghanistan, and the effects of the financial crisis at home. And yet, the United States oozed with optimism. The exceptional American people were producing incomparable ideas and innovations. The Wright brothers' flying machine whipped through the skies at Kitty Hawk; Henry Ford's Model T, "stronger than a horse and easier to maintain," zoomed through the streets; Frederick Cook's dogsleds plowed through the Arctic ice to reach the North Pole; Howard Hughes's drilling bit bore deep into rocks to release petroleum; and every day people snapped one another's pictures with Eastman Kodak's Brownie, danced at home to music on Edison's phonograph, and vacuumed their rugs with a Hoover.

If the United States was flying high, New York was soaring in superlatives. The twenty-five-story New York Times Tower reigned over triangular Times Square; downtown the forty-five-story Singer Building scraped the sky; and in Madison Square, the Metropolitan Life building ascended higher than any other edifice in the world. At night the lights in the granite buildings glittered like Christmas trees in the dark. In the daytime uniformed men in their lobbies stood ready to swoop the workers up in elevators and discharge them onto their floors. And the workforce rode the longest subway system in the world, rumbling underground or hurtling along on elevated tracks. Not only the subway linked Manhattan to the surrounding parts: beneath the East River, the Battery Tunnel opened the way to Brooklyn; the Williamsburg and Manhattan bridges spanned above; the Queensboro Bridge stretched to its namesake; and a brand-new tunnel connected New York to New Jersey.

Manhattan bubbled over with wealth and possessions. Imposing mansions filled with fine furnishings lined Fifth Avenue. Elegant ladies wrapped in furs stepped into brightly colored Buicks that raced like thoroughbreds through Central Park. Flags flew from the buildings, flanks of pedestrians charged through the streets, and fashionable homes proudly showed off the scenes painted by Childe Hassam. Henry James was entranced by "the extent, the ease, the energy." H. G. Wells extolled the "lively air, gigantic buildings, incessant movement, sporadic elegance." Another English author thrilled to the city's feel: "I have driven rapidly in a fast car clinging to my hat and my hair against the New York wind from one end of Fifth Avenue to the other, and what with the sunshine, and the flags wildly waving in the sunshine, and the blue sky and the cornices cutting into it, and the roofs scraping it, and the large whiteness of the stores, and the invitation of the signs, and the display of the windows, and the swift sinuousness of the other cars and the proud opposing processions of American subjects," said Arnold Bennett, "I have been positively intoxicated!"

The United States boasted the highest per capita income in the world. Two percent of the people owned 60 percent of the wealth—highly skewed toward the top but not nearly as bad as a century later, when 1 percent of the people would own 90 percent of the wealth. In New York, where people of lesser means still suffered the loss of jobs, the princes of privilege recovered swiftly from the financial crisis, and prosperous men clutched wads of money as fondly as they clasped their mistresses' breasts. At Delmonico's and Sherry's, at the Waldorf-Astoria, the Hotel Astor, the Hotel Knickerbocker, and the brand-new Plaza Hotel, society feasted its way through the season. With more than 150 functions in the Waldorf's grand ballroom alone, and thousands more in the other hotels, the maître d's of the city's top dining spots declared it a record year: their patrons spent $1 million on dinner parties in 1908. From a dinner at the Knickerbocker that featured a duck pond with live ducks to the dinner for the Duchess of Marlborough complete with a rose garden, and rosebushes running the length of the tables, hosts and hostesses outdid one another with extravagant decorations, expensive entertainment, exotic food, and rare wines.

As for the former Consuelo Vanderbilt, now a duchess, or her cousin Gladys Vanderbilt, soon to be married to a Hungarian count, their titles meant little to Hetty. She dismissed them like cheap perfume: "I am glad Miss Gladys Vanderbilt is not my daughter. Girls who go to Europe to get their husbands deserve what they get and more. If my son married a foreign woman because the union would bring him a title, I would disown him," she declared. "The mother who will pay a million pounds for a title for her daughter should not expect to get a son-in-law of any account. Further, the woman who pays a million pounds for a son-in-law should have a guardian appointed to care for her."

Hetty's attitude may not have surprised those who knew her, but the note about her in *Town Topics* took the public aback. On February 27, 1908, society's favorite rag ran its scoop: Countess Leary and Mrs. Hetty Green, it said, "have managed one of the greatest matrimonial engagements of the decade." After successive failures at arranging a marriage for the spinsterly Sylvie, who stood timidly in her mother's shadow, the gossip sheet congratulated Annie Leary for introducing the new couple and proclaimed Sylvia Green, age thirty-seven, and Matthew Astor Wilks, age fifty-six, to be engaged.

"Despite Miss Green's lack of modern proclivities in her indifference to week-end parties, bridge, and cigarettes," said *Town Topics*, she had the "proper appreciation of her family's ramifications" in the choosing of a husband. As for her lover, it approved: "Though Mr. Wilks is no longer in the first blush of adolescence, he is still very nimble on his legs, and able to hold up a figure in a cotillion with many of the men not half his age."

Matthew Astor Wilks, great-grandson of John Jacob Astor and longtime bachelor, was shy in the eyes of some, but "suave of manner with a store of small talk that enables him to bewitch many from more ambitious places than Hoboken," said the paper. A scion of a real estate family with an eponymous building on Wall Street, he maintained his own house on Madison Avenue, was well known in New York and Newport, and belonged to all the right clubs. He was a Patriarch; an officer of the Knickerbocker; a member of the Union Club, the Metropolitan Club, Turf and Field, Fencers, Badminton, and the New York Yacht Club; and a long-standing member of the New York Society Library, where every Christmas he gave the librarian a pair of gloves. He was a friend of the late Arthur Leary, a guest at fashionable dinners and balls, and had often dined at Annie Leary's home. He had been acquainted with Ned and Sylvie for years. And one night in Newport, Sylvie told her friend Mamie Bolles, she and Matthew took a walk in the moonlight through the Trinity Churchyard. The two, who had circled each other for years, were now entwined. But when asked about the story, all involved denied it.

Astors, Goulds, Vanderbilts, and other prominent members of New York society were among the first to entertain at the new Plaza Hotel or to ensconce themselves in its suites. Mrs. Waldorf Astor hosted lavish dinners; Alfred Gwynne Vanderbilt was the first to sign the hotel's register; George Jay Gould resided there with his family; and Diamond Jim Brady lived in the hotel with Lillian Russell. But of all the rich who stayed at the Plaza, no one ever dreamed that Hetty Green would be in their midst.

The French Renaissance fortress, with dormers, gables, turrets, and towers, was drenched in old-fashioned elegance and modern luxury. The $12 million palace on the park featured a vast restaurant and summer dining room facing Fifth Avenue where guests drank their wine from Baccarat crystal and ate their food off china crested in gold. Ladies nibbled cucumber sandwiches and sipped their afternoon tea in the Tiffany-skylighted tearoom; men drank stronger stuff in the oak-paneled bar; couples danced in the white and gold wedding-cake ballroom; and all could speculate with their money in the six branches of stock brokerage firms on the first floor. Financed in large part by the Wall Street gambler John Gates, managed by Fred Sterry, the country's best hotelier, it was the most sumptuous lodge in America.

On May 1, 1908, Hetty Green had arrived at the Plaza. She had come, at Annie Leary's urging, to reassure Matthew Astor Wilks—to

enhance Sylvie's standing, to pay her daughter's social debts, to entertain the couple's friends, to prove her own worth. She may have lived
in a Hoboken flat, but she was the Queen of Wall Street.

Accompanied by her daughter and maid, with the aid of a uniformed footman, she emerged from a cab at the hotel's columned
entrance and stepped inside. Welcomed by gold-braided doormen, she
swirled through the revolving doors, rushed across the Oriental rugs,
and, after registering at the desk, was sped by the elevator boy in a
bronze-doored lift to her suite on the second floor. Several rooms with
views of the park were fitted with plush furnishings to sit on, Irish
linens to sleep on, marble baths to bathe in, telephones in every room,
and buzzers to summon waiters and maids. What do all these people
do? she wanted to know when she saw the size of the staff.

The surprises just kept coming. "A woman has failed to do her
duty to humanity when she fails to be attractive," proclaimed *Good
Housekeeping* magazine. Readers regularly found their pages filled
with tips such as standing for twenty minutes after meals to aid diges-
tion and prevent the flesh from settling around the waist. Newspaper
ads promoted plastic surgery, beauty potions, and other cures. But no
one expected the headline "Hetty Green Taking Beauty Treatments,"
which appeared in the *New York Times*.

Walking across Fifth Avenue soon after her arrival at the Plaza,
wearing a black wool dress and modest hat, Hetty entered the well-
known world of Madame LeClair. "What do you do here?" she asked
as she peered inside the mecca of beauty. A young woman escorted her
into a drawing room and showed her to a seat. Among potted palms on
pedestals and green silk walls filled with portraits of pretty women, the
beautician assured her of the artful ways of Madame LeClair. Peeling
away the layers, they could erase her wrinkles and reinstate her youth.
Hetty wanted to know the price. A series of sessions would cost her
$300. Undaunted, she demanded to know what the regime entailed.
Informed of the wondrous results of miraculous potions, she declared
at last, "I think I'll try this treatment." With that, she reached under
her skirts, pulled out a thick wad of bills, and announced, "I'll pay for
this now." Asked her name and address, she identified herself as Mrs.
Green and gave her residence as the Plaza.

With that she was led from the reception area to a private room in the rear. Wrapped in a dustcoat and reclined in a chair, she succumbed to the magical hands of the cosmetician. Steam puffed onto her face and perspiration saturated her skin as the hot air opened her pores. Next, thick layers of black unguent were smoothed on and left for twenty minutes to do their work. Ordered to abandon her thoughts, she lay in the chair and tried to relax as much as she could. When at last the mud was removed and her skin refreshed with scented oils, she was allowed to look in the mirror. Pleased enough with the results, Hetty returned five more times to the salon.

The rejuvenated Hetty showed herself off at a series of small dinners; toward the end of May, she entertained on a grand scale in her suite. She invited friends to dine on Tuesday, May 26, 1908, in the Plaza's state apartments. That evening, dressed in a fashionable directoire gown of black satin trimmed with lace, but no jewels, her hair newly thickened and coiffed in a modish manner, her skin gleaming, she took her place to receive her guests in the green and gold suite. Sylvie, dressed in gray with a string of pearls, stood beside her.

Promptly at 7:30, the guests arrived, dropped off their wraps in the dressing rooms, straightened their clothes, smoothed their hair, and entered the drawing room. In the swirl of frescoed panels and Louis XVI furnishings, they spoke with their hosts, sipped their drinks, and chatted. One of the men gushed over the transformed Hetty: "You resemble an eighteenth century Marquise," he said, to his hostess's delight.

Hetty led the guests into the Louis XIV dining room. Embossed cards filled out in her own hand marked their places. Their names a roster of society, their fortunes rooted in finance, real estate, and railroads, they included Mr. and Mrs. Howland Pell; Mr. and Mrs. Amory Carhart; Rear Admiral and Mrs. George Ide; Mr. and Mrs. Philip Livingston; Mr. and Mrs. A. F. Eno; and Annie Leary. The array of young heirs and heiresses included Miss Louise Hoyt, Miss Margaret Waldo, Miss Ruth Lawrence, Mr. Shipley Jones, Mr. Stephen Pell, and Mr. Matthew Astor Wilkes.

The Plaza's gold service glittered, its crystal sparkled, its silver shone on the hotel's crisp damask cloths. The hostess had gone all out: asparagus at sixty cents a plate, a ten-course feast, and three kinds of wine. After partaking of the soup, the fish, the meat, and the fowl and conversing with their chosen partners on the left and the right, and having swallowed the last bite of dessert, at 10 p.m. the guests left. Slipping their place cards into their pockets, they savored the proof that anything, indeed everything, was possible.

"Dinner was said to have cost $200 a plate," declared the *Washington Herald*. The story appeared in newspapers from New York to New Zealand. Hundreds of letters poured in, most of them pleading for money, but Hetty pushed them aside. Instead, she hired a clipping service and a secretary to paste the articles into a scrapbook: at a nickel apiece, one newspaper estimated, it was costing her a thousand dollars a month.

After almost six weeks at the Plaza, on June 12, 1908, she paid her bill and left. She returned to the boardinghouse on Madison Avenue where she and Sylvie had stayed the year before, where well-respected guests dwelled in comfortable rooms and dined on comforting food. George, the black man in the starched white jacket who stood at the door, smiled and welcomed her back. She was always generous, he told a reporter, tipping the maid two dollars and often giving him a coin or two. The location, in walking distance of Matthew Wilks's house, was convenient, the two rooms fine, but when hot weather arrived, the women left for Newport and later headed for Bellows Falls; by October they were on their way back to a flat in Hoboken.

Hetty was tired of living in hotels, she said, hounded by people begging for money, accosted by men with business ventures or philanthropy schemes. "I'm back, Twink," she told the janitor of her old building on Washington Street, "and I'm mighty glad to be back. I want my old flat. When can I move in?" To her terrible disappointment he informed her that two women had taken the apartment; Hoboken, thanks to her, had become a popular place to live. Despite her offers to pay $100 for the key, Twink could not help. Instead, she took an apartment around the corner on Bloomfield Street.

She returned to her old routine. But instead of the Chemical Bank, she had moved to the National Park bank and set up her office next to that of Stuyvesant Fish, former head of the Illinois Central Railroad and an officer of the bank. Asked why she had changed venues, she accused her old allies of trying to poison her. She had been at the Chemical, she said, to collect nearly $4 million due her, and after she signed some papers she stayed for lunch. "There were a dozen others at the table, set in the directors' room, and the funniest thing was that there was no one else but me taken sick. I thought I was going to die," she disclosed. The doctor said it may have been ptomaine poisoning, or, as her son suggested when he came up to visit, indigestion. Nonetheless, she collected her money and left. The fear of being poisoned plagued her all her life.

For several months rumors of Sylvie and Matthew continued to swirl, but no reliable news was released. Except for the passing of Mrs. Caroline Astor, marking the end of an era, and the noting of Matthew Astor Wilks as one of the pallbearers at her funeral, the couple's names did not appear in the papers—until Matthew's sister broke the silence.

"Mrs. Hetty Green, New York, announces the engagement of her only daughter, Miss Sylvia, to Matthew Astor Wilks of New York, eldest son of the late Matthew Wilks of Cruickston Park, Galt, Ontario," declared newspapers around the world.

The announcement, made on February 12, 1909, by Katherine Wilks, who lived on the family's estate in Canada, was simply not true, said Hetty; she had not even given her approval. But the word was out: Matthew Astor Wilks had given Sylvia Green a solitaire diamond ring, and the wedding would be in June. When Hetty was questioned, she shook her head with vigor; but in a moment of weakness, she slipped and said she and Sylvia were busy at home sewing clothes.

The soap opera continued. Reporters stalked the neighborhood, hoping to catch Hetty and toss her a question. But she knew how to dodge the press: she slipped out of basement doors and scurried through alleys, while Sylvie wore a disguise when she went out to walk the dog. The neighbors kept watch through the peepholes. Several times Matthew Wilks appeared in the vestibule and waited for Sylvie to come down; the two often stayed there and chatted.

In the mornings when the housewives compared notes, calling out through the building's dumbwaiter from one floor to another, Hetty heard them and sometimes joined in. When were they getting married? the women asked. Where would the wedding be? Who would be invited? Knowing the press had offered the neighbors money for their news, Hetty had a laugh: "Mind you, although I say I'd like to kill all reporters, I wouldn't murder them. But oh! I would like to pull their hair a little bit now," she divulged, and was duly quoted in the papers.

A few days later it was learned that Matthew and Hetty had had a meeting at the Chemical Bank. Unbeknownst to the outside world, a prenuptial agreement had been arranged. When the question was asked once more, "When will they be married?" Hetty repeated the words with a chuckle. Finally she gave an answer: "Now, I will tell you a secret," she said. "You mustn't breathe it to a soul." The week before, she revealed, she and Sylvie and Mr. Wilks had gone over to Morristown and had the wedding. She described the event and the cake and exclaimed: "My, but Sylvie looked fine in her new gown! But," she reported, "she's caught a dreadful cold wearing it."

The neighbors spread the story like busy bees. More reporters swarmed the house and police were called to stand guard. On February 23, 1909, at 9 a.m., a cab arrived in front of the building on Bloomfield Street. Hetty, Sylvie, and a female friend rushed down to the cab and hopped in; reporters quickly followed their trail. Twenty minutes later the threesome arrived at the Delaware, Lackawanna & Western Railroad station and, with a dash for the platform, joined friends who were already waiting on the Ivorydale, a private Pullman attached to a regular train. When they emerged at Morristown they rode by carriage to the local inn. At noon the group, including Matthew Astor Wilks, was driven to St. Peter's Episcopal Church.

The small party of family and friends, including Matthew's sisters and brother, but lacking Sylvia's brother Ned, scarcely filled the front rows of the church. A flock of reporters and curious townsfolk crammed the rear. The organ rumbled, heads turned, and, escorted by Howland Pell, the bride appeared. Sylvie, thirty-eight, tall and stout, wearing a brown dress and huge white feather boa, and a large white hat and veil, made her way down the aisle. The mustachioed groom, fifty-seven, in a dark vested suit, stood at the altar with his best man and the priest. After Reverend Sturges said the appropriate words and pronounced the couple man and wife, the stodgy pair marched off to the carriages and rode to the Morristown Inn.

A wedding brunch welcomed the two dozen guests. The menu, printed in French, included filet de boeuf and pigeons grille, and champagne from Moët et Chandon. After the toasts the couple posed for pictures on the porch of the hotel: the balding Matty stood stiffly between his bride and her mother; a frowning Hetty, formidable in a black silk gown covered with white lace, was seated on his right, while Sylvie, smiling slightly, bespectacled, and clutching a big bouquet, sat on his left.

The following day the official announcement appeared:

"Wilks-Green On Tuesday, February 23 at St. Paul's Church, Morristown N.J. by the Reverend Sturges, D.D., Sylvia Howland, daughter of the late Edward H. and Hetty Robinson Green, to Matthew Astor Wilks."

Mrs. Green, said the *New York Times*, "seemed in excellent spirits." After so many tries and disappointments, Sylvie had married an acceptable man. Asked if she approved of the marriage, Hetty replied, "I am happy if my daughter is happy."

Chapter 22

═══

Home

etty Green wasn't happy. The daughter she had glued to her side for so many years had finally come unstuck. The marriage that marked the start of a new life for Sylvie marked the start of the end for Hetty. Her health declined; her spirits dropped; her drive decreased. She bit her lip and did the best she could.

When Sylvie and Matty came back from their honeymoon to live in his house on Madison Avenue, Hetty took a room close by. She stayed first at the Plaza, then around the corner from the couple, at the St. Regis. But as much as she yearned to be near her daughter, hotel life felt wrong. She returned with her dog to Hoboken, glad to be back with her friends. She still commuted by ferry to Wall Street, and still made loans at favorable rates. At the end of the year she was lending New York much of the money it needed at below the market cost. And she was generous to Annie Leary: in March 1910 it was reported she was donating half a million dollars to help her build an art school on Fifth Avenue near the Metropolitan Museum. When asked, Annie Leary's lawyer revealed that an anonymous donor had given the land. But neither woman divulged any news. What's more, rumors spread that all was not well, that Hetty was ill.

Come to New York, she wrote to her son. She needed his help. Ned, dubbed a Texas Colonel by the new Democratic governor, arrived in his private railroad car. "I just dropped everything in Texas, when mother wrote for me to come and relieve her of some of her financial cares," he told reporters at the Waldorf-Astoria Hotel. Denying stories she had been seriously ill, he said she had just been out for a ride in his automobile.

In truth, wistful over the loss of her husband, alienated by the distance of her son, alone after the marriage of her daughter, and, most recently, despondent over the death of her beloved dog, Hetty was weighed down with grief. Nonetheless, as Ned had promised, she was on the mend. By summer 1910 she was off to Bellows Falls, spending the days at Tucker House and the nights at the home of her friend Mrs. Herbert Bancroft. In August she was out and about in Newport, shuttling between the houses of her daughter and Annie Leary.

She seemed to have regained her full strength. And the *Times* declared a few months later that Hetty Green had given the lowest-rate loan in many months on a mortgage in New York City. She offered the money to the Church of St. Ignatius Loyola—the place, the paper neglected to mention, where Annie Leary went to pray. But Hetty was executing far fewer deals than before. Although no one may have been surprised at news the following spring concerning the sale of some land in Chicago for five times what she had paid, the story came with a twist. "Million for Hetty Green," the headline said. The arrangement had been made, not by Hetty, but by her son. "Colonel Green is now in complete control of all his mother's vast interests," said one of the men involved in the sale.

Ned left behind his new Wright Brothers flying machine and brought his secretary, Walter Marshall, his parrot, Toper, and his Pierce Arrow car up from Texas. He moved with his girlfriend, Mabel, to the Waldorf-Astoria Hotel and kept her away from Hetty. He managed the deals for his mother, negotiating the loans in real estate, collecting the interest on her holdings, seeking opportunities to buy and sell. And while he did all that, she handed out a list of "Don'ts":

Don't cheat in our business dealings, for sooner or later your conscience will trouble you and you will worry yourself into your grave.
Don't fail to be fair in all things, business and otherwise, and don't kick a man when he is down.
Don't envy your neighbors.
Don't overdress, whether you have the means or not, causing envy.

Don't fail to go to church for the church needs you and you need
   the church.
Don't forget that riches dishonorably gained must be left behind
   some day, and when you depart you will find the gates of heaven
   doubly bolted against you.
Don't forget to be charitable, and don't falsify.
Don't forget to obey the laws of God for they were the first laws.
   By so doing you will as God wishes you to, giving unto Caesar
   that which is Caesar's and unto God that which is God's.

For years Hetty boasted her healthy habits would help her live
to be eighty-five. Now, at seventy-seven, her heart was weak and a
hernia she had had for years was making her wince. She wrapped herself in anonymity, put on a faded old dress, and went to see a doctor.
He advised the impoverished woman that an immediate operation was
needed; she shuddered when he told her the cost. "You're all alike.
You're just a bunch of robbers," she said. Instead, she took the stick
she had used for years to press against the swelling and put it back
inside her underwear to keep it in place. Some weeks later at a party at
Annie Leary's, the same physician noticed the elegant woman in the
fine-looking dress.

The pain had diminished but the threat of mortality increased. She
asked Ned to send for their lawyer in Texas, and in her son's elaborate
suite at the Waldorf, she and Mr. Ogden spent several days drawing
up her will. Aside from a few thousand dollars she left as "tokens of
esteem"—to Amory Lawrence, a banker friend from Boston; Mrs.
Herbert Bancroft, her friend from Bellows Falls; Miss Ruth Lawrence,
a longtime friend in New York; and Matthew Astor Wilks, her son-
in-law, who had relinquished rights to his wife's estate—Hetty left all
her money, jewelry, property, paintings, and personal effects to her
children, including a ten-year trust for Sylvia. The trust fund would
be overseen by her son, the income would go to her daughter, and after
ten years they would divide the principal.

The $5 million trust included bonds in the Main Line Houston and
Texas Central Railroad, the Great Northern Railroad, and New York
City, and a mortgage on property at 572 Fifth Avenue. True to her-

self, she left no money to charity; her children would do that in years to come. Worried the public might learn the details, she insisted on signing the papers in Hoboken. She put on a proper dress, fixed her hair, filled a bowl with sugar cookies, and invited her friends James Smith, the neighborhood butcher, and his brother Michael, the city treasurer, to serve as witnesses in her flat.

Stories of Hetty changed from tales of financial hell-raising to snippets of fashion tastemaking. When an acquaintance, Mrs. George Kemp, held a hat-trimming contest for a children's charity, Hetty snubbed her nose at the fussy styles. "I like simple hats for children," she said. "I wouldn't like to send children out into the streets with all those filigree things on them."

Still, she was not averse to something pretty. When Mrs. Kemp showed her some pearls being sold for a raffle, Hetty took a second look at the fakes. "I must have those pearls, although it would not do for me to wear anything imitation," she confessed. After a moment thinking it over, she said: "But they are going so cheap. Please hand me the raffle book. I will take two chances."

In an interview with a female reporter, she talked about her clothes: "This hat," she pointed out, "isn't in style. I've worn it for nearly ten years and it's going to do ten more years' service. I'm too old a lady to care about clothes. You know," she said, explaining her priorities, "when it comes to spending your life, there have to be some things neglected. If you try to do too much, you can never get anywhere. As I was naturally made for work, I just as naturally wasn't made for a fashion plate. I have never bothered about what to wear." But, she confessed, "I like to see what other people are wearing. It does me good sometimes and gives me a laugh."

She dismissed the notion of fashion but had a sentimental need to keep the effects of her youth. She stored them in a wooden loft on Broad Street: like so many of her holdings, run-down and neglected, she left the building unimproved to avoid paying property taxes. Up the rickety flights of stairs she climbed with Walter Marshall to the sixth floor. In a dirty, dusty, airless room she kept locked, she showed her secretary the remembrances of her past: the white muslin dress and pink sash she had worn to the ball for the Prince of Wales; dancing shoes, ballet programs, opera tickets, jewelry, and photographs of herself as a girl, all tucked away. "People said I was good looking then," Hetty recalled as she riffled through the boxes.

An old sleigh with a buffalo robe thrown inside sat on one side of the room. "That sleigh was my father's," she explained. "I used to ride with him behind a black horse that beat anything on hoofs in New Bedford. Black Hawk Robinson's daughter was the envy of all the other girls in town." She found a daguerreotype of her father that displayed his sharp eyes and determined jaw. Her face turned pale. "He was murdered, Marshall," she said as she lowered her voice. "As sure as you were born. With poison. He told me so on his deathbed. And so was my Aunt Sylvia. It was all part of a conspiracy to get their money and cheat me out of it. They intended to kill me, too, but I fooled 'em."

Her fear of being killed was heightened by the real death threats and blackmail notes she received in the mail. An attempted murder of Russell Sage years before, the assassination of President McKinley, and an attempt to assassinate Teddy Roosevelt increased her fears. Scary incidents, her son said, kept her up at night and drove her to live under assumed names. True or imagined, she claimed she found ground glass in her coffee when she was living on Pierrepont Street; that burglars had tried to enter a house she had rented in Hempstead; that strangers were following her in New Bedford; that a fallen brick from a building in downtown New York had been deliberately dropped on her; that her dog had been poisoned; that a train she was on had been sabotaged.

She was even suspicious of the call for women to vote; she had no use for the suffragists. The president of the National American Woman Suffrage Association announced the presidential Cabinet of her dreams: Jane Addams as secretary of state and Hetty Green as treasurer. Said Hetty, without explanation: "I don't believe in suffrage, and I haven't any respect for women who dabble in such trash." Later, Ned told the *Dallas Times Herald* that although he approved of women's suffrage, he was wary of making it universal: "If our wives and sisters and mothers vote we can easily trust them with the ballot," he said. But big cities, like Chicago, Pittsburgh, and New York, populated with "foreign and unintelligent women," as well as "occupants of the underworld," made the situation untenable. "There must ultimately be someone there to control this class of people." However, he added, "in cities the size of Dallas, and in all rural sections of the nation, woman suffrage would be safe."

Hetty felt safe with Ned. At nearly seventy-eight, she placed her holdings in a joint trust with her son and agreed to move their offices to the Trinity Building on lower Broadway. On a Saturday afternoon in July 1912, at their new Westminster Company, she straightened her papers and rose from her desk. Together with her son and the Reverend Augustine Elmendorf, she left the office and rode in a chauffeured limousine to Jersey City. For five or six years, her husband's nephew said, he had been trying to get her attuned to a more spiritual life. At the Holy Cross Episcopal Church, with no one else as witness, the woman so proud of her Quaker heritage was baptized. Her confirmation in her husband's Episcopal church would allow her to be buried beside him.

For the moment, she had no intention of joining him. On the eve of her birthday that November, she sat in her office and spoke with a reporter. Her mouth was full and odorous, and she apologized for the smell. "Pardon this onion I'm chewing," she said, "but it's the finest thing in the world for health. Perhaps that's why I live so long. I had a big tenderloin steak for breakfast, with fried potatoes, a pot of tea, and the top of a bottle of milk." Questioned about her rosy cheeks, she answered angrily, "That's not rouge and don't you think so for a minute. That's because I always chew a baked onion." When the writer asked if anything else helped her maintain her health, she replied, "Well, I walk all I can."

She continued to walk to work for several more years, holding on to the myth that she was in charge. Birthdays took on more significance, and instead of brushing them aside as she had in the past, she savored them with her children. Asked a year or two earlier if she planned to celebrate by taking time off, she exclaimed, "What! Waste a whole day? I guess not. I'll be in my office before 10 o'clock tomorrow morning, and I shall remain there until 4 o'clock."

But on her eightieth birthday she breakfasted with Ned and told him, "Colonel, you will have to look after everything today. I'm going to have a real holiday. My friends are to give me a birthday party.

Maybe," she teased, "the girls will let you attend when you come uptown." Lighthearted, she went for her morning walk, hosted some friends at Ned's place, motored with Annie Leary in Ned's limousine, and lunched with friends at Annie's Fifth Avenue house.

As Hetty celebrated her birthday in November, Americans played their phonographs and danced to Irving Berlin's new ragtime song, "Society Bear": "Millionaires, so the papers tell / learned a dance we all know well. . . . / Doing that Society Bear / Hetty Green and Rockefeller / Threw their shoulders up in the air / Rocking like a big propeller . . . / It's a bear, it's a bear."

Not everyone was making merry. The sinking of the Cunard line's *Lusitania* by German torpedoes earlier that year brought shivers down America's spine. Alfred Gwynne Vanderbilt, son of the Commodore, was among the 130 Americans killed on board. In Europe, the German attacks on Russia and France and their invasion of neutral Belgium shrouded the continent in war. "The lamps are going out all over Europe; we shall not see them lit again in our lifetime," said the British foreign minister Sir Edward Grey.

The fighting in Ypres that November marked the start of the four years of trench warfare that would keep them in the dark. The following year, as the Great War in Europe worsened, Hetty bought a million dollars' worth of war bonds to support the Allies against the Central powers. She would have bought more if her enemy Joseph Choate were not spearheading the drive.

Strong-minded and stalwart, it was reported she showed "a firmness of carriage, a quickness of movement, a poise of the head and a flash of the eye that belie her age." She ferried from Hoboken, took the streetcar up Madison Avenue to Eighty-sixth Street, transferred to another car to Central Park West, and walked briskly up to Ned's to celebrate her eighty-first birthday. Afterward, she headed back to Sylvie's at Madison Avenue and Forty-ninth Street. Still "hale and hearty," she tried to continue working as Americans danced to a new tune, "At the Million Dollar Tango Ball": "Millionaires gave a tango ball / the other night at the Wall Street Hall / Hetty Green and old John D / Vanderbilt and Carnegie." But Hetty was slowing down. Ned moved her office to West Ninetieth Street in the brownstone next to his. Sylvie and Matthew bought a townhouse a few blocks away. Age was creeping up on their mother and her heart was grow-ing frail.

In April 1916, when reporters asked if she was ill, Ned assured them in his protective way that his mother had only caught a cold. In fact, after an argument with Annie Leary's cook, who drank a lit-tle too much for Hetty's liking, his mother had suffered a stroke. A series of smaller strokes left her paralyzed on one side. With Ned's help, Hetty spent her days in comfortable rooms in the brownstone on Ninetieth Street. The professional nurses he hired—he asked them to wear regular clothes so as not to upset his mother—wheeled her about. Sitting at the window, she watched life go by.

On better days she was lifted into Ned's limousine for a drive around the park. Her son insisted she was feisty as ever. Asked if she still concerned herself with business, he said with a laugh, "If you heard her put me over the jumps every day, you'd think so. She scolds me for the way I handle her affairs and says she surely made a mistake in my education or I would be doing things better." But the strokes had taken their toll.

Early in the morning of July 3, 1916, Ned and Sylvie were called to her bed. She was not worried, she had said; she had led a good, clean life. In the Quaker spirit, she added, "I do not know what the next world is, but I do know that a kindly light is leading me, and that I shall be happy after I leave here." With her children by her side, eighty-one-year-old Hetty bade farewell. Her body, placed in a plain coffin wrapped in a simple cloth, was put on a private train, and with her son and daughter, along with Matthew Wilks and Mrs. Bancroft to accompany her, she made her final trip to Bellows Falls.

The Texas Midland Railroad honored her with a five-minute rest. The town of Terrell stopped its business for an hour. Two hundred people turned out for her funeral in Vermont. Flowers poured in, pinned with cards from friends and business colleagues around the country. Headlines around the world told the tale: Hetty Green—the "Wizard of Finance," the "Feminine Croesus," the "Queen of Money," the "Richest Woman in America"—was dead.

A millionaire a hundred times over, she had made her mark beside Carnegie and Morgan, Vanderbilt and Rockefeller. But she was dif-ferent: she was a woman. She was an enigma, a blue-blooded heiress who identified with the common folk; an interloper, a female who triumphed in the male world of finance; an independent who answered to no one but herself; a renegade, a moneymaker who thumbed her nose at what money could buy; a pariah, like Ishmael, cast out in her youth. Now her family and friends in the pews of the Immanuel Church heard the organist play "There Is a Blessed Home." The woman who had wandered all her life from place to place could rest in peace. At long last, Hetty was home.

Epilogue

If a man had lived as did Mrs. Hetty Green," wrote the *New York Times,* "devoting the greater part of his time and mind to the increasing of an inherited fortune that even at the start was far larger than is needed for the satisfaction of all such human needs as money can satisfy, nobody would have seen him as very peculiar—as notably out of the common. He would have done about what is expected of the average man so circumstanced, and there would have been no difficulty in understanding the joys he obtained from participation in the grim conflicts of the higher finance."

"To the popular attention, she was 'the richest woman in the world' and nothing else," said the *Times.* "Yet it was known that the great experiences of wifehood and motherhood had been hers, and there were occasional rumors of kindly and generous acts. . . . Probably her life was happy. At any rate, she had enough of courage to live as she chose and to be as thrifty as she pleased, and she observed such of the world's conventions as seemed to her right and useful, coldly and calmly ignoring all the others."

Added the *New York Sun,* "Mrs. Green matched her wits with the sharpest and made her way. The magnitude of her interests, their situation in widely separated sections of the country, index her vigor, mental and physical. She contributed to the development of the country, a service not to be held 'in contempt.' "

. . .

Hundreds of people and dozens of individuals benefited from Hetty Green's wealth. Her estate had been clearly laid out before her death: The trust fund left by Aunt Sylvia, worth just over $1 million in 1916, was divided among hundreds of descendants of Gideon Howland; some received as much as one forty-fifth, others a minuscule one 8,640th. The rest of Hetty's money, the equivalent of some $2 billion today, was distributed as stipulated in her will: aside from the $25,000 to friends, it all went to her offspring.

With no heirs to inherit their money, the solid fortune that Hetty made was scattered like confetti in the wind. The bequests were as random as $10,000 to Robert Moses, in appreciation of his work creating public parkways, to $1.2 million to the church where Sylvia and Matthew were married; half a million dollars to the Boston Public Library, and gifts for the library in New Bedford; a new hospital in Bellows Falls; and donations to schools of higher learning, including Harvard, Vassar, Columbia, and Yale.

Hetty Green's money is long gone, and with it, her fame. What remains is her legacy: a woman who stood her ground, who defied the crowd and refused to follow its whims. Making her way in a hostile male world, she was never hesitant to look a man in the eye, never reluctant to say what she thought, never afraid to act as she saw fit.

Before deciding on an investment, seek out
every kind of information about it.

Watch your pennies and the dollars will take care of themselves.

After your business is over you may take your colleague to dinner
and the theater, or allow him to take you, but wait until the
transaction has been closed and the money paid.

Before making a deal, if anyone is fool enough to offer you the
full amount, take it. If you are offered less, tell the man
you will give him the answer in the morning.
Think the matter over carefully in the evening. If you decide that it
will be to your advantage to accept the offer, say so the next day.

In business generally, don't close a bargain until you have
reflected on it overnight.

The secret of good nursing is common sense, just as common sense
is the secret of making money.

What man has done, women can do.

❧

It is the duty of every woman to learn to take care of
her own business affairs.

❧

An ordinary gift to be bragged about is not a gift
in the eyes of the Lord.

❧

Some young women do better in business than men.

❧

A girl ought to be careful about the man she marries,
especially if she has money.

❧

A girl oughtn't to marry until she's old enough to
know what she's doing.

❧

When good things are so low that no one wants them, I buy
them and lay them away in the safe; when owing to some new
development, they go up and my shares are so needed that men
will pay well for them, I am ready to sell.

❧

I am always buying when everyone wants to sell,
and selling when everyone wants to buy.

❧

If one can buy a good thing at a lower cost than it has ever sold for
before, he may be fairly sure of getting it cheap.

❧

Every girl should be taught the ordinary lines of
business investment.

❧

Railroads and real estate are the things I like.
Government bonds are good, though they do not pay
very high interest. Still, for a woman safe and low
is better than risky and high.

～❧～

Common sense is the most valuable possession
anyone can have.

Acknowledgments
===

This book would never have been written without the suggestion of Susana Kraglievich. I am grateful to her and to Mahnaz Ispahan, Jane Geniesse, Mike Kandel, Barbara Bedell, Elaine Abelson, Lee Gruzen, and Michael Wallach for their enthusiasm and support from the beginning, and especially to Robert Menschel, whose continual encouragement and curiosity kept me going even when Hetty remained at her most elusive.

My thanks to the dedicated librarians and archivists around the country who dug through their collections for material: the staff of the New Bedford Free Public Library; Laura Peraira at the New Bedford Whaling Museum Research Library; Elaine Grubin at the Massachusetts Historical Society; reference librarian Emily Zervas and the staff at the Rockingham Free Public Library in Bellows Falls; James McCord at the Terrell Historical Society; Greg Ames of the Mercantile Library in St. Louis; the staff of the Morristown Library; Marsha Bissett and others at the Barnard Archives of Columbia University; the library staff at the New-York Historical Society; Kirsten Aguilera of the Museum of American Finance; Kristin McDonough, director of the SIBL branch of the New York Public Library, and the librarians of the NYPL; Patrice Kane of the Fordham University Archives; the librarians at the Tamiment Library of New York University and the Brooklyn Historical Society; and the staffs of the British Library and the British Newspaper Library in London. My enormous gratitude to Mark Bartlett, Carolyn Waters, and the incredible staff of the

New York Society Library. Thanks also to David Kelso of JPMorgan Chase, and to Ronay Menschel for her introduction to Sarah Henley at the Museum of the City of New York.

In Bellows Falls the spirited Shirley Capron put me in touch with Ann Fitzgerald, Arthur Bolles, Betty Johnson, Robert Adams, and others whose families had known Hetty Green. Ann Collins of Village Square Books, Michael Reynolds, and the clerks Brenda and Doreen at Town Hall were all helpful.

Many people informed me on different parts of Hetty's life: Llewyn Howland shed light on her Quaker background and how it affected her. Susan Yohn of Hofstra University gave me perspective on Hetty's importance as a woman and the price she paid for it. Dr. Mary Elizabeth Brown of Marymount helped with information on Annie Leary; Richard Sylla at New York University opened my eyes to *The Wizard of Oz*; John Steel Gordon helped with the Union Club and Wall Street; Maury Klein was informative on the Louisville and Nashville Railroad; Scott Reynolds Nelson at William and Mary College advised me on nineteenth-century finance; Melanie Gustafson at the University of Vermont made excellent suggestions on Hetty Green's childhood and her relationships; Andrew Ross Sorkin was enlightening on the contemporary financial panic.

My thanks to the autograph dealers and collectors Scott Winslow, Scott Trepel, David Beach, and Ron Terlizzi. Richard John at the Columbia Journalism School led me to valuable sources. Lavinia Briggs Abel, whose family were friends of Sylvia and Matthew Wilks, shed light on Hetty's children.

Credit goes to Carol Bundy, Alyson Greenfield, Alex Karp, and Susan Sawyers for their research assistance. Catherine Talese did great scouting for the photographs.

I am grateful to Lynn Nesbit for her encouragement in shepherding this project through. My appreciation for the work of all the staff at Doubleday. Ronit Feldman was incredibly patient with my endless questions and technology fears. Daniel Meyer was always ready to help. Nan Talese is an author's dream.

Notes

═══

CHAPTER 1: THE SPIRIT WITHIN

5 New Bedford, Massachusetts: Herman Melville, *Moby-Dick* (New York: Oxford University Press, 1998). Melville drew on his time in New Bedford to describe the narrator's experience as he waits for the *Pequod* to sail (chapters 1–7).

5 Along the bustling waterfront: For descriptions of the whaling industry in New Bedford, see Samuel Eliot Morison, *The Maritime History of Massachusetts, 1783–1860* (Cambridge: Riverside Press, 1923); Louis Menand, *The Metaphysical Club: A Story of Ideas in America* (New York: Farrar, Straus, and Giroux, 2001).

7 Everyone in New Bedford: For descriptions of the town and its inhabitants, see Daniel Ricketson, *The History of New Bedford, Bristol County* (New Bedford: published by the author, 1858); William Allen Wall, *New Bedford Fifty Years Ago* (New York: Charles Jabert, 1858); New Bedford Preservation Society archives; Charles T. Congdon, *Reminiscences of a Journalist* (Boston: J. R. Osgood, 1880).

8 Howland and Robinson families: Llewyn Howland offered insights into Hetty Green, her family, and the Quakers of New Bedford in a telephone interview with the author in 2009.

8 Almost everyone he dealt with: For an excellent account of New Bedford and its Quaker community, see Everett S. Allen, *Children of the Light: The Rise and Fall of New Bedford Whaling and the Death of the Arctic Fleet* (Hyannis, MA: Parnassus Imprints, 1973). The Old Sturbridge Village website describes the atmosphere at a Friends meeting, http://www.osv.org/explore_learn/document_list .php?A=LA&T=P.

CHAPTER 2: A POLISHED REFLECTION

12 As Hetty grew up: The following books offer many anecdotes about Sylvia Ann Howland and Hetty Robinson as well as sketches of the Howland and Robinson families: William M. Emery and William W. Crapo, *The Howland Heirs*

(Whitefish, MT: Kessinger Publishing, 2007); Robinson Genealogical Society, *The Robinsons and Their Kin Folk* (New York: Robinson Family Historical and Genealogical Association, 1902).

Testimony from the Howland Will trial, as well as the following books, includes detailed descriptions of Hetty's childhood. See *Hetty H. Robinson, in Equity, vs. Thomas Mandell et al.*, Circuit Court of the United States: Massachusetts District (Boston: Alfred Mudge & Son, 1867). Boyden Sparkes and Samuel Taylor Moore conducted numerous interviews for their book *Hetty Green: A Woman Who Loved Money* (Garden City: Doubleday, Doran, 1930), as did Arthur Lewis for *The Day They Shook the Plum Tree* (New York: Harcourt, Brace & World, 1963), but neither book cites sources. Charles Slack provides more updated information on her life in *Hetty* (New York: HarperCollins, 2004).

13 Quakers viewed anger: For explanations of the Quaker attitude and descriptions of New Englanders' emotions, see Hugh Barbour and Jerry Williams Frost, *The Quakers* (Westport, CT: Greenwood Press, 1988); Nicole Eustace, *Passion Is the Gale: Emotion, Power and the Coming of the American Revolution* (Chapel Hill, NC: University of North Carolina Press, 2008); Thomas Low Nichols, *Forty Years of American Life, 1821–1861* (London: Longsman, Green, 1874).

13 "Hetty, daughter": *Hetty Green: A Woman Who Loved Money* (Garden City: Doubleday, Doran, 1930).

13 Young Hetty's rage exploded: Charles Slack, *Hetty* (New York: HarperCollins, 2004), 15.

14 Round Hills: Barbara Bedell has a wonderful description of Round Hills in her book *Colonel Edward Howland Robinson Green* (self-published, 2003).

17 The one who gained: For good descriptions of Edward Mott Robinson, see John T. Flynn, *Men of Wealth* (New York: Simon & Schuster, 1941), chapter 6; *New Bedford and Fairhaven Directory*, 1918 (Boston: W. A. Greenough, 1909).

19 Anna Cabot Lowell: For a description of life at Anna Cabot Lowell's school, see Elizabeth Rogers Mason Cabot, *More Than Common Powers of Perception: The Diary of Elizabeth Rogers Mason Cabot*, ed. P. A. M. Taylor (Boston: Beacon Press, 1991).

19 their classmate who had gone home: Carol Bundy, *The Nature of Sacrifice* (New York: Farrar, Straus & Giroux, 2005), chapter 3.

20 her reply to an invitation: Hetty Green's Manuscript Book included letters pertaining to her social life. Quotes from the letters are courtesy of its current owner, David M. Beach.

20 "A woman, old or young": Mrs. Burton Harrison, *The Well-Bred Girl in Society* (Philadelphia: Curtis Publishing Company, 1905).

CHAPTER 3: A CITY OF RICHES

22 Walt Whitman's beloved city: Whitman was born on Long Island and educated in Brooklyn. He wrote for several local newspapers and worked for two years as editor of the *Brooklyn Eagle*.

23 The city founders: For descriptions of New York in the mid-nineteenth century, see Isabella Bird, *The Englishwoman in America* (1856; repr., Whitefish, MT: Kessinger Publishing, 2004); Fredrika Bremer, *The Homes of the New World: Impressions of America* (New York: Harper, 1853); and *America of the Fifties: Letters of Fredrika Bremer* (New York: American-Scandinavian Foundation, 1924).

24 social rules: On social rules, New York society, and young women, see Maureen E. Montgomery, "The Female World of Ritual and Etiquette," *Displaying Women* (New York: Routledge, 1998). For more information on social rules, see Mabel Osgood Wright, *My New York* (Norwood, MA: Berwick & Smith, 1926); Mrs. Burton Harrison, *The Well-Bred Girl in Society* (Philadelphia: Curtis Publishing, 1898); Charles Astor Bristed, *The Upper Ten Thousand: Sketches of American Society* (London: J. W. Parker and Sons, 1852).

26 at the homes of friends: The description of the furnishings and daily routines is based on the Merchant House Museum, New York City.

28 Hostesses sent an endless stream: For an incomparable view of life among the upper crust of New York from 1820 to 1875, see Allan Nevins and Milton Halsey Thomas, eds., *The Diary of George Templeton Strong, 1835–1875* (New York: Macmillan, 1952). The diarist's notes cover everything from his role as a trustee of both Columbia University and the Philharmonic Orchestra to his work for the Sanitation Commission during the Civil War, to his disdain for some of his rich clients.

Edwin G. Burrows and Mike Wallace provide myriad details about New York City in *Gotham: A History of New York City to 1898* (New York: Oxford University Press, 2000), parts 4 and 5.

29 her husband's cousin Caroline: Eric Homberger, *Mrs. Astor's New York: Money and Power in a Gilded Age* (New Haven: Yale University Press, 2002), chapter 6; various *New York Times* articles from 1894 to 1914.

CHAPTER 4: AMERICA BOOMING

32 A fortunate few took trains: For excellent information on the railroads, see John F. Stover, *American Railroads* (Chicago: University of Chicago Press, 1997); Albro Martin, *Railroads Triumphant* (New York: Oxford University Press, 1992); Robert Selph Henry, *This Fascinating Railroad Business* (New York: Bobbs-Merrill, 1942); Jack Beatty, *Age of Betrayal* (New York: Knopf, 2007); Ron Chernow, *The House of Morgan* (New York: Grove Press, 1990).

36 Henry David Thoreau's Lyceum lecture: Henry David Thoreau, *Walden, or Life in the Woods* (New York: Heritage Club, 1939).

CHAPTER 5: IRRATIONAL EXUBERANCE

39 And then the bubble burst: For descriptions of the financial crisis, see James L. Huston, *The Panic of 1857 and the Coming of the Civil War* (Baton Rouge, LA: Louisiana State University Press, 1987); Robert Morris, *The Banks of New York,*

Their Dealers, the Clearinghouse, and the Panic of 1857 (New York: D. Appleton, 1859); Robert Sobel, *Panic on Wall Street* (Frederick, MD: Beard Books, 1999); Chernow, *House of Morgan*; Jean Strouse, *Morgan: American Financier* (New York: Harper Perennial, 2000).

42 "the most violent": Robert Morris and James Sloane Gibbons, *The Banks of New York* (New York: D. Appleton, 1859).

42 "all the bubble, blunders and dishonesties": Quoted in Sobel, *Panic on Wall Street*.

44 the South's slaves: *New York Times*, August 26, 2001.

48 organizing a ball: Descriptions of the Prince of Wales Ball taken from Lloyd Morris, *Incredible New York* (Syracuse University Press, 1996); Edward N. Tailer, diaries, October 6–7, 1858 (New-York Historical Society); Helen Lansing Grinnell diary, 1861 (New York Public Library); Maunsell B. Field, *Memories of Many Men & of Some Women* (New York: Harper & Brothers, 1874); Kate Simon, *Fifth Avenue: A Very Social History* (San Diego: Harcourt, 1979).

Chapter 6: A Willful War

50 But it was Lincoln's attitude: In reference to New York's connection to the Civil War, see Wallace and Burrows, *Gotham*; Thomas Kessner, *Capital City* (New York: Simon & Schuster, 2006); Sven Beckert, *The Monied Metropolis* (New York: Cambridge University Press, 2003).

51 plot to derail his train: *Harper's New Monthly*, June 1868.

52 he had become a partner: *New York Times*, July 1, 1860.

53 Sylvia had given her niece: Testimony from the Howland Will trial.

56 "Americans speak of a man": Nichols, *Forty Years of American Life*. In *Capital City*, Kessner quotes two other observers of New York: Anthony Trollope remarked, "Every man worships the dollar, and is down before his shrine from morning to night." The essayist James McCabe said, "Here, as in no other place in the country, men struggle for wealth. They toil, they suffer privations, they plan and scheme and execute with persistence that often wins the success they covet. . . . Elsewhere poverty was a misfortune; in New York, poverty was an enemy to be defeated."

60 "he dried snow in his oven": Mark Twain and Charles Dudley Warner, *The Gilded Age* (New York: Oxford University Press, 1996).

60 pledged $500 for Lincoln's reelection: Coleman's story about Robinson was reported in *Harper's Magazine*.

Chapter 7: A Will to Win

63 "He was the coolest man I ever saw": George Francis Train, *My Life in Many States and in Foreign Lands* (New York: Appleton, 1902).

63 "rather a pleasant place": E. H. Green to H. A. Wise, New-York Historical Society.

64 Edward Mott Robinson died rich: Description of Edward Mott Robinson's last will and testament, *New York Times,* October 19, 1865.

66 Standing alone in the parlor: C. W. de Lyon Nichols told the story of Hetty's return to New Bedford for Sylvia Ann's funeral in "Hetty Green: A Character Study," *Business America,* May 1913.

67 she was afraid to be alone: Leigh Mitchell Hodges, "The Richest Woman in America: Mrs. Hetty Green as She Is Seen in Her Home and in the Business World," *Ladies' Home Journal,* June 1900.

68 a landmark case: *Hetty H. Robinson, in Equity, vs. Thomas Mandell et al.* Circuit Court of the United States: Massachusetts District (Boston: Alfred Mudge & Son, Printers, 1867). The transcript of the entire Howland will trial is available online at Google Books.

71 "We've put a lot of money": Warren Buffet, annual letter to Berkshire Hathaway shareholders, as reported in the *New York Times,* February 27, 2010.

72 Dressed in a Victorian gown: Description of Hetty and Edward's wedding photograph, *Collier's* magazine, February 19, 1946.

CHAPTER 8: A NEW LIFE

74 boarded the steamship: Weekly transatlantic passenger lists, *New York Times* archives.

74 With the reliable Captain T. Cook: Descriptions of life on board can be found in Stephen Fox, *Transatlantic: Samuel Cunard, Isambard Brunel, and the Great Atlantic Steamships* (New York: HarperCollins, 2003).

77 During the Civil War: For the impact of the railroads, see Albra Martin, *Railroads Triumphant* (New York: Oxford University Press, 1992) and Bradley G. Lewis, *Railroads and the Character of America, 1820–1887* (Knoxville: University of Tennessee Press, 1986). For a history of the Louisville and Nashville and the people involved in the line, see Kincaid A. Herr, *The Louisville and Nashville Railroad, 1850–1963* (Lexington, KY: University Press of Kentucky, 2000), and Maury Klein, *History of the Louisville and Nashville Railroad* (Lexington, KY: University Press of Kentucky, 2003).

78 "a magic wand": John Roebling, *American Railroad Journal Extra: The Great Central Railroad from Philadelphia to St. Louis* (Philadelphia, 1847).

78 "As yet, no portion of the world": Henry Adams, *The Education of Henry Adams* (New York: Modern Library, 1931).

78 "Eureka!": Andrew Carnegie, *The Autobiography of Andrew Carnegie* (Boston: Northeastern University Press, 1986).

79 Abigail used her pin money: "Women of Wall Street" (exhibit), Museum of American Finance, New York, June 2009.

79 Opportunists in London: In a lengthy telephone interview with the author, Professor Scott Reynolds Nelson of the College of William and Mary explained the buying and selling of greenbacks.

80 The completion of the route: Nevins and Thomas, *Diary of George Templeton Strong*.

80 "Pittsburg Fort Wayne & Chicago Railroad": Letters courtesy of David Beach.

82 Hetty gave birth to a daughter: Census report for England, 1871, Westminster City archives, London.

85 Victoria Woodhull, a spiritualist: See Barbara Goldsmith, *Other Powers: The Age of Suffrage, Spiritualism and the Scandalous Victoria Woodhull* (New York: Knopf, 1998).

86 "Everybody seemed to be making money": James Ford Rhodes, *History of the United States from the Compromise of 1850* (New York: Harper, 1899).

87 Henry Bischoffsheim and E. H. Green: The *Times* of London ran articles referring to E. H. Green on September 13, 1869, December 1870, April 11, 1872, July 6, 1872, and July 10, 1872. See also the *New York Times*, March 12, 1872.

88 Europeans held 80 percent: Mira Williams, *The History of Foreign Investment in the U.S.* (Cambridge: Harvard University Press, 2004).

91 "The panic of 1873": The causes and effects of the financial panic in 1873 are described in Matthew Hale Smith, *Bulls and Bears of New York* (Hartford: J. B. Burr, 1875); Kessner, *Capital City*; Sobel, *Panic on Wall Street*. For a portrayal of life in the city before the crisis, see James McCabe Jr., *Lights and Shadows of New York Life* (New York: Farrar, Straus & Giroux, 1970), chapter 15, "Wall Street."

CHAPTER 9: RETURN TO AMERICA

94 "It takes a clear, cool head": McCabe, *Lights and Shadows*. McCabe wrote about New York in 1872: "All over the world to be poor is a misfortune. In New York it is a crime."

94 "If you had bought": *Harper's New Monthly*, vol. 48.

95 While government officials: Scott Nelson, historian and professor at William and Mary College, has written extensively about this period. For a description of the panic of 1873, see "The Real Great Depression," *Chronicle Review of Higher Education*, October 17, 2008.

96 Rich New Yorkers: For descriptions of the atmosphere on Wall Street, see *New York Times* City Room blog (http://cityroom.blogs.nytimes.com/); Nevins and Thomas, *Diary of George Templeton Strong*. On the causes of the crisis and the relationship between railroads and the financial markets, see James Rhode, *History of the United States* (London: Macmillan, 1920).

97   The town thrived: For descriptions of Bellows Falls, see Lyman Simpson Hayes, *History of the Town of Rockingham* (Bellows Falls, VT, 1907); Anne L. Collins, *Around Bellows Falls* (Charleston, SC: Arcadia Publishing, 2002); Blanche Adaline Webb, *A History of the Immanuel Church of Bellows Falls* (Bellows Falls, VT: Immanuel Church, 1953).

CHAPTER 10: A FORCEFUL WOMAN

103   Outdoors in the Central Park: Ishbel Ross, *Crusades and Crinolines* (New York: Harper & Row, 1963).

103   But when young Ned: There are various versions of what happened to Ned's leg, including stories in several newspapers and books and one in an unpublished book by John Nicholas Beffel and Walter Marshall (John Beffel Papers, Walter P. Reuther Library, Wayne State University).

105   the family traveled together: The *Chicago Tribune* reported the comings and goings of Hetty and Edward Green, and on the pillow fight.

CHAPTER 11: CHANGING TIMES

108   "Our country's prosperity": *USA Today*, March 25, 2010.

108   each decided on its own time: Concerning the confusion over time zones, see the following sources: Jackson Lears, *Rebirth of a Nation* (New York: Harper Perennial, 2010); Warren TenHouten, *Time and Society* (Albany: State University of New York Press, 2005); Patricia Murphy, *Time Is of the Essence* (Albany: State University of New York Press, 2001); Beatty, *Age of Betrayal*.

110   The railroads' dynamic potential: Describing the ups and downs of the railroad and the role of Edward H. Green: Kindcaid Herr, *The Louisville and Nashville Railroad* (Lexington, KY: University of Kentucky Press, 2000); Klein, *Louisville and Nashville Railroad*.

112   his reputation as a bachelor: The Beffel/Marshall Papers, John Beffel Papers, Wayne State University.

114   "Do you buy long or short?": Henry Watterson, *Marse Henry: An Autobiography* (New York: D. H. Doran, 1919), 208.

115   she demanded the house: For records of ownership, see Town Hall records, Bellows Falls.

CHAPTER 12: AGAINST THE TREND

119   Union Club: Descriptions of the Union Club taken from Greg King, *A Season of Splendor* (Hoboken, NJ: Wiley, 2008).

121   "They light up and tell me a story": "Women of Wall Street," Museum of American Finance, June 2009.

121 "I know of no profession": Lloyd R. Morris, *Incredible New York: High Life and Low Life from 1850 to 1950* (New York: Random House, 1951).

122 no one could outshine: Mrs. Astor's entertaining is well covered in Jerry Patterson, *The First Four Hundred* (New York: Rizzoli Press, 2000), and Homberger, *Mrs. Astor's New York.*

123 "The highest luxury": Henry James, *The American Scene* (1907; repr., New York: Penguin Classics, 1994).

123 "is not the place for a lady": Henry Clews, *Twenty-Eight Years in Wall Street* (New York: J. S. Ogilvie, 1901).

123 Instead, Hetty boarded: For information on boardinghouses, see Gunther Barth, *City People* (New York: Oxford University Press, 1982); Harriet Beecher Stowe, *We and Our Neighbors* (Buffalo, NY: J. B. Ford, 1875); Ross, *Crusades and Crinolines*; Wendy Gamber, *The Boarding House* (Baltimore: Johns Hopkins University Press, 2007).

124 a young woman defended her residence: *New York Times*, August 6, 1908.

128 "She went for him like a tigress": *New York Times*, July 1, 1888.

130 Hetty's choice of Brooklyn: Bremer, *Homes of the New World*; see also Bird, *Englishwoman in America.*

131 "a kind of sleeping place": John Forster, *The Life of Charles Dickens* (New York: Dutton, 1990).

133 modern billionaire Alice Walton: "Alice's Wonderland," *New Yorker*, June 20, 2011.

CHAPTER 13: THE EDUCATION OF CHILDREN

136 "interminable vistas": Rudyard Kipling, *American Notes* (New York: Brown, 1899).

136 Teasing and practical jokes: In a telephone interview in June 2011, Lavinia Abel told me about the family's love of teasing.

137 Relaxing in his office: Ned's grandiose plans were reported in the *New York Times*, the *New York Sun*, and the *Chicago Daily Tribune*, among other newspapers. Hetty's activities were frequently described in the *Chicago Herald* and *Chicago Daily Tribune*.

138 Not only was the city: Descriptions of Chicago in Lears, *Rebirth of a Nation*; Henry Smith, *Chicago's Great Century* (Chicago: Consolidated Publishers, 1933); Bessie Pierce, *As Others See Chicago* (Chicago: University of Chicago Press, 2004).

139 the town of Colehour: *Chicago Tribune*, December 31, 1890.

140 "Loans on Distressed Properties": *New York Times*, December 24, 2008.

141 "the Rome of the Great West": Lears, *Rebirth of a Nation*.

142 The fair brought to life: Alexis de Tocqueville, *Democracy in America* (New York: Harper & Row, 1966).

143 Like Henry James's character: *Washington Square* (Boston: G. K. Hall, 1980).

143 Witty or not: The duties of debutantes of the period are portrayed in Maureen Montgomery, *Displaying Women* (New York: Routledge, 1998).

144 The Patriarchs' Ball: A detailed description can be found in the *New York Times*, January 14, 1892.

144 "not unlike Dante's description of Paradise": Alexander Klein, *The Empire City: A Treasury of New York* (New York: Rinehart, 1955).

145 "the long cold agony": Edith Wharton, *A Backward Glance* (New York: Scribner, 1964), 78.

145 "If you die before the dinner": Ward McAllister, *Society as I Have Found It* (New York: Cassell, 1890).

145 August in Newport: Gail MacColl and Carol Wallace give a description of the daily routine in Newport in *To Marry an English Lord* (New York: Workman, 1989).

147 "I want to say": *New York Tribune*, December 31, 1894.

CHAPTER 14: TEXAS

149 wanted badly to outwit Huntington: Beffel/Marshall Papers, Wayne State University, describe Hetty Green's dealings with Collis Huntington and the Texas railroads as well as Ned Green's extensive activities in Texas.

153 "He is generous, though level-headed": *Dallas Morning News*, October 17, 1897. The Dallas newspapers reported continuously on the activities of Ned Green.

CHAPTER 15: THE GLITTER OF GOLD

155 "mortgaged to the railways": *The Education of Henry Adams* (New York: Modern Library, 1931).

156 With not enough gold: For descriptions of the financial panic of 1893, see Matthew Josephson, *The Robber Barons* (New York: Mariner Books, 1962); Jett Lauck, *The Causes of the Panic of 1893* (Boston: Mifflin, 1907); Kessner, *Capital City*; Douglas Steeples, *Democracy in Desperation* (New York: Greenwood Press, 1998); Alexander Noyes, *Forty Years of American Finance* (New York: Ayer, 1980); Beatty, *Age of Betrayal*; Thomas Kane, *The Romance and Tragedy of Banking* (Boston: Bankers Publishing, 1922).

156 The rich still imported: In *The Theory of the Leisure Class* (New York: B. W. Huebsch, 1912), Thorstein Veblen explores the need of the rich to spend money.

156 "Everyone is in a blue fit": *Education of Henry Adams*.

157 Referring to 2008: Conversation with Andrew Ross Sorkin, August 2011, Easthampton, NY.

158 sold to a former adviser: *Brooklyn Eagle*, August 1896.

158 "Ex Judge Hilton": *New York Times*, August 27, 1896.

159 an adult allegory: Hugh Rockoff, "The 'Wizard of Oz' as a Monetary Allegory," *Journal of Political Economy* 98 (1990): 736–60. See also works by Professor Richard Sylla (New York University), Henry Littlefield, Gretchen Ritter, and Taylor Quentin.

Chapter 16: Crazy as a Fox

162 "folks can't find me out": The story of Hetty Green in Bellows Falls was published in the *Chicago Daily Tribune*.

163 "tall and stately" figure: *Godey's*, November 1895.

165 The trustee Henry Barling: Accounts of the trial appeared in all the New York newspapers in 1895, including the *New York Times*, the *New York Tribune*, the *New York World*, the *Sun*, and the *Brooklyn Eagle*.

165 "She is the brightest woman": *New York Tribune*, December 26, 1894.

170 "Because she devoted her surplus": James Gerard, *My First Eighty-Three Years in America* (New York: Doubleday, 1951).

170 "Hetty Green has in secret": Nichols, "Hetty Green."

170 "For him, it is a vocation": Sue Halpern, "Making It," *New York Review of Books*, May 28, 2009.

Chapter 17: A New Hetty

173 "I only need $75": Beffel/Marshall Papers, Wayne State University. The papers also include extensive information about Ned Green's political activities.

174 after dinner she held court: Beatrice Fairfax, *Ladies Now and Then* (Boston: E. P. Dutton, 1944). The *Brooklyn Eagle* reported on Hetty Green's comings and goings.

175 "We are all slaves": Jay Gould, quoted in Homberger, *Mrs. Astor's New York*.

176 In New York, she dined with friends: George A. Plimpton folders, Barnard College.

178 Hetty arranged dinner parties: Gerard, *My First Eighty-Three Years*.

180 "A woman hasn't as many chances": *Women's Home Companion*, February 1990.

180 "Most women are afraid": Hetty Green, article on women and investing, *Success* magazine, April 1901.

180 "She has reduced money-making": *Wisconsin Labor Advocate*, December 10, 1886.

CHAPTER 18: FAMILY MATTERS

185 "A girl should be brought up": Hodges, "Richest Woman in America."

186 she had attended an auction: *New York Herald*, April 10, 1899.

187 "Hetty Green is smart": *New York Times*, July 28, 1901.

CHAPTER 19: A COOL HEAD

190 The Spanish-American War: Describing America at the time of the Spanish-American War: Samuel Forman, *Advanced American History* (New York: Century, 1914); H. W. Brands, *American Colossus* (New York: Doubleday, 2010).

190 John Gates . . . led the merger mania: Describing the creation of trusts: Beatty, *Age of Betrayal*.

192 a prominent art collection: The S. D. Warren Collection. Coverage in the *New York Times*, January 10, 1903.

193 "I keep them just as I keep": *New York Times*, November 5, 1905.

193 "The captains of industry": Roosevelt, State of the Union speech, 1901.

193 "Great corporations exist": Roosevelt, first annual message to Congress, December 3, 1901.

193 "shake the largest trusts and corporations": Thomas Lawson, *Frenzied Finance* (New York: Ridgway-Thayer, 1905).

195 "Every girl should be taught": Frank Carpenter interview, 1904.

195 "There is no reason why": "Words of Wisdom from the Wealthiest Woman in America," *Women's Home Companion*, February 1900.

196 "I enjoy being in the thick of things": Hetty Green, as told to Frank Carpenter.

196 "God gave me my money": Quoted in Flynn, *Men of Wealth*.

CHAPTER 20: PANIC AGAIN

199 With the economy flourishing: Noyes, *Forty Years of American Finance*. In *Fifth Avenue* (San Diego: Harcourt, 1979), Kate Simon quotes Paul Bourget, a Frenchman who visited New York in 1895: "It is too evident that money cannot have much value here. There is too much of it. The interminable succession of luxurious mansions which line Fifth Avenue proclaim its mad abundance. . . .This avenue has visibly been willed and created by sheer force of millions, in a fever of land speculation, which has not left an inch of ground unoccupied."

199 the cost of land skyrocketed: See "Land Values Always Increasing," *Moody's*, December 1906.

199 "If this condition of affairs": *New York Times,* January 5, 1906.

199 "the solidest men in Wall Street": *New York World,* February 17, 1908.

200 Opportunities emerged: Carol Ford, *National Magazine,* September 1905.

200 There, in the marble house: The description is by C. W. de Lyon Nichols in *Business America*. Nichols was an author, theologian, and observer of society.

202 "It had been a cardinal doctrine": Noyes, *Forty Years of American Finance.*

202 J. P. Morgan took a sandwich: Article in the *New York Times,* May 12, 1907, on the lunch habits of leading businesspeople. "J. Pierpont Morgan eats his luncheon on his desk, and this luncheon consists of a single sandwich and a glass of water." August Belmont had "a modest luncheon" in his private office. "William Schieffelin, the millionaire head of a drug trade in America, frequently takes from a little tin box in his desk drawer a soda cracker and a lump of chocolate and calls that luncheon." As for Hetty Green, "the richest woman in the land goes regularly to a dairy lunch place in Broadway, just below Fulton Street, and her midday meal consists of a cup of custard and a glass of milk."

206 "Mr. Roosevelt has not made good": *Town Topics,* February 27, 1908.

206 The United States could continue to prosper: Noyes, *Forty Years of American Finance.*

206 "There's one reason why": *Farm Journal,* November 1908.

207 "We had a big financial crisis": Paul Volcker made these comments in an interview with Charlie Rose in New York, September 2011, at a dinner in honor of the newly established Paul Volcker Chair in Behavioral Economics at the Maxwell School of Syracuse University.

CHAPTER 21: REMARKABLE CHANGES

208 "Anything, everything is possible": James Rasenberger, *America 1908* (New York: Scribner, 2007).

208 Newspapers reported talk of war: *The Sun,* June 14, 1908.

209 Henry James was entranced: James wrote about New York in *The American Scene* (1907).

209 H. G. Wells extolled: Bayrd Still, *Mirror for Gotham* (New York: Fordham University Press, 1994).

209 Another English author thrilled: Arnold Bennett, *Your United States* (New York: Harper and Brothers, 1912).

209 highest per capita income: Rasenberger, *America 1908.*

210 "I am glad Miss Gladys Vanderbilt": *Washington Times,* October 12, 1907.

210 A scion of a real estate: Marion King, *Books and People* (New York: Macmillan, 1954).

211 The French Renaissance fortress: Curtis Gathje, *At the Plaza* (New York: Macmillan, 2000); Simon, *Fifth Avenue*; Eve Brown, *The Plaza* (New York: Meredith Press, 1967).

211 Financed in large part: Henry Clews, *Twenty-eight Years in Wall Street*.

212 "A woman has failed": Rasenberger, *America 1908*.

214 she hired a clipping service: *New York Daily Tribune*, June 4, 1908.

214 "I'm back, Twink": *Washington Times*, October 6, 1908.

Chapter 22: Home

219 Ned left behind: Beffel/Marshall Papers, Wayne State University.

219 list of "Don'ts": Nichols, "Hetty Green."

221 not averse to something pretty: Ibid.

221 a wooden loft: Beffel/Marshall Papers, Wayne State University.

222 presidential Cabinet: *McCall's*, July 1911.

224 million dollars' worth of war bonds: Beffel/Marshall Papers, Wayne State University.

Bibliography

ARCHIVES

Beffel, John Nicholas. Papers. Walter P. Reuther Library, Wayne State University, Detroit.

Bullard, John M. "The Greens as I Knew Them." John M. Bullard Papers. Harvard Law School Library, Cambridge.

Fravert, John B. Railroad Collection. University of Louisville Archives and Record Center.

Grinnell, Helen Lansing. Diary. New York Public Library.

Holbrook, Stewart Hall. Papers. Special Collections, University of Washington Libraries.

Howland, Emily. Family Papers. Friends Historical Library of Swarthmore College.

Logan, Andy. Papers. New York Public Library.

Plimpton, George Arthur. Papers. Barnard College, New York.

Tailer, Edward N. Diaries. New-York Historical Society.

Wise, H. A. Letterbook #80, Box 32/22/1865. New-York Historical Society.

Heritage Auctions. School Book, 1850.

NEWSPAPERS

The Advertiser Journal
The Boston Evening Transcript
The Brooklyn Eagle
The Chicago Daily Tribune
The Deseret Evening News
The Hazel Green Herald

The Illustrated London News
The Jerseyman (Morristown, NJ)
The New Bedford Evening Standard
The New Bedford Newspaper
The New Bedford Standard Times
The New Orleans Bee (*L'Abeille de la Nouvelle-Orléans*)
The New York Daily Tribune
The New York Herald
The New York Times
The New York World
The North Eastern Reporter
The San Francisco Call
The St. Paul Daily Globe
The Sun (New York)
The Thrice-a-Week-World
Town Topics: The Journal of Society
The Washington Times

JOURNAL AND MAGAZINE ARTICLES

"Are we a happy people?" *Harper's Magazine*, January 1857, 207–11.

Cummings, Joseph E. "United States Government Bonds as Investments." *Annals of the American Academy of Political Social Science* 87 (January 20, 1920): 158–67.

Ford, Carol. "Hetty Green: A Character Study." *National Magazine*, September 1905.

Green, Hetty. "Why Women Are Not Money Makers." *Harper's Bazaar*, March 10, 1900.

Halpern, Sue. "Making It." *New York Review of Books*, May 28, 2009.

Hamer, John H. "Money and the Moral Order in Late Nineteenth and Early Twentieth Century American Capitalism." *Anthropological Quarterly* 71, no. 3 (July 1998): 138–49.

Heath, Kingston William. "The Howland Mill Village: A Missing Chapter in Model Worker's Housing." *Old-Time New England* 75 (1997): 64–111.

Hodges, Leigh Mitchell. "The Richest Woman in America: Mrs. Hetty Green as She Is Seen in Her Home and in the Business World." *Ladies' Home Journal*, June 1900.

Jepson, Jill. "Women's Concerns: Twelve Women Entrepreneurs of the Eighteenth and Nineteenth Century." *American University Studies*, Series XXVII ("Feminist Studies"), Vol. 11.

Kramer, Rita. "Cathedrals of Commerce." *City Journal*, spring 1996.

"Letters from New York." *Wisconsin Labor Advocate*, December 10, 1886.

Meier, Paul, and Sandy Zabell. "Benjamin Peirce and the Howland Will." *Journal of the American Statistical Association,* Vol. 75, no. 371 (September 1980): 497–506.

Nichols, C. W. de Lyon. "Hetty Green: A Character Study." *Business America,* May 1913.

"Words of Wisdom from the Wealthiest Woman in America." *Women's Home Companion,* February 1900.

Wyckoff, Peter. "Queen Midas: Hetty Robinson Green." *New England Quarterly,* June 1950.

Yohn, Susan M. "Crippled Capitalists: Gender Ideology, the Inscription of Economic Dependence and Female Entrepreneurs in Nineteenth Century America." *Feminist Economics* 12, no. 1 (2006): 85–109.

———. " 'Men That Wouldn't Cheat Each Other . . . Seem to Take Delight in Cheating Women': Court Challenges Faced by U.S. Businesswomen in the Nineteenth Century." Conference presentation, Hofstra University, Hempstead, New York, August 21, 2006.

INTERVIEWS

Abel, Livinia. Telephone interview by author, summer 2011.

Bedell, Barbara (author of *Colonel Edward Howland Robinson Green and the World He Created at Round Hill,* 2003). Interview by author, July 2009, Round Hill, Dartmouth, Massachusetts.

Howland, Llewyn. Telephone interview by author, 2009.

Lowe, James. Telephone interview by author, 2010.

McCord, James. Telephone interview by author.

Nelson, Scott Reynolds. Telephone interview by author, August 27, 2010.

BOOKS

Ackerman, Kenneth D. *The Gold Ring: Jim Fisk, Jay Gould, and Black Friday, 1869.* New York: Carroll & Graf, 1988.

Adams, Henry. *The Education of Henry Adams.* New York: Modern Library, 1931.

Allen, Everett S. *Children of the Light: The Rise and Fall of New Bedford Whaling and the Death of the Arctic Fleet.* Hyannis, MA: Parnassus Imprints, 1973.

Almond, Gabriel A. *Plutocracy and Politics in New York City (Urban Policy Challenges).* Boulder, CO: Westview Press, 1997.

Amory, Cleveland. *Who Killed Society?* New York: Harper, 1960.

Anderson, Bonnie S., and Judith P. Zinsser. *A History of Their Own: Women in Europe from Prehistory to the Present.* New York: Harper & Row, 1988.

Attie, Jeanie. *Patriotic Toil: Northern Women and the American Civil War.* Ithaca, NY: Cornell University Press, 1998.

Bakewell, Michael. *Fitzovia: London's Bohemia (Character Sketches).* Bellevue, WA: Robert Hale, 1999.

Barbour, Hugh, and Jerry Williams Frost. *The Quakers.* Westport, CT: Greenwood Press, 1988.

Beard, Patricia. *After the Ball: Gilded Age Secrets, Boardroom Betrayals, and the Party That Ignited the Great Wall Street Scandal of 1905.* New York: HarperCollins, 2003.

Beatty, Jack. *Age of Betrayal: The Triumph of Money in America, 1865–1900.* New York: Knopf, 2007.

Beckert, Sven. *The Monied Metropolis: New York City and the Consolidation of the American Bourgeoisie, 1850–1896.* Cambridge, UK: Cambridge University Press, 2003.

Beebe, Lucius Morris. *Boston and the Boston Legend.* New York: Appleton-Century, 1935.

Bennett, Arnold. *Your United States.* New York: Harper, 1912.

Bird, Isabella L. *The Englishwomen in America.* Whitefish, MT: Kessinger Publishing, 2004. First published 1856.

Borden, Alanson. *Our Country and Its People; A Descriptive and Biographical Record of Bristol County, Massachusetts.* Boston: Boston History Company, 1899.

Brands, H. W. *American Colossus: The Triumph of Capitalism, 1865–1900.* New York: Doubleday, 2010.

Braynard, Frank O., and William H. Miller Jr. *Picture History of the Cunard Line 1840–1990.* Mineola, NY: Dover Publications, 1991.

Bremer, Fredrika. *The Homes of the New World: Impressions of America.* Ann Arbor, MI: University of Michigan Library, 1853. Reprint, Whitefish, MT: Kessinger Publishing, 2007.

Bristed, Charles Astor. *The Upper Ten Thousand: Sketches of American Society.* London: J. W. Parker and Sons, 1852.

Brooks, John. *The Go-Go Years: The Drama and Crashing Finale of Wall Street's Bullish 60s.* Hoboken, NJ: Wiley, 1999.

Brown, Eve. *The Plaza.* New York: Meredith Press, 1967.

Brown, William H. *The History of the First Locomotives in America.* New York: D. Appleton, 1874.

Bundy, Carol. *The Nature of Sacrifice: A Biography of Charles Russell Lowell, Jr., 1835–64.* New York: Farrar, Straus & Giroux, 2005.

Burke, John. *A Genealogical and Heraldic History of the Landed Gentry: Or Commoners of Great Britain and Ireland Enjoying Territorial Possessions or High Official Rank: But Uninvested with Heritable Honours*. London: R. Bentley, 1835.

Burrows, Edwin G., and Mike Wallace. *Gotham: A History of New York City to 1898*. New York: Oxford University Press, 2000.

Burstyn, Joan N., ed., and Women's Project of New Jersey. *Past and Promise: Lives of New Jersey Women*. Syracuse, NY: Syracuse University Press, 1997.

Cabot, Elizabeth Dwight. *Letters of Elizabeth Cabot*. Vol. 1. Charleston, SC: BiblioLife, 2009.

Cabot, Elizabeth Rogers Mason. *More Than Common Powers of Perception: The Diary of Elizabeth Rogers Mason Cabot*. Edited by P. A. M. Taylor. Boston: Beacon Press, 1991.

California Louisiana Purchase Exposition. *California, Its Products, Resources, Industries, and Attractions: What It Offers the Immigrant, Homeseeker, Investor and Tourist*. 1904. Reprint, Charleston, SC: Nabu Press, 2010.

Catton, Bruce. *The Civil War (American Heritage Book)*. Wilmington, MA: Mariner Books, 2004.

Chancellor, Edward. *Devil Take the Hindmost: A History of Financial Speculation*. New York: Plume, 2000.

Chernow, Ron. *The House of Morgan: An American Banking Dynasty and the Rise of Modern Finance*. New York: Grove Press, 1990.

Churchill, Allen. *The Upper Crust: An Informal History of New York's Highest Society*. New Jersey: Prentice-Hall, 1970.

Clark, Arthur Hamilton. *The Clipper Ship Era: An Epitome of Famous American and British Clipper Ships, Their Owners, Builders, Commanders and Crews*. New York: G. P. Putnam and Sons, 1910.

Collins, Anne L. *Images of America: Around Bellows Falls*. Charleston, SC: Arcadia Publishing, 2002.

Collins, Gail. *America's Women: 400 Years of Dolls, Drudges, Helpmates, and Heroines*. New York: HarperCollins Publishers, 2003.

Congdon, Charles T. *Reminiscences of a Journalist*. Boston: J. R. Osgood, 1880.

Cowles, Virginia. *The Astors: Story of a Transatlantic Family*. London: Weidenfeld & Nicolson, 1979.

Craven, Wayne. *Gilded Mansions: Grand Architecture and High Society*. New York: Norton, 2009.

Crowninshield, Frank. *Manners for the Metropolis*. New York: Arno Press, 1975. First published 1908.

Depew, Chauncy M. *My Memories of Eighty Years*. New York: Charles Scribner's Sons, 1921.

de Toqueville, Alexis. *Democracy in America*. New York: Harper & Row, 1966.

Drachman, Virginia. *Enterprising Women: 250 Years of American Business*. Chapel Hill: University of North Carolina Press, 2002.

Dreiser, Theodore. *Sister Carrie*. New York: Doubleday & McClure, 1900.

Emery, William M., and William W. Crapo. *The Howland Heirs: Being the Story of a Family and a Fortune and the Inheritance of a Trust*. Whitefish, MT: Kessinger Publishing, 2007.

Eustace, Nicole. *Passion Is the Gale: Emotion, Power, and the Coming of the American Revolution*. Chapel Hill, NC: University of North Carolina Press, 2008.

Fairfax, Beatrice. *Ladies Now and Then*. Boston: E. P. Dutton, 1944.

Field, Maunsell B. *Memories of Many Men & of Some Women: Being Personal Recollections of Emperors, Kings, Queens, Princes, Presidents, Statesmen, Authors, and Artists, the Last Thirty Years. 1822–1875*. New York: Harper & Brothers, 1874.

Fite, Emerson David. *Social and Industrial Conditions in the North During the Civil War*. New York: Macmillan, 1910.

Fitzpatrick, Terry, and Bruce Nash. "The Stock Exchange." *Modern Marvels*. The History Channel, October 12, 1997.

Flynn, John T. *Men of Wealth: The Story of Twelve Significant Fortunes from the Renaissance to the Present Day*. New York: Simon & Schuster, 1941. Reprint, Ludwig von Mises Institute, 2007.

Forester, John. *The Life of Charles Dickens*. New York: Dutton, 1990.

Forman, Samuel. *Advanced American History*. New York: Century, 1914.

Fox, Stephen. *Transatlantic: Samuel Cunard, Isambard Brunel, and the Great Atlantic Steamships*. New York: HarperCollins, 2003.

Friend, Tad. *Cheerful Money: Me, My Family, and the Last Days of Wasp Splendor*. New York: Little, Brown, 2009.

Gamber, Wendy. *The Boarding House*. Baltimore: Johns Hopkins University Press, 2007.

Gary, Ralph V. *Following in Lincoln's Footsteps: A Complete Annotated Reference to Hundreds of Historical Sites Visited by Abraham Lincoln*. New York: Carroll and Graf, 2001.

Gathje, Curtis. *At the Plaza*. New York: Macmillan, 2000.

Geisst, Charles. *Wall Street: A History: From Its Beginnings to the Fall of Enron*. New York: Oxford University Press, 1997.

George, Henry. *The Menace of Privilege: A Study of the Dangers to the Republic from the Existence of a Favored Class*. New York: Macmillan, 1905.

Gerard, James W. *My First Eighty-Three Years in America: The Memoirs of James W. Gerard*. New York: Doubleday, 1951.

Goldsmith, Barbara. *Other Powers: The Age of Suffrage, Spiritualism, and the Scandalous Victoria Woodhull*. New York: Harper Perennial, 1999.

Gordon, John Steele. *The Great Game: The Emergence of Wall Street as a World Power: 1653–2000*. New York: Scribner, 1999.

Grant, James. *Money of the Mind: Borrowing and Lending in America from the Civil War to Michael Milken*. New York: Farrar, Straus and Giroux, 1995.

Greenough, W. A. *New Bedford Directory: Of the Inhabitants, Business Firms, Institutions, Streets, Societies*. Boston: W. A. Greenough & Co., 1909.

Habberton, John. *My Country 'Tis of Thee: Or, Great National Questions*. Chicago: Prospect, 1895.

Hargreaves, George Milton. "History of the Quakers in New Bedford and Vicinity." MA Thesis, University of Maine, Orono, 1936. http://www.library.umaine .edu/theses/theses.asp?Cmd=abstract&ID=ocm50214284

Harris, Luther S. *Around Washington Square: An Illustrated History of Greenwich Village*. Baltimore: Johns Hopkins University Press, 2003.

Harrison, Constance Cary (Mrs. Burton). *The Well-Bred Girl in Society*. Philadelphia: Curtis, 1898.

Hayes, Lyman Simpson. *History of the Town of Rockingham: Including the Villages of Bellows Falls, Saxtons River, Rockingham, Cambridgeport and Bartonsville, 1753–1907*. Bellows Falls, VT: The Town, 1907.

Hemp, William. *New York Enclaves*. New York: Clarkson Potter, 2003.

Henry, Robert Selph. *This Fascinating Railroad Business*. New York: Bobbs-Merrill, 1942.

Herr, Kincaid A. *The Louisville and Nashville Railroad, 1850–1963*. Lexington, KY: University Press of Kentucky, 2000.

Homberger, Eric. *The Historical Atlas of New York City: A Visual Celebration of Nearly 400 Years of New York City's History*. New York: Holt Paperbacks, 1998.

———. *Mrs. Astor's New York: Money and Power in a Gilded Age*. New Haven: Yale University Press, 2002.

Huston, James L. *The Panic of 1857 and the Coming of the Civil War*. Baton Rouge, LA: Louisiana State University Press, 1987.

James, Henry. *The American Scene*. New York: Penguin Classics, 1994. First published in 1907.

Jones, Richard. *Walking Dickensian London: Twenty-Five Original Walks Through London's Victorian Quarters*. London: Interlink Books, 2005.

Josephson, Matthew. *The Robber Barons*. New York: Mariner Books, 1962.

Kane, Thomas. *The Romance and Tragedy of Banking*. Boston: Bankers Publishing, 1922.

Kessner, Thomas. *Capital City: New York City and the Men Behind America's Rise to Economic Dominance, 1860–1900*. New York: Simon & Schuster, 2006.

King, Greg. *A Season of Splendor*. Hoboken, NJ: Wiley, 2008.

Kipling, Rudyard. *From Sea to Sea: Letters of Travel*. Garden City, NY: Doubleday, 1911.

Klein, Alexander, ed. *Empire City: A Treasury of New York*. New York: Rinehart, 1955.

Lamas, Rosmarie W. N. *Everything in Style: Harriet Low's Macau*. Hong Kong, China: Hong Kong University Press, 2006.

Lamoreaux, Naomi R. "Entrepreneurship in the United States, 1865–1920." Working paper, UCLA/NBER, August 19, 2007.

Laurence, Anne, Josephine Maltby, and Janette Rutterford. *Women and Their Money 1700–1950: Essays on Women and Finance*. New York: Routledge, 2008.

Lears, Jackson. *Rebirth of a Nation: The Making of Modern America 1877–1920*. New York: Harper Perennial, 2010.

Lebrun, George P. *It's Time to Tell*. New York: William Morrow, 1962.

Lefevre, Edwin. "Mr. Williams and the Chemical National Bank," In *The World's Work*, Vol. III. New York: Doubleday, Page & Co., 1902.

———. *Reminiscences of a Stock Operator*. Hoboken, NJ: Wiley, 2006.

Leonard, John William, and Albert Nelson Marquis. *Who's Who in America*. Chicago: Marquis, 1901.

Lewis, Arthur. *The Day They Shook the Plum Tree*. New York: Harcourt, Brace & World, 1963.

Lewis, Bradley G. *Railroads and the Character of America, 1820–1887*. Knoxville: University of Tennessee Press, 1986.

Lowell, Anna Cabot Jackson. *Thoughts on the Education of Girls*. Boston: Ticknor, Reed, and Fields, 1853.

The Manhattan Company. *Manna-hatin: The Story of New York*. I. J. Friedman, Inc., 1968.

Martin, Albro. *Railroads Triumphant: The Growth, Rejection, and Rebirth of a Vital American Force*. New York: Oxford University Press, 1992.

McCabe, James. *Lights and Shadows of New York Life: or The Sights and Sensations of the Great City*. New York: Farrar, Straus and Giroux, 1970.

McColl, Gail, and Carol Wallace. *To Marry an English Lord*. New York: Workman, 1989.

Melville, Herman. *Moby-Dick*. New York: Oxford University Press, 1998.

Menand, Louis. *The Metaphysical Club: A Story of Ideas in America*. New York: Farrar, Straus and Giroux, 2001.

Milton, Allan and Thomas. Edited by Halsey Nevins. *The Diary of George Templeton Strong, 1835–1875; In Four Volumes*. New York: Macmillan, 1952.

Mitchell, Wesley Clair. *A History of the Greenbacks, with Special Reference to the Economic Consequences of Their Issue: 1862–1865*. Chicago: University of Chicago Press, 1903.

Monaghan, Jay. *Diplomat in Carpet Slippers: Abraham Lincoln Deals with Foreign Affairs*. New York: Bobbs-Merrill, 1945.

Montgomery, Maureen E. *Displaying Women: Spectacles of Leisure in Edith Wharton's New York*. New York: Routledge, 1998.

Morison, Samuel Eliot. *The Maritime History of Massachusetts, 1783–1860*. Cambridge, MA: Riverside Press, 1923.

Morris, Lloyd. *Incredible New York: High Life and Low Life from 1850–1950*. New York: Random House, 1951.

Morris, Robert, and James Sloan Gibbons. *The Banks of New York, Their Dealers, the Clearinghouse, and the Panic of 1857*. New York: Appleton, 1859.

Moss, Frank. *The American Metropolis: From Knickerbocker Days to Modern Times*. New York: P. F. Collier, 1897.

Murphy, Patricia. *Time Is of the Essence: Temporality, Gender and the New Women*. Albany, NY: State University Press of New York, 2001.

Nasaw, David. *Andrew Carnegie*. New York: Penguin Press, 2006.

Nichols, Thomas Low. *Forty Years of American Life, 1821–1861*. London: Longsman, Green, 1874.

Noyes, Alexander. *Forty Years of American Finance*. New York: Ayer, 1980.

Old Dartmouth Historical Society. *Old Dartmouth Historical Sketches*. Vol. 4. New Bedford, MA: New Bedford, 1903.

Oppel, Frank. *Tales of Gaslight New York*. Edison, NJ: Castle Books, 2000.

Parton, James. *Captains of Industry*. New York: Cosimo Classics, 2005.

Patterson, Jerry E. *First Four Hundred: New York and the Gilded Age*. New York: Rizzoli Press, 2000.

Pease, Zephaniah. *New Bedford Massachusetts: Its History, Industries, Institutions, and Attractions*. New York: Lewis Historical Publishing, 1918.

Phalon, Richard. *Forbes Greatest Investing Stories*. Hoboken: Wiley, 2001.

Pink Dandelion, Ben. *The Quakers: A Very Short Introduction*. New York: Oxford University Press, 2008.

Pullum-Piñón, Sara Melissa. "Conspicuous Display and Social Mobility: A Comparison of 1850s Boston and Charleston Elites." PhD dissertation, University of Texas at Austin, 2002.

Rae, John W. *Morristown: A Military Headquarters of the American Revolution.* Mount Pleasant, SC: Arcadia, 2003.

Rasenberger, Jim. *America 1908: The Dawn of Flight, the Race to the Pole, the Invention of the Model T, and the Making of a Modern Nation.* New York: Scribner, 2007.

Rhodes, James Ford. *History of the United States: From the Compromise of 1850 to the McKinley-Bryan Campaign of 1896.* Vol. 7. New York: Macmillan, 1920.

Ricketson, Daniel. *The History of New Bedford, Bristol County, Massachusetts: Including A History of the Old Township of Dartmouth and the Present Townships of Westport, Dartmouth, and Fairhaven from their Settlement to the Present Time.* New Bedford, MA: Published by author, 1858.

Robinson Genealogical Society. *The Robinsons and Their Kin Folk.* New York: Robinson Family Historical and Genealogical Association, 1902.

Rodman, Samuel. *The Diary of Samuel Rodman.* Edited by Zephaniah Pease. Dayton, OH: Reynold's Printing, 1927.

Ross, Ishbel. *Crusades and Crinolines.* New York: Harper & Row, 1963.

Sarnoff, Paul. *Russell Sage: The Money King.* New York: I. Obolensky, 1965.

Schroeder, Alice. *The Snowball: Warren Buffett and the Business Life.* New York: Random House, 2008.

Scudder, Horace Elisha. *James Russell Lowell: A Biography.* Boston: Houghton, Mifflin, 1901.

Sharp, Robert M. *The Lore and Legends of Wall Street.* New York: Dow Jones-Irwin, 1989.

Simmons, James C. *Castaway in Paradise: The Incredible Adventures of True-Life Robinson Crusoes.* Dobbs Ferry, NY: Sheridan House, 1993.

Simon, Kate. *Fifth Avenue: A Very Social History.* San Diego: Harcourt, 1979.

Slack, Charles. *Hetty: The Genius and Madness of America's First Female Tycoon.* New York: HarperCollins, 2004.

Smith, Henry. *Chicago's Great Century.* Chicago: Consolidated Publishers, 1933.

Smith, Matthew Hale. *Bulls and Bears of New York; With the Crisis of 1873, and the Cause.* Hartford: J. B. Burr, 1875.

Sobel, Robert. *The Big Board: A History of the New York Stock Market.* Frederick, MD: Beard Books, 2000.

———. *Panic on Wall Street: A History of America's Financial Disasters.* Frederick, MD: Beard Books, 1999.

Sparkes, Boyden. *The Witch of Wall Street*. Garden City, NY: Doubleday, Doran, 1930.

————, and Samuel Taylor Moore. *Hetty Green: A Woman Who Loved Money*. Garden City, NY: Doubleday, Doran, 1935.

Still, Bayrd. *Mirror for Gotham: New York as Seen by Contemporaries from Dutch Days to the Present*. New York: Fordham University Press, 1994.

Stover, John F. *American Railroads*. The Chicago History of American Civilization. Chicago: University of Chicago Press, 1997.

Stowe, Harriet Beecher. *Uncle Tom's Cabin, or, Life Among the Lowly; The Minister's Wooing; Oldtown Folks*. New York: Literary Classics of the United States, 1982. (Distributed by Viking Press.)

————. *We and Our Neighbors*. Buffalo: J. B. Ford, 1875.

Strouse, Jean. *Morgan: American Financier*. New York: Harper Perennial, 2000.

Tifft, Susan E., and Alex S. Jones. *The Trust: The Private and Powerful Family Behind the New York Times*. New York: Back Bay Books, 2000.

Trachtenberg, Alan. *The Incorporation of America: Culture and Society in the Gilded Age*. New York: Hill and Wang, 1982.

Trager, James. *The New York Chronology: The Ultimate Compendium of Events, People and Anecdotes from the Dutch to the Present*. New York: Collins Reference, 2003.

Train, George Francis. *My Life in Many States and in Foreign Lands*. New York: Appleton, 1902.

Van Rensselaer, John King, Mrs., and Frederic Franklyn Van de Water. *The Social Ladder*. New York: Holt, 1924.

Wachtel, Howard M. *Street of Dreams—Boulevard of Broken Hearts: Wall Street's First Century*. London: Pluto Press, 2003.

Wall, William Allen, Endicott Lith, and Charles Jabert. *New Bedford Fifty Years Ago*. New York: Charles Jabert, 1858.

Waugh, Joan. *Unsentimental Reformer: The Life of Josephine Shaw Lowell*. Cambridge: Harvard University Press, 1998.

Wells, Richard A. *Manners, Culture and Dress of the Best American Society, Including Social, Commercial and Legal Forms, Letter Writing, Invitations, &C.* Published 1923. Reprint, Charleston, SC: Nabu Press, 2010.

Werth, Barry. *Banquet at Delmonico's: Great Minds, the Gilded Age, and the Triumph of Evolution in America*. New York: Random House, 2009.

Wharton, Edith. *A Backward Glance*. New York: Scribner, 1964.

Wharton, Phillip and Grace. *The Wits and Beaux of Society*. Vol. 1. Philadelphia: Porter and Coates, 1860.

Wilkins, Mira. *The History of Foreign Investment in the United States 1914–1945.* Cambridge: Harvard University Press, 2004.

"Women of Wall Street." (Exhibit.) The Museum of American Finance, New York. June 2009–March 2010.

Wright, Mabel Osgood. *My New York.* Norwood, MA: Berwick & Smith, 1926.

Yarnall, James L. *Newport Through Its Architecture: A History of Styles from Postmedieval to Postmodern.* Lebanon, NH: University Press of New England, 2005.

Zuckerman, Mary Ellen. *A History of Popular Women's Magazines in the United States, 1792–1995.* Westport, CT: Praeger, 1998.

WEBSITES

Abraham Lincoln's Classroom. The Lincoln Institute. http://www.abraham lincolnsclassroom.org.

Carnegie Hall Archives. http://www.carnegiehall.org/History/Carnegie-Hall -Archives/.

Cultural History Database. Lone Star College, Kingwood, TX. http://lonestar .edu/kingwood.htm.

Extrapolations from the Kouroo Contexture. www.kouroo.info/.

Financial Inspiration Café. www.financial-inspiration.com.

G. H. LaBarre Galleries website. http://labarregalleries.blogspot.com/.

Heath, Kingston Wm. "The Howland Mill Village: A Missing Chapter in Model Workers' Housing." http://www.historicnewengland.org/preservation/your-older -or-historic-home/articles/pdf78.pdf.

The History Box Database. http://thehistorybox.com.

"Howland Descendants," American Ancestors (New England Historic Genealogical Society database). http://www.americanancestors.org/home.html.

Jewish Virtual Library Database. https://www.jewishvirtuallibrary.org/.

Marin History Museum. http://marinhistory.org.

Merchant's House Museum. http://merchantshouse.org.

Museum of American Finance. http://www.moaf.org.

The Nantucket Historical Association. http://nha.org.

New Bedford Preservation Society website. http://nbpreservationsociety.org /index.html.

New York City History. http://www.cosmopolis.ch/travel/newyorkcity_e.htm.

New York Social Diary. http://www.newyorksocialdiary.com/nysd/archive.

Old Sturbridge Village website, historic documents. http://www.osv.org/explore _learn/document_list.php?A=LA&T=P.

Paine, Albert Bigelow. "Mark Twain, A Biography." Great Literature Online. http://paine.classicauthors.net/twainbio/.

Texas Transportation Archive. http://www.ttarchive.com.

Walden Woods Project Database. http://www.walden.org/Thoreau.

WhalingCity.net website. www.whalingcity.net.

The White House. http://www.whitehouse.gov/.

Illustration Credits

Index

═══

Page numbers beginning with 235 refer to notes.

Janet Wallach is the author of nine books, including *Desert Queen: The Extraordinary Life of Gertrude Bell,* which has been translated into twelve languages and was a *New York Times* Notable Book of the Year.

This book was set in Fournier, a typeface named for Pierre Simon Fournier *fils* (1712–1768), a celebrated French type designer. Coming from a family of typefounders, Fournier was an extraordinarily prolific designer of typefaces and of important typographic ornaments.

Fournier's type is considered transitional in that it drew its inspiration from the old style, yet was ingeniously innovational, providing for an elegant, legible appearance. In 1925 his type was revived by the Monotype Corporation of London.